Diary of an Immigrant

Colin Templeman

Copyright © 2025 Colin Templeman

All rights reserved.

This book is a memoir. It reflects the author's present recollections of experiences from the time. Some names and characteristics have been changed to protect the privacy of those depicted. Some events have been compressed, and some dialogue has been re-created from memory.

Warning: Contains some explicit language

No part of this book may be reproduced, or stored in a retrieval system, or transmitted in any form or by any means, electronic, mechanical, photocopying, recording, or otherwise, without express written permission of the author.

Printed book ISBN: 978-1-7385342-2-7
eBook ISBN: 978-1-7385342-3-4

DEDICATION

For my Mum
Ethel Margaret (Maggie) Templeman

And to my best friend Jack.
Border Terrier, pub buddy and devourer of pork scratching's.
Missed but never forgotten.
"Your lead is still on its hook lad."

CONTENTS

Acknowledgments	i
INTRODUCTION	1
PART ONE – Ironing out the wrinkles	6
PART TWO – The end of the beginning	40
PART THREE – Clear for take-off	61
PART FOUR – A balancing act	76
PART FIVE – The anticlimax of a climax	139
PART SIX – The final move	159
PART SIX (and a half) – Bonee Annee!	243
PART SEVEN – Shifting sands	347
PART EIGHT – April 2018 - the point of return	352
EPILOGUE	359
BEFORE YOU GO	362

ACKNOWLEDGMENTS

To my bold and daring co-conspirator, Clare – navigator of life's twists, tamer of my grand delusions, and the only person who truly understands the peculiar mechanics of my mind. Without you, I'd be an untethered balloon, drifting aimlessly into the stratosphere of mediocrity.

To the unwitting cast of this tale, whose very existence has now been repurposed for my literary ambitions. Whether they suspect it or not, they now reside in the hallowed halls of my story – immortalised, for better or worse, in these pages.

And lastly, to my tireless band of critics, word-wranglers, and patience-stretchers – Martin B and Simon J – who have endured my efforts with stoic resolve and only occasional threats of submission. You have my profound gratitude... and my deepest sympathies.

INTRODUCTION

This book has been over four years in the making. Not for lack of effort, nor out of apathy, but because of an ever-present companion: self-doubt. I questioned myself endlessly – do I have the skill this story deserves? Will my words do justice to the tale, and will anyone even care to read it? But despite my hesitation, I pushed through. And here you are now, the final arbiter of this journey – the reader.

Though, let me begin with a confession: this isn't some grand epic spun by a master wordsmith. Far from it. I'm just a bloke – a slightly older one – who finds pleasure in putting pen to paper. Mostly about life, my life; the meagre escapades and (mis)adventures that dot this so-called 'winter of our years.' A time, they say, for reflection and taking things easy, savouring the simple joys and quiet moments.

I've always had a knack for spotting life's absurdities, capturing the humour that people unknowingly serve up every day. Retirement, at last, has granted me the chance to pause and really take it all in – to examine not just the world as it is now, but the echoes of its past and the faint outlines of what might lie ahead. Through this reflective lens, I've uncovered a few truths, chief among them being the myth of the so-called 'good old days.' Let's be clear: they don't exist.

What we have are simply days, months, and years – some memorable, some forgettable, and others that simply drift by.

To any young reader who's stumbled upon this book, let me offer you a bit of hard-earned wisdom: if someone of my vintage – or, heaven forbid, someone even older – starts waxing lyrical about those 'good old days' of endless sunshine and storybook winters, don't be fooled. Smile, nod politely, and make your escape.

Nostalgia has a funny way of gilding the mundane, but in reality, life is a mixed bag, always has been.

And with that, I welcome you to step into my world.

Adventures come in an endless assortment of shapes and sizes, each with its own brand of flair. Some are rollicking escapades teeming with derring-do, while others might be humble road trips where ordinary folk end up doing the most extraordinary deeds, or perhaps, the unlikely quest of scaling Mount Kilimanjaro with a horde of elderly relatives in tow. Yet, the tale that unfolds within the following pages? Now, that's a different beast entirely.

You are invited to join my wife Clare and I on less of a quest and more of a yarn. Though could be regarded as being most definitely a voyage of discovery. This tale is peppered with humour, steeped in a fair share of uncertainty, and unfolds through anecdotes and stories from the period following the immediate aftermath of my decision to retire. Or rather, Clare's gracious decision to allow me to retire.

As for me? Well, apart from being a cantankerous old sod, I don't take much in life too seriously. After all, life's too fleeting, and for me, the finish line is drawing nearer with each passing day.

Well into my sixth decade now – closer to my seventh, if we're being frank – I suppose I've packed quite a bit into my brief time on this planet. Or perhaps more accurately, life has packed a lot into me. But truth be told, I haven't really notched up any remarkable achievements. Mostly, I've just managed to trudge along a well-trodden and rather predictable path.

Be born, go to school, leave school, dabble in a bit of romance, start working, indulge in slightly more romance, climb the professional ladder – mostly by sheer luck – get married, get divorced, tie the knot again, father three children, experience a decline in romance, and finally, retire.

Getting old for me has been a somewhat creeping phenomenon. In spite all the tell-tale signs, such as my increasingly aching joints, ear hair, a need to sleep during the middle of the day and a burgeoning intolerance for, well, nearly everything.

When I retired, I thought of getting old as little more than a shadow hovering just out of sight – something distant and for the time being, inconsequential. After all, I had spent nearly four decades climbing the professional ladder in Facilities Management, accumulating an impressive collection of lofty titles along the way.

I'm guessing most of you don't know what Facilities Management is either. Don't worry, you're in good company. Even my kids never quite figured it out. Over the years, they asked me time and again what my job entailed. Each time, I struggled to explain it in a way that made sense, until they eventually lost interest or decided I was making it all up. For a moment, I considered turning to the internet to find some clever definition from the so-called experts to help you out. But as it turns out, while there's a faint common thread, there's no universally agreed-upon explanation. Much like my career itself, it seems Facilities Management is best described as something I made up as I went along.

But there's something to be said for the comfort of a corporate security blanket, especially one that paid so handsomely. So, casting it aside and stepping into a world where the only blanket I would have was the one I'd have to make for myself – by way of retirement planning – was quite a leap.

But lofty titles and comfort blankets aside, the truth is I was struggling to keep pace with the influx of bright young things joining the business, who had the audacity to interrupt and even worse, share their opinions on my otherwise cushy existence. My energy levels were dipping, and boredom was creeping in. Actually, that's a bit of an understatement – I'd been bored for quite a while. The perpetual travelling didn't help either. My body having no clue what time zone it was in.

To many, flying around the globe might seem glamorous, and it was for a while, but after accumulating hundreds of thousands of airmiles I had no intention of using, my carbon footprint a disgrace, I was utterly exhausted. When I wasn't jet-setting – how about that for a 1960's term? – I often found myself getting out of bed at ridiculous hours for conference calls spanning multiple time zones. In short, I was constantly tired.

There was something else going on as well. Our personal situation was also changing. Kids were growing up, moving out and on. Meaning that we – when I wasn't in the air – had time to ourselves, to think. Which was both liberating and dangerous.

For years, in both our professional and personal lives, we were constantly encouraged to *'think outside the box'*. Now, it was time to find opportunities within the box. This newfound enlightenment brought about a seismic shift in our perspectives. I was no longer just a cog in the corporate machine; almost overnight, I transformed into a dedicated member of our very own escape committee. A committee of two – Clare and me.

As it happened, our escape was anything but swift. On the contrary, it was a slow burn. The journey from planning to execution to eventual completion spanned several years. Even reaching the planning stage was a lengthy affair.

At the outset we really had nothing concrete, aside from some outline ideas, which above all needed to include – according to Clare – something that didn't involve me going to the pub every day. Along with a whole host of other pastimes and businesses that I might be inclined to invest both my time and money in.

With no previous experience, this is the tale of how two novices set out to decode the mystery of retirement – from a standing start.

PART ONE

IRONING OUT THE WRINKLES

Lesson number one for soon to be retirees – courtesy of yours truly: Sure, you can sort out the practicalities of retirement, like financial planning or escaping from a job that I was, frankly, struggling to keep up with. But preparing for the grand adventure of retirement itself, one that you hope will endure for many years, is almost an impossibility. At least, it was for us.

Our starting point was to embrace a simple truth: a lack of strategy shouldn't stop us from at least attempting to put together some kind of plan to fill the impending void between now and when we check out for good.

An obvious notion being to consider doing something we've never had time for before?

I'm sure, like me, you've noticed countless adverts promising endless ways to spend your time – and your money. Mainly found in the back pages of Sunday newspapers, selling us *'holidays of a lifetime'*.

Cruises are a popular choice, onboard one of those colossal liners that look ready to tip over with their towering accommodations. For just a few thousand pounds, you can find yourself confined at sea with hundreds, if not thousands, of other old-timers.

There's also the luxury hotels and resorts tailored specifically for the over-the-hill mob, offering unlimited hot tub access and a choice of masseuse or masseur, being set the impossible task of trying to iron out your wrinkles – including the extra ones from spending too much time in the hot tub. The reality is, even a flat iron couldn't smooth out my wrinkles, so I couldn't justify spending money on letting someone else try.

To be frank, I'm not convinced any of what I've just outlined qualifies as serious retirement planning. At least, not in my book. Unless, of course, our aim was to spend our twilight years perpetually on the move. Sleeping in beds that weren't our own, endlessly packing and unpacking, and eating at set times – often with complete strangers...

But we had no plans to travel on the high seas, because thankfully Clare doesn't care for cruises. Or boats of any description for that matter, being that she's a sufferer of sea sickness. She's also afflicted with 'going round a corner too fast in the car sickness,' 'funfair ride sickness,' and even 'turning her head too quickly sickness.' Luckily, she's fine standing still or travelling in a straight line – on solid ground, that is. As for flying? That's another nausea-inducing affair. She often talks about places she'd like to visit, but those destinations seem to change almost weekly.

As for me, having already clocked up extensive travel during my career – though barely glimpsing any of the sights in the countries I'd visited – I had little enthusiasm for getting on a plane.

Anyway back to retirement. That time of our lives in which we moved, almost seamlessly, from being mum and dad to a pair of old biffers. According to our children that is.

As I have already – and wisely – suggested, as much as

you can plan for your retirement I was not convinced you can actually prepare yourself for it.

To those yet to reach the venerable age, it's no easy feat to convey what it's truly like to transition from one stage of life to another. The best I can do is liken it to other major life shifts – like moving from being a childless couple to becoming parents. By all means, read the books, seek the advice of those who've trodden the path before you. But the truth is, nothing prepares you for the reality that will eventually unfold.

Though the actual date of our retirement was yet to be pinned down, we both agreed it was high time to start considering it seriously. After taking stock of our modest investments, we concluded that our finances were reasonably sound. In other words, if we were cautious with our spending, our pensions could see us comfortably through our twilight years. And a brief message to our children who might be reading this; Spending what *you* consider to be *your* inheritance is not an issue for us.

Being reasonably fit and healthy for a couple of fifty somethings (at the time), we reckoned, at least on paper, that we could look forward to quite a few more years on this planet. With that settled, the next item on our agenda was to cobble together some sort of plan, or at least a vision, that could serve as the foundation for said plan.

As a couple, we share the belief that merely drifting from one day or one week to the next is a bit of a waste. We've always tried to avoid it, even when the kids were growing up and we were tied to all those necessary routines. Retirement wasn't going to change that outlook.

This doesn't mean to say we feel the need to be constantly on the go, or fill our lives with endless projects. We've come to recognise that doing nothing, even for a short time, can be quite rewarding. Our stance isn't about coming up with grand ideas all the time – that would be exhausting – but rather, finding a good reason to get out of bed in the morning. Even if that reason is simply for me to go make the tea and bring it back to bed while we figure out the rest of the day.

When our family was younger, getting out of bed had different imperatives – certainly not the optional luxury it is now.

We've always believed, and impressed upon our children, that stepping out of your comfort zone at least once in your life is a must. And that's precisely what this is I guess: our tale of stepping out of our comfort zone, hoping our dream would blossom into a blissful reality.

However, as we set out on our new adventure, we hadn't accounted for the anxiety, feelings of inadequacy, and uncertainty that would accompany us – often clashing with a thrilling pit-of-the-stomach excitement. But I digress, because at the start, we had little idea where this dream of ours would lead or what shape it would take.

When all's said and done, I was just a bloke in that awkward phase of life: too young to be old, too old to be middle-aged – unless I was planning on living to a sprightly 114, which, even with modern advances, seems a tad unlikely.

Having missed the mark at proper middle age – opting for a Saab convertible over a big Triumph motorbike – I was determined to master old age with gusto.

So, there we were, Clare and I, spinning on the wheel of life where two out of our three kids had flown the coop. Our youngest daughter, blissfully unaware, was soon to follow suit in a couple of years' time, despite her vehement protests to the contrary. We contented ourselves with this arrangement, along with the inevitable and frequent door slamming – an art form exclusive to teenage daughters.

As a father of teenagers, past and present, I've

experienced both ends of the popularity spectrum. I've been hated and hugged in equal measure – often with one quickly following the other. Clare learned that "no" was never an acceptable answer to any query or request from our children. As for me, I deftly avoided using the dreaded "no" word by directing all such inquiries to their mother.

I'm pleased to report that we are no longer considered as the obstructive force we once were. We've graduated to just being annoying.

Another point, tied directly to our advancing years, was that our mortgage term had dwindled to single digits, though still at the higher end. Additionally, our debts and expenses were decreasing, primarily due to reduced household bills. With these costs fading, we were gradually becoming what some might call 'solvent' – a state we hadn't known for decades.

Suddenly, our lives weren't dictated by the necessity of having to bring home the bacon for the brood – or, in the case of our vegetarian daughters, having to bring home some plant based foodstuffs. Our responsibilities, obligations, and priorities, once imposed by our circumstances, were shifting. Of course, there were still mouths to feed (albeit only three, plus a dog and cat) and bills to pay, but the relentless treadmill we'd been on for so many years was starting to slow. To the point where we could seriously consider stepping off.

So, aside from the occasional door slamming by our very own 'She Devil,' we found ourselves in a rare state of peace. This afforded us a bit of thinking time – a luxury we were not accustomed to, and as I've mentioned before, was quite liberating. But, as it turned out – largely due to us being novices at this free-thinking lark – quite dangerous.

HATCHING THE PLAN

With shifting priorities and ample time to ponder, we swiftly realised that coasting into old age wasn't for us. Simply waiting for grandchildren to fill a self-imposed void seemed pointless. Not the arrival of grandchildren themselves, but the act of sitting and waiting for them. Trust me, I was eagerly looking forward to having grandchildren – and still am. Teaching them how to use a chainsaw, light fires... all those indispensable, practical life skills.

Despite our ageing bodies, we knew there was still time for one more grand adventure. Whatever that adventure entailed, it had to be more than just painting a new picture over an old canvas. That old canvas being our current house and life – a place that, though good and safe, was likely chosen more for convenience and practicality.

Don't get me wrong, we have some wonderful memories and had some great times in our family home, which is why the thought of moving was never going to be easy. But we always knew it wasn't our forever home. For one, it wasn't near enough to the sea. It was a small town in rural North Dorset, which was fine if you liked rural living with all of its associated challenges.

That combined with the thought of being held to a mortgage for another eight years or so, was something we really didn't want to do anymore, if we could possibly avoid it that is.

It was time to hatch our escape plan. So we sat down, repeatedly, to try and figure out exactly what it was we wanted to get out of the next period of our life together.

At the top of our list, as I mentioned, was becoming mortgage-free. Additionally, we needed to settle various other debts that had built up over time. Ultimately, we desired a location closer to the sea, somewhere secluded yet not entirely remote. Thus, our preference was not for a seaside town, nor the Hebrides, and certainly not France.

So, why not France? Aside from some visits to our dear friends Alan and Hélène in Brittany, where I've had some of the best times, I've never really felt a connection with France. For the record – and this isn't just my opinion but that of the Bretons – Brittany isn't regarded as being part of France. Our friends say it's similar to the Cornish perspective and their relationship with the rest of the UK: they don't particularly desire one, feeling it has been foisted upon them.

Over the years, I believe I've given France ample chances to impress me, yet it has never quite managed to do so. Our holidays have taken us to the south of France, the southwest, central regions, and even the north. We've rented homes with and without swimming pools, gone touring (much to the kids' dismay), tried camping (which they disliked even more), and even combined flying with car rental. Admittedly, there were enjoyable moments, but even through the lens of a vacation, I always found comfort in returning home. Though in hindsight, maybe it wasn't so much about France after all, but rather the two uninterrupted weeks spent with my wife and children. They weren't troublesome, at least not all the time, but it seemed that being 'the dad' came with certain unspoken expectations. Specifically, there was a presumption that I possessed unique skills unknown to me, yet somehow acknowledged by my family. With no previous experience, I had become an adept at driving on the opposite side of the road. I was, by all accounts, also skilled at deciphering French food menus, articulating them for our group, and understanding everyone's preferences, including, but not limited to, the inevitable requests for no mushrooms or dairy. Consequently, I was expected to order our meals in fluent French, or so it seemed. In the supermarket and open-air markets my family's expectations continued, as I was pressed forward to order actual quantities and count out the money in French. The truth is I did manage to grasp the driving – it's actually quite intuitive – but in everything else I made a complete arse of myself. Then in doing so, and give my family their due, when a French waiter or stall holder threw their hands up in frustration, often leaving me hanging, much to the amusement of any of the natives in the vicinity, they were there for me. Laughing louder than anyone else, making sure to point at me, in case there was any doubt as to who the ill spoken Lugg was.

But that wasn't the only reason France and I never saw eye to eye. There wasn't *one* single thing that got under my skin; it was a multitude of little things that, when piled together, just irked me. Nothing was open on Sundays (apart from the occasional supermarket until lunchtime) or at any convenient time. And don't get me started on the alleged delights of French gastronomy.

In my opinion and in the grand gastronomic theatre, the myth that French cuisine effortlessly outshines British fare deserves a profound debunking. An illusion, as dazzling and fleeting as a soufflé, likely to collapse when faced with the robust, hearty truth of a proper British roast. There it is – said and served!

Furthermore, the whole concept of grammatical gender left me bewildered. Why does cheese, wine, fish – or anything, really – need to be labelled as masculine or feminine? I'd often find myself shaking my head, muttering, "Why does it matter? It's just a fish!" And then I discovered an amusing twist – beer, a drink commonly associated with men, is feminine in French. Even more surprising? So is the chainsaw (*la tronçonneuse*).

Yep, the French are overrated and mad, and I had no desire to engage with them any more than was absolutely necessary.

Ireland, on the other hand, boasting an undeniable charm, became a contender. Having visited multiple times, I must confess there's an elusive quality about the country that strikes a chord with me – a connection that's easy to feel but hard to define. Yes, they have their social issues, but where doesn't? They speak English, in their unique way, and offer excellent beer, delicious food, and plenty of open space. What's not to like?

Then there's Cornwall. We've always had a soft spot for it. We holidayed there a few times and even went house hunting once, back when we were younger and more foolish. What we loved about Cornwall was its relative isolation, sparse population, dramatic coastline, and of course, the pasties and beer – more my preference, mind you.

Sure, in the summer, it's teeming with holidaymakers (guilty as charged) and coach parties. But as we often reminded each other during our planning sessions, the English summer only lasts about three days, so it seemed manageable. Plus, Cornwall is one of the few holiday spots I've been genuinely reluctant to leave.

So, here's where we were thus far.

Our grand plan involved selling our house and using any accrued equity to settle our debts, including the mortgage. Ideally, this would leave us with enough funds to purchase a charming fixer-upper in a picturesque location. We knew our plan needed more refinement, but those were the broad strokes we aimed to flesh out over time. As I've mentioned before, we were novices at this free-thinking lark, so baby steps were the order of the day.

However, there were a couple of hitches to consider, during what we termed our planning phase. Both would undoubtedly impact the immediate execution of our developing plan. The big hitch was my business commitments, which would last at least another two years. The small one, our youngest daughter, who still needed to finish her schooling. After that, we agreed we needed to gently encourage her to leave the nest – by renting out her room, cutting off her food supply, or if push comes to shove move house while she was at school. Only kidding, of course. She would be nudged towards independence in a loving and supportive way.

Either way we would still need a base, that was geographically convenient for us all. In other words, we couldn't just sell up and move out to Cornwall or Ireland straightaway. Nevertheless plans are plans and we needed to maintain the small amount of momentum we'd created. So it was agreed that the best course of action would be to go ahead and sell the house, bank whatever money we had left – after debts had been paid – and move into a rental. Giving ourselves some breathing space to go find the right house in the right place.

Time to check some boxes; No debts ✓, mortgage free ✓, ability to look for the right type of house ✓, in one of our preferred places ✓, kid free X (work in progress).

After we sobered up the doubts did start to creep in.

But then, no matter how much we deliberated or tried to find a reason to preserve our stable, predictable lives, we always ended up with two key conclusions. First, there was no compelling reason not to do it. Second, if we didn't at least give it a try, embracing whatever outcomes may follow, we would likely regret it later on.

Even if it all blew up in our faces, at least we tried.

So, there we were, eyeing Cornwall or a quaint Irish country cottage near the coast. Watch out world, we were on a mission! No, it was more than that – we were setting out on an adventure! One that would last for the rest of our lives.

And so it was that almost eighteen months to the day after

selling our house and moving into a rental, we signed on various dotted lines and took the keys to our wonderful, landlocked house, in France!

SHORT INTERMISSION

Having decided on our French adventure – please, hold your "How on earth did you end up in France?" because all will be revealed soon – I was determined to chronicle as much of it as possible. However, it turns out that diarising one's life requires something I have always been woefully short of: discipline.

So, what you're about to get are the stories, narratives, experiences, and the many characters that have provided us with a lifetime of memories. These are drawn from actual journal entries, random notes scribbled at the time of an event – often on a piece of torn cardboard with a pencil – and our combined recollections. Many of which we still reflect on fondly today.

In taking this approach, I was determined to ensure that these notes remained unsanitised by professional editing, as such interference could have compromised their authenticity. I recognise that this may not align with conventional publishing standards, but the result is a genuine reflection of my experiences. Therefore, any notable stylistic differences between the journal entries and the ensuing tales are entirely by design.

We also took hundreds of photographs, many of which I've shared as our story unfolds. And, where it felt right, I've included snippets of French dialogue – pieced together from memory and my own limited grasp of the language. While they may not be perfect, they reflect the reality of those moments, just as they were.

HOUSE HUNTING, AND A VISIT THAT CHANGED OUR LIVES

I recall hearing, through some grapevine or other, that the prime time for house hunting is when the leaves are falling, not when the flowers are blooming. It's all too easy to get swept off your feet by a charming garden under the summer sun, but it's the drizzly days that really test your love for a place. So, armed with this wise advice, we held off on our property search until the autumn of 2013, giving us plenty of time to mull over our retirement plans.

With a spanking new Land Rover Defender at our disposal, we were primed and ready to tackle any terrain in pursuit of our dream home.

So it was that one day we found ourselves looking over a particularly remote house nestled within the rugged confines of Dartmoor National Park. At that juncture, France still remained decidedly off the itinerary. Not quite Cornwall, but it was certainly en route. Our prospective neighbours were none other than the residents of Princetown, whose most famous establishment is the formidable HMP Dartmoor.

The house, a perfect example of off-grid living, was equipped with its own generator for electricity, a borehole for water, and naturally, a cesspit for waste.

As it turned out the place was a bit of a shit-hole to be perfectly honest – quite literally in many respects. The owners ran some kind of sheep dog breeding business and had clearly underestimated the amount of excrement a pack of dogs and their progeny could produce.

Seemingly unaware of the extensive accumulation of excrement around the perimeter and, to a lesser yet equally repugnant extent, within the house itself. Though one might still find the remote location appealing, nestled as it was in one of England's most picturesque landscapes. However, the prospect of savouring Dartmoor's famed fresh air became decidedly less appealing until we had placed a considerable distance between ourselves and the property.

According to the estate agents' rather enthusiastic description, the house was a bit of an old dame of about two hundred years, created from the stout local granite, and appearing as though it could endure another two centuries without so much as a shudder. Its wooden sash windows and solid wooden doors exuded a certain rustic charm, and the vast garden – richly manured, I might add – was encircled by an equally sturdy, waist-high stone wall.

Sadly, that's where the rural fantasy came to an abrupt halt. Though not averse to the idea of a 'doer-upper', but this particular house and all its appendages were in a state of woeful disrepair. The dream, it seemed, being sold by the estate agents was with rather more gloss and considerably less reality than we might have hoped.

The chap who lived there with his lady companion gave us the grand tour, beginning with the contraption they called an electricity supply. Perched under a ramshackle corrugated metal canopy, the ancient diesel generator seemed precariously supported by four rickety wooden posts. The diesel fuel tank, however, was situated some distance away, just off the track we had driven down to get to the property. Evidently, the reason for its remote position, was that it was the nearest point to the place to which the diesel oil delivery driver could get to.

Our trusty Land Rover had no difficulty making its way to the house, but it soon dawned on us that hosting visitors, particularly those with regular road cars, would be a logistical nightmare. When I inquired how the fuel made its journey from the tank to the generator, the bloke pointed to a large Jerrycan. Not just any Jerrycan, mind you, but one of those safari-sized ones you'd expect to see strapped to the side of a rugged off-roader like ours.

However, there was no need for us to fret over fuel logistics, as it turned out the generator had been out of commission for years. And as for the pump that was supposed to whisk waste and sewage uphill to the septic tank, it was described as "a bit dicky". In this context, "dicky" apparently meant it functioned intermittently, though I couldn't fathom how it managed to work at all without a reliable electricity supply.

The interior of the house, as one might predict, was downright appalling. The proprietors, it appeared, had abandoned the practice of wiping canine excrement off their footwear years ago, resulting in a pervasive and rather unsavoury environment. Undeterred, we ploughed ahead with our inspection, desperately seeking some redeeming feature to justify the visit.

The solitary glimmer of hope? The place, as far as we could ascertain, was watertight.

Emerging from the kitchen, which boasted a solid fuel cooker, we were ushered into what had once been a grand reception room. In its heyday, it must have been a splendid sitting room, complete with a cosy fire nestled in a huge Victorian fireplace and offering enviable views across the countryside. Today, however, it had been relegated to a dumping ground for an assortment of paraphernalia – car parts, firewood, and a plethora of other items I chose to ignore. To add to the charm, most of the panes in the large bespoke arched windows were broken, inviting all the weather Dartmoor National Park could muster into the room. With a cheerful grin, our host informed us that they no longer used this room. Though, like the rest of the house, it was amply adorned with canine excrement.

Upstairs offered no respite, so we, having no doubt set a new world record for breath-holding, graciously took our leave. We decided to spare ourselves the customary handshake and left the couple to the peculiar existence they had carved out for themselves.

We drove into Princetown and made a beeline for a quaint little pub, hoping to scrub off the remnants of our ordeal and reflect on the day's particular adventure. But not before swapping our sullied shoes for some sturdier walking boots we had wisely packed. Over a pint and something with fries, we dissected our visit and, believe it or not, began listing the Herculean tasks required to restore the house to its former glory.

It was all about location, location, location – as that respected Channel 4 programme often reminds us. Though in this instance, even the show's intrepid presenters might have reconsidered, opting for a different perspective and a change of footwear.

Certain in our decision, we phoned the estate agent and connected with the same young lady who had provided the details earlier. Informing her that we would not be proceeding, she quickly countered with an eager suggestion: the owners were prepared to negotiate on the price. Lacking a sharp answer, I settled for a straightforward, "No thank you," before we drove off towards Cornwall, contemplating whether we should set fire to our dog excrement covered shoes and purchase new ones in Truro.

'Our trusty Land Rover had no difficulty making its way to the house...'

'To add to the charm, most of the panes in the large bespoke arched windows were broken, inviting all the weather Dartmoor National Park could muster into the room...'

***

Journal entry from February 2014 – *So I've started a journal. I had hoped that my initial, significant journal entry would carry a positive tone. I've been jotting down some notes since we embarked on this house-hunting adventure, yet I haven't fully transcribed them until now. It still surprises me how challenging it can be to find the right house. If Clare shares my feelings, she masks them well. As for myself, I must admit I'm feeling somewhat disheartened, though I try to keep such sentiments to myself. Clare frequently reminds me that we've only been searching for a few months, and given that we're planning for a lifelong home, patience is key. Yet, it's evident that her sighs echo my own as we repeatedly encounter misleading property descriptions from estate agents. Tomorrow, we return to Cornwall, hopeful once more.*

***

During the autumn of 2013 and the winter of 2014, we made several pilgrimages to Cornwall and uncovered its two contrasting personas. There's the vibrant, sun-drenched Cornwall, teeming with life – and tourists – that we had frequently enjoyed with our children. Then, there's the authentic Cornwall, which transforms into a veritable ghost town in the autumn and winter months.

This transformation is largely due to the exodus of second-home and holiday property owners who close up shop for the winter, leaving entire villages and large sections of towns virtually deserted. The local businesses, consequently, suffer from this seasonal slump, their cheerful facades masking the grim reality of dwindling clientele.

Having said all that, there's no denying that Cornwall is one of the most geographically enchanting and contrasting places you'll ever encounter. The landscape is a fascinating patchwork of rugged and undulating terrain, green and granite, barren and fertile all at once. The people, too, are equally diverse – friendly yet offhand, welcoming yet chilly, chatty yet reserved.

Perhaps it's the same everywhere, but for me, the distinct impression lingered that Cornwall is quintessentially for the Cornish. You're welcome to visit (for a brief spell), just be sure to bring your purse.

That aside we still viewed numerous houses and spent considerable time in various locations, but nothing floated our boat. Either the right house was in the wrong place or vice versa. We would still go back there to visit, but as a place to live, we both agreed, that it wasn't for us. And to be honest with you we had the distinct feeling that it really didn't want us either.

So, what about Ireland? Well, we conducted an extensive online investigation and, despite finding one or two properties that piqued our interest, it was the sheer faff of getting there that deterred us. Journeying from middle England to Ireland is a real bugger, especially by car. The thought of making multiple trips, as house hunting often requires, seemed like more trouble than it was worth.

We concluded that if we weren't willing to jump through these hoops, our passion for relocating to Ireland wasn't as fervent as we imagined. Thus, we shelved the notion and, despite growing reservations, kept a watchful eye on the West Country.

***

And so it was, after yet another futile journey westward, that we resolved to take a brief rest which included a vacation to visit our dear friends, Alan and Hélène, in Brittany. It was a chance to recharge our batteries.

As it happened, this visit was destined to change our lives.

The most gracious of hosts and dearest of friends – Alan being English and Hélène French – we stayed in their charming mill house, or moulin, as the locals call it. Nestled in a small commune in the Morbihan region of Brittany, it's a picturesque retreat.

Alan and Hélène had packed up their lives in England years ago to establish a small business in Brittany. Both were teachers, but Alan, ever the man of the land, found this part of France to be his perfect playground. Swapping the protractor for a tractor was an easy transformation for him, though, in fact, he was actually a drama teacher. Nonetheless, I couldn't resist the protractor/tractor analogy.

Hélène, one of life's truly lovely people, had discovered a talent for natural healing, which she put to good and grateful use within the local community.

Over aperitifs – which we have enthusiastically adopted and highly recommend – we regaled our hosts with tales of our travels, the sights we'd seen, and the places we'd visited. Reflecting on that evening, it's fair to say it turned into something of an emotional purge – not quite frustration, but pretty close.

While our discussions weren't solely driven by our inability to find the perfect house (we remained doggedly optimistic despite the setbacks), our patience was wearing extremely thin. Much of what was gnawing at us had less to do with the elusive dream home and more with the conduct of the people involved. Chief among the culprits were the estate agents, that peculiar breed unto themselves. Equally bothering though were the outright fabrications spun by sellers eager to offload their properties.

Now, don't get me wrong, when it came to selling our own place, we weren't holier-than-thou, happily withholding a few of our home's quirks. But nothing to the extent of the deception we encountered, which seemed practically endemic.

Here are just a couple of examples for you.

We had a standard set of questions for most house sellers. One query focused on any proposed planning in the area –

houses, roads, that sort of thing – and another on the general vibe of the neighbourhood. Naturally, we could always check out planning information ourselves, but these questions seemed like fair game during an initial chat with a seller. We hoped to gain a different perspective from what the local authority records might show us.

When it came to the neighbourhood, we were wholly reliant on the seller's honesty, keeping in mind their primary objective was to sell their house. That's life, and we believed we were prepared for it – or so we thought.

Regarding future development plans, we were reassured by a worm farmer in Cornwall – yes, I too was surprised such a vocation existed – along with the accompanying agent, that there were no known plans. They saw no reason why we wouldn't have an idyllic, quiet life in the old house – minus the worms, of course.

However, the truth we unearthed was rather different. A significant trunk road was being expanded and rerouted to come within a few hundred yards of the property. We were quite certain the owner had known about this development, especially since the property boundary was set to receive a new ten-foot-high noise-dampening fence, courtesy of the local authority as part of the construction project.

The other notable incident involved the neighbours of a house we were set to view. Had we not taken a leisurely stroll through the village beforehand and struck up a conversation with a local chap, we would have remained blissfully ignorant of the fact that the neighbours of the house we were about to inspect were avid car breakers. They dealt in selling scrap and second-hand car parts to all and sundry.

The gentleman we spoke to was gushingly complimentary about the service provided by this family – mum, dad, and their four industrious sons. He had recently procured a replacement starter motor for his old Rover Metro from them. Whether his tune would have changed had the scrappy clan been his next-door neighbours, we did not delve into.

When we posed our queries to both the homeowner and the estate agent, they simply shrugged, as though we were making an unnecessary fuss. This, despite the cacophony of disc cutting, hammering and the pervasive smell of old engine oil that saturated our conversation as we ambled through their so-called country garden.

I won't bore you with anymore.

In hindsight, it might have been one of the dullest dinner evenings our dear friends had ever endured. They had prepared a delightful meal and offered supreme company, while we responded with endless grumbles.

As the evening progressed and we settled into the warmth of their hospitality, Alan posed a question: had we ever considered moving to France – or more precisely, Brittany?

Given my preconceived notions of France, shaped by numerous disappointing holidays, I was quick to dismiss the idea. However, Alan explained that Brittany, much like Cornwall, didn't consider itself French. He pointed out that local schools still taught Breton as a language and shared many unique aspects of Brittany. My initial thoughts were that we had considered Cornwall and found it unwelcoming to outsiders. I struggled to see how Brittany would be any different. Nonetheless, overnight, we found ourselves reconsidering France, or rather Brittany, in a new light. Despite numerous glasses of wine, we stayed wide awake, mulling over the idea well into the early hours.

The next day, after a very English breakfast, Alan mentioned he had a neighbour's fallen tree to deal with, and Hélène had some errands to run, which we were invited to join. Instead, we opted to drive the short distance to the Blavet (pronounced Blavé) and take an extended walk along its banks. The Blavet, one of many wide rivers, now a canal, running throughout Brittany, had been transformed under Napoleon's orders to form part of an extensive network for transporting goods and people, due in part to the British blockade of their seaports. It's a beautiful and serene place to walk, with the only sound being, our feet on the gravel path, the breeze through the trees, birdsong, and the occasional fish breaking the surface of the gently flowing water. It was so serene that conversation was unnecessary. We just walked, hand in hand, with nothing more than each other and our own thoughts for company – perfect.

To top it all off, the sun made an appearance, and considering the time of year – early March – it was surprisingly warm. Just what we needed to clear our heads and further open up our minds to the prospect of a possible move to Brittany – but not France.

'It's a beautiful and serene place to walk...'

Saint-Gildas 15th Century chapel on the banks of the Blavet has been built into the rock.

***

We extended our stay at Alan and Hélène's for a few more days, during which we not only continued to flesh out what was rapidly becoming our plan B, but also took some time to explore a few Estate agents. To our surprise, we discovered that Estate agents, as we know them in England, were a relatively recent addition to France. Before the British influence on French house buying, one would typically search for properties for sale in the office of the local Notaire. We were soon to learn that the Notaire is the single point of contact for everything related to house buying in France – but I'll explain more about that later.

With Hélène happy to accompany us and Alan content to transform a fallen tree into perfectly sized logs for one of their many open fireplaces, we set out to visit one of the few Notaire's offices in Baud. Like many places and words in the French language – at least to us Brits – there's often little connection between how we perceive the word and how it's pronounced. Take the town of Baud, for instance; you might be forgiven for assuming it's pronounced like 'board' or 'bode'. But no, it's pronounced 'Bo'. I guess much like our own linguistic challenges for tourists (both domestic and foreign) such as Worcestershire, Bicester, Cholmondeley, and my personal favourite, Featherstonehaugh – I'll leave you to decipher that one.

Anyway, back to Baud, a reasonably sized town just a short drive from Alan and Hélène's place. While we were there, we managed to get the details of a few houses for sale in the local area. Or rather, Hélène asked for the details, and we stood a half-step back, as English dummies abroad tend to do, not daring to try out our primary school French for fear of appearing, well, 'dummies'. The reality is that while the French – and many other countries – might chuckle at our language struggles, they often appreciate us at least making an effort. But we are what we are, and so we opt instead to speak English louder and louder, perhaps because of some preconceived notion that loud English is more universally understood than normal volume English.

Despite my family's unwarranted confidence in my foreign language skills, thanks in no small part to our family holiday exploits where I was pushed forward as the multilingual expert, I was happy to leave this piece of business to our host. Back in the car, Hélène gave us a brief induction into the house-buying process in France, which we learned was considerably different from England. I won't go into all the details right now; you'll get all of that, and more, a little later on. But the key takeaway for me was that once you have an offer accepted on a house, you must, following a very short cooling-off period, stump up your ten percent (nonrefundable) deposit. This amount can sometimes be less, by negotiation, depending on the property's value. But in the price range we were looking at, it would most likely be the whole ten percent. If you decide not to proceed with the purchase after the cooling-off period, for whatever reason, your deposit is forfeit. Oh, and all fees associated with buying a house come out of the buyer's pocket.

As we sailed back home on the ferry, our conversations buzzed with excitement. We were now fully committed to the idea of a future in Brittany – not France. In just a few days, our original plan A had been tossed aside, and we found ourselves with a brand-new plan B – or maybe even D. I was having trouble keeping up. But the important thing was, we had a plan. Now we just needed to break the news to friends and family, and I needed to get back to work.

CLARE FLIES SOLO HOUSE HUNTING IN BRITTANY

Over the next few weeks, Alan and Hélène forwarded us several properties for sale. I got the distinct impression they were almost as excited as we were at the prospect of us moving to Brittany. With my limited availability due to work commitments, it largely fell to Clare to make the numerous house-hunting and viewing trips. And not being someone who enjoys sea travel at the best of times, doing it alone took immense courage on her part – and a lot of sick bags.

It was during this time that I was starting to have some doubts about the whole thing, or was it just cold feet? To be honest I wasn't sure. Looking back through my newly started, though barely populated, journal I found the following entry.

Journal entry from April 2014 – *Clare's away and I'm having some niggling doubts about this plan to up sticks and move to another country. She's looking for our dream house in Brittany and I'm here having second thoughts. Should I say something or just hope that these feelings are just a temporary cold feet thing? All I know is that if these feelings persist then I need to say something sooner rather than later. This could end up being the shortest adventure journal, ever.*

***

It was an incredibly tough time for us for a variety of reasons, but for me, it was more about those nagging doubts. Mostly driven, I think, by the prospect of leaving my home country – for which, to be honest, I had no ill will – so why was I leaving? I found myself constantly asking that question. Much later, Clare revealed to me that, on more than one of her many ferry crossings, it wouldn't be unusual for her to contemplate doubts along the lines of, "What the hell are we doing?" But she never let on, and I never picked up on it.

We now had a new norm to our lives.

I wasn't letting on to anyone at work about our plans and did what I thought was a decent job of delaying business trips, allowing my wife to continue with the Brittany house hunt. Back home, we still had a teenage daughter to water, feed, and generally take care of, ensuring her education wouldn't be disrupted by all our comings and goings. Another of our dependents, a small Border Terrier named Jack, was oblivious to all the upheaval until now. He hadn't yet made the trip to Brittany, but his time would come soon enough, and it became quite a frequent event for him – which he hated every single time. For now, though, he seemed content as long as his regular daily walks were provided, he got his regulation quantity of 'in-between meal' snacks, and he was allowed to sleep anywhere and everywhere. And of course, his main meal of the day was always on time. We would never say our Jack was spoiled, just indulged. As for our cat, Nettle, a small wiry tabby female, she had no care nor opinion on what we were doing such was her aloof nature. In the unlikely event that she had no food – because Jack had eaten it – she would simply go hunt something. Depositing any unwanted detritus on the floor for one of us to clear up. Other times she would hunt something, bring it into the house, still alive, and let it go. Possibly her way of telling us that we should think twice in future before we let the pesky dog eat her food. Our Nettle was very much the pintsized matriarch with a natural gift for scorn.

'Jack – ...never spoiled, just indulged.'

***

Despite my work commitments, I still managed to squeeze in one or two trips across the Channel, mostly during school half terms. It was always a delight to see my dear friends, Alan and Hélène. More importantly, I was able to lend some genuine support – and assuage my guilt – to this grand adventure by accompanying Clare on a few house viewings. This also provided us with some much needed quality time together, although the bulk of the house hunting was done without me.

Now, let me offer a bit of advice to any of you considering

a similar journey. You will undoubtedly face numerous logistical hurdles and quite a few unexpected twists. "Expect the unexpected" may be a cliché, but it's sound advice nonetheless. However, there are a couple of things you can always rely on: estate agents will invariably stretch the truth – or at the very least, obscure it – and the full English breakfast on a Brittany ferry is an absolute travesty.

***

Journal entry from May 2014 *– This is now her third solo visit and she's really getting into it. When we speak she is so animated, so positive, even when the houses she's visited aren't up to much. I'm pretty sure that if I was able to be there with her more often, then much of the guilt I'm feeling right now would just melt away. But I need to continue to divide my thinking time between work and not work. Which is a bit of a challenge because work is proper mad just now. I'm so busy and not sure how much longer I can put off another inevitable trip to Seattle. Thing is daughter and dog can't be left home alone. I've completely underestimated how difficult this was going to be – the plan to up sticks and retire I mean.*

There's no doubting that having Alan and Hélène there for us, with both their language and local knowledge, has been a real God send. Interestingly they seem equally as excited at the prospect of us moving to France, Brittany. To be honest I'm not so sure we could have pursued this hunt had we been left to our own devices. Especially with Clare having to do most of this on her own right now. Young'uns been good and getting herself up for school. She's even been cooking for us both (veggie of course). Most of which I've eaten.

I received another bunch of photos from her recent house hunting expeditions, but I know from the tone of her emails that none of the properties are particularly floating her boat. It appears that as much as you can buy an awful lot more for your money in Brittany compared to say, where we live now, we still seem to be financially just outside of that perfect property. Fingers crossed for next week and then she'll need to come home because I can't leave Maggie here on her own. A bit like old times this.

'I received another bunch of photos from her recent house hunting expeditions, but I know from the tone of her emails that none of the properties are particularly floating her boat...'

***

Journal entry from May 2014 – *A Phone call and an email in quick succession told me that she's found 'the' house. The Notaire (I'm still unclear as to what this bloke's role in all this is, but he seems to have his fingers in all the pieces of the pie) a Maître Gonon, suggested that she might want to go look at an old farmhouse which I'm told was way too expensive for our budget. She initially thought that he might be just showing her because he liked this particular property himself. But no, it turns out that it has been on the market for a considerable time and the family are keen to move it on. So, if we liked it enough to make an offer then he would be quite prepared to take that offer to the family. We had a long conversation on the phone because quite frankly having trawled through the many photographs she sent me, the place, including its numerous outbuildings, needs some serious investment. I don't know how much to be honest, but a lot.*

I've done some sums and considering that neither of us want to make a huge hole in our pension pots, the amount that we can realistically offer would be derisory by comparison to the asking price. Over here we'd been used to making cheeky offers on the many houses we've bought together but not to this extent, which is why I think I might tell her to leave it.

***

The whole property search and move to Brittany nearly ground to a halt at this juncture, thanks in no small part to my impeccable sense of fair play. As you've read from my journal, we'd made cheeky offers on houses in England and sometimes got away with it. But in my very English way of thinking, the amount we could afford was beyond cheeky – it was downright rude. However, you already know we persisted, leading to our eventual move to France. What you might not know – as we didn't at the time – is that cheeky offers are the norm in France. And it's not just limited to houses; it applies to anything up for sale.

Anyway, I suggested to Clare that she ought to leave it and move on to the next one. She politely acknowledged my request and then promptly ignored it.

***

Journal entry from May 2014 (mid-week entry) – *I wouldn't normally revisit this journal / diary call it what you like, until the weekend. It's now Wednesday and I've just come off the phone with Clare (she decided to stay on for another couple of days) with Alan & Hélène. And I just felt that I needed capture this moment. Mainly because the last time I felt this nervous I was waiting for my bride to be to show up at the registry office all those years ago. The current Mrs Templeman.*

They all agree that if we liked the house enough to want to own it then we have nothing to lose by putting in an offer, regardless. They have a point but after taking everything into account the amount we have left to offer was a little over half the asking price. And no matter how much we tried to rework the numbers we just couldn't squeeze anymore out, given the minimum amount that I'd calculated we'd have to spend on the place.

I've also learned a bit about who this Notaire is, and what his role is in all of this. Not only does his office, the Notary, act as an estate agency, selling properties and so on, but they also represent both parties from a legal perspective. So doing all the conveyancing, for both sides. Now I'm kind of getting why the fees are so high compared to England – upward of 10% of the value of the house plus one or two other disbursements. And all to be paid for by the buyer, us! Which of course is another hit on our budget.

With my concerns duly noted, or rather brushed over, Clare (with Hélène by her side) is going to speak with the

Notaire in the morning and make the offer.

I'm not building my hopes up to be honest, but good for her for having the nerve to do what I probably wouldn't have the nerve to do.

***

The offer was submitted, and we were left teetering on tenterhooks, waiting for a response. Honestly, we both expected a resounding "no." After all, if the roles were reversed, we would have kicked such an offer straight back across the Channel.

***

Journal entry from End of May 2014 – *Thursday evening and most of the way through a bottle of Spanish red – So much for doing this journal on a Sunday. I have to say that I struggled to concentrate on work these last couple of days waiting for the call, which I fully expect to be a disappointing one given how far away our offer was from the asking price. Despite the place – as understatements go – needing a good deal of TLC, I'm still left wondering how the family could consider dropping the price by nearly half for a house set in over an acre of what was previously a working pig farm complete with a barn, orchards, a hangar (for all the agricultural toys I'd need to have), and multiple other buildings? None of which I've ever owned before and, if I'm being perfectly honest, none of which I'm sure I'd know what I would use them for anyway. But let's wait and see how this plays out. As they say it'll be a nice problem to have.*

PART TWO

THE END OF THE BEGINNING

Twenty-four hours later and a response was received from the owner, together with an apology from the Notaire for the delay. Seemingly the whole family, as being the beneficiaries from the sale, needed to be consulted, and they were spread far and wide across France.

***

__Journal entry from End of May 2014__ – Friday, finished off the red wine from last night. Clare phoned this morning, to tell me, or rather squeal at me down the phone, that they have accepted our offer and if everything goes through smoothly we could be the proud owners of our own piece of Brittany by early summer, latest. All we have to do now is figure out the French buying process which I'll need to bone up on some more. Once again Alan and Hélène have been invaluable, not just in translating documents and acting as interpreters but also walking us through the whole process so far, which seems remarkably straightforward. Clare also went on to tell me that as much as our offer has been accepted the Notaire found it odd and was a bit uncomfortable, insofar as she (the wife) being his primary *point of contact. To the point where when we have to go across to do some initial signing and so on, I'm being expected to make an official visit to the house, with Maître Gonan in tow, and give the purchase my own (husbandly) green light. Could the French still be a tiny bit sexist?*

But I trust my wife implicitly and I'm now looking forward to seeing the house proper, and strangely enough those cold feet, the same ones I was talking about just a couple of weeks ago, have all but thawed. And indeed my guilt complex regarding the cheeky offer is now a distant memory. I'm genuinely excited and a bit nervous in equal measure. Even so I can't wait for Clare to get back tomorrow.

***

The answer to my own question above – Could the French still be a tiny bit sexist? – is a categoric YES! All documentation regarding the purchase of our house in Brittany referred to Clare as *Monsieur et Madam Colin TEMPLEMAN*. Or sometimes simply as *M. et Mme TEMPLEMAN Colin*. Every single document, including bills and formal correspondence, bore this curious nomenclature. One might think, in the 21st century, we'd have moved past these ancient quirks, but clearly not in France.

***

June 2014 arrived, and Clare was back home while I needed to be overseas for business. But not before a lightning visit to Brittany so I could see exactly what we were committing to buy. This short visit also put the Notaire's mind at rest, clearly happier that a man was now in the picture to take over proceedings. He had no idea of the tour de force that is my wife. Any assumed authority on my part in this transaction was a gross misunderstanding. As much as this whole process was a learning curve for us, our Maître Gonan was also in for an education regarding my wife, but he didn't know it yet.

On this particular trip, we embarked on the all important opening of our French bank account. This being a crucial financial basecamp from which we could transfer funds and make payments in this foreign land. We even had the foresight to include Hélène as a signatory, allowing her to command financial operations in our absence. With this strategic move, we were primed and ready for whatever lie ahead.

We were also still in the ten-day cooling-off period, a time of introspection and suspense. After this interlude, we would have to demonstrate our commitment to the purchase, by handing over a princely ten percent of the agreed price to the Notaire. As the days ticked by, my thoughts began to wander towards my grand exit strategy from the world of gainful employment – though it was to be a leisurely and prolonged departure. In doing so I naively imagined it would be straightforward. But if my time on this spinning rock has taught me anything, it is this: If something appears straightforward on paper, reality will inevitably conspire to prove otherwise. Life, after all, cannot be confined to mere paper.

Amid the countless tasks of purchasing and preparing for life in our new French haven, we also had our youngest daughter to think about. With roughly eighteen months of full-time schooling still ahead of her, thoughts of planning her transition to independence hadn't yet surfaced. As a result, it was clear that none of us would be settling in Brittany permanently anytime soon.

But what exactly had we committed to buying?

As it turned out, we were buying a house with the potential to be a gem amidst the French countryside. A broken barn standing stoically, bearing scars of past glories. A neglected orchard (*verger*) with a variety of, yet to be determined, fruit trees. Though I'm sure I could discern apple, pear, possibly plum, and a large walnut tree, waiting patiently for someone to care once more. Some equally neglected land, which once thrived and hopefully would flourish again under our ownership.

There was also an oak framed, corrugated sheet topped hangar, a garage, and numerous other smaller buildings, each with their own secrets and stories. In short, we were buying a treasure trove of possibilities, and while the path ahead was not fully mapped out, it promised an adventure worthy of any pioneers tale.

As for my first impressions? Beyond the veneer of neglect, it was clear this was once a cherished home. The faded remnants of flower beds, the rows of fruit trees – all in dire need of a good pruning. The strategically grown laurel hedge, three metres high, running the perimeter and serving as a natural weather screen for what was once a sizable allotment (*potager*). And which, given the chance, would be again. But more than anything, it was the calmness of the place. Waiting patiently, accepting its situation with no regrets or malice, just a graciousness that whispered, "I may be a bit run-down, but my promise is limitless." I completely understood it. There was no shame, no embarrassment, no false modesty or vanity. It was telling me that we could do as much or as little as we pleased. Because no matter what, it would still be our home.

The birdsong – none of which I recognised – the myriad trees, and the creak of the frail corrugated tin roof on the hangar. The same roof that had probably looked frail from the moment it was installed decades ago. Yet there it was, still, creaking defiantly in the breeze.

Later, I found myself standing by an old well, pondering the mysteries of what shape our lives will take hereon in.

I was transported back to those months before, when our plans were fluid, strolling along the Blavet, the peace and quiet allowing us to reflect on our future. But even that serenity didn't compare to this. The calm that enveloped me during that first visit touched my soul deeply. It was a feeling that, despite times of frustration, relentless hard work, and the storms that threatened our dreams, stayed with me throughout our time there. This, I knew, would become my special place. A landlocked island of tranquillity. And at that moment, more than anything, I wanted to be there. No, that's not quite right. At that moment, I wanted to be there, with the love of my life, Clare, more than anything.

Life had handed me a mystery wrapped in a challenge, which I hoped would be served up with a side of humour. And as with any good story, it was the journey, not the destination, that held the greatest appeal. So, with a grin, I stepped away from the well, ready to embrace the unknown, with the firm belief that the best tales are those yet untold.

'...we were buying a house with the potential to be a gem amidst the French countryside...'

'A broken barn standing stoically, bearing scars of past glories...'

'...a garage, and numerous other smaller buildings, each with its own secrets and stories.'

'A neglected orchard (*verger*) with apple, pear, plum, peach, and walnut trees, waiting patiently for someone to care once more.'

'The strategically grown laurel hedge, three metres high, running the perimeter and serving as a natural weather screen for what was once a sizable allotment (*potager*).'

'...the creak of the frail corrugated tin roof on the hangar.'

Waiting patiently, accepting its situation with no regrets or malice, just a graciousness that whispered, "I may be a bit run-down, but my promise is limitless."

'Later, I found myself standing by an old well, pondering the mysteries of what shape our lives will take hereon in.'

THE HOUSE PURCHASE ROLLS ON

What was originally assumed to be a quick and uncomplicated process revealed itself to be anything but. It was now getting towards the end of the summer – September, to be precise – and everything had gone eerily quiet with no real end in sight. It seems that buying a house in France is straightforward, as long as you're not purchasing what was once a working pig farm. The Notaire, in his infinite wisdom (and with a tone suggesting we ought to have known), informed us that he is required to put a notice of the impending sale out to the farming community. If a bona fide farmer wishes to, they can swoop in and claim the property at the same price as our offer.

In an attempt to put a positive spin on this minor oversight, he cheerfully advised that if no one comes forward within twelve weeks, we can proceed. And, as if to add a trace of suspense to our lives, he mentioned that the notice had been out for quite a few weeks already – although he conveniently omitted when "quite a few weeks" actually began. As yet, no one had come forward. The only thing missing from his letter was a patronising smiley or thumbs up emoji.

However, although we were on tenterhooks and keeping our fingers crossed, we remained positive and decided to get on with our lives back in England. Clare, undeterred by the looming uncertainty, busied herself with grand plans for kitchen layouts, bathrooms, and numerous other improvements. Whenever time allowed, I found myself being carted off to all manner of showrooms to gather ideas for when we found ourselves in a position to buy. I attempted to explain that France likely had similar establishments, but Clare was having none of it. Thus, I could see us becoming one of those couples who arrive at the ferry port with vans and trailers loaded to the brim with building materials. As if France were some remote outpost where you couldn't procure wood, paint, or any other such necessities.

Meanwhile, I made a valiant effort to appear engaged in the mundane business-as-usual tasks. The allure of our future French home and the impending adventure had me daydreaming far too often. Every trip to a showroom, every discussion about tiles and fixtures, and even the routine workday were all just stepping stones toward our grand plan becoming a reality.

***

***Journal entry from September 2014** – I've bought a trailer. Never had one before. It's another one of those things that blokes are supposed to have a natural aptitude for. I've often wondered why it is that when we become husbands and fathers, we're expected to magically adopt a whole range of skills that we'd previously had no experience of. Professionally carving a Sunday joint, mending toys, all the trades – plumbing, electrics, woodwork etc – barbequing, putting up a tent, ability to speak the local language when on holiday (no matter what the country) and a whole lot of other stuff. And now I can add trailering to my repertoire. Consequently, with a confidence that I had no right to have, I went to the trailer shop and bought myself what I thought to be an adequately sized one. "Will it be big enough?" Clare asked as we drove it home. I had no idea, but it'll have to do. Keeping my thoughts to myself.*

Such was my low level of confidence in how to manoeuvre this new addition onto our drive, I let Clare get out of the car to go into the house, telling her that I just needed to do some last-minute checks before reversing. I'm pretty sure she never believed a word of it.

To start with, the idea of turning the steering wheel in one direction in order to get the trailer to turn in the other just didn't compute. It defied logic. But then it somehow worked because after multiple attempts, going back and forth on the drive I managed to get the darned thing pretty much where I wanted it. But not necessarily at the angle I wanted it.

Note to self: Make sure you don't put yourself in any situation where you're going to have to reverse the trailer – in public. And avoid tight spots. The Defender has the turning circle of an oil tanker so how it'll be with a loaded trailer on the back lord only knows. Off next week to get a roof rack fitted. Should be alright with that.

***

The trailer wasn't as grand as some of the behemoths I had seen at the ferry port, but it was a modest size and more than capable of meeting our anticipated needs. However, I immediately regretted my purchase when, fully hitched and loaded to the back of our Land Rover, it received no attention whatsoever from the other trailer owners at the ferry port, all waiting to board. Unlike many of the others being fawned over.

Small groups would gather around various trailers, discussing the finer points of jockey wheels, twin axles, and drop sides, with special reverence for anyone fortunate enough to own a 'tipping' trailer. Trailer envy wasn't something I had considered before, but it was clearly alive and well. My six by four, despite having drop sides, was woefully lacking in envy.

There I stood, beside my humble trailer, feeling like the poor cousin at a family gathering. The conversations around me were akin to secret societies, each trailer owner with their own code and jargon. And there I was, on the outskirts, with my modest sized trailer, which no one seemed to notice or was keen to admire.

It was a moment of both amusement and introspection,

realising that even in the world of trailers, there was a hierarchy, and my place in it was decidedly at the bottom. But no matter, for this little trailer was ours – trailer envy be damned!

***

Other items that would find their way onto my growing list of 'must-haves' included a small tractor with multiple accessories, a chainsaw (despite its feminine designation in French), and a sit-on lawnmower. Oh, and a log splitter. With wood being taken so seriously in Brittany – possibly more important than learning the language, having children, and breathing – there was no way I was going to be considered the English dummy abroad. Though how to use any of this kit was a question for another day.

Now, circling back to wood for a moment because it truly is serious business in Brittany. Wood was more than just a currency – a fallen tree was like striking gold. The number of logs you owned was a badge of affluence and masculinity, proudly displayed for all to see. This is why you often see carefully and precisely erected wood stacks, purposefully placed and visible from the roadside. There is pride and a particular art in stacking wood, and it was something I needed to learn quickly and do well.

During those early days, Alan was on hand to share his knowledge, and he did so willingly and enthusiastically by allowing me to split and stack a winters worth of timber. His reward was the many wood stacks erected on his land – in public view, of course – by yours truly.

Although the house sale was stalled, we still made the occasional trip to Alan and Hélène's for long weekends, that sort of thing. This meant that we quickly became regular travellers on Brittany Ferries, privy to all the antics of Brits sailing abroad.

One particularly amusing observation involved the

curious habit of some travellers who felt the need to put their hazard warning lights on as they joined the queue to board the ferry. It seemed to be a contagious phenomenon, but only among men of a certain age – let's be honest, old! Despite making numerous trips across the Channel, I could discern no actual requirement for this hazard warning light ritual. The only exception might be if it were particularly foggy at the port, but that was a rarity. Nonetheless, these elderly gents took it upon themselves to lead this peculiar charge, and inexplicably, others followed suit.

Furthermore, there are others who appear utterly flabbergasted by the audacity of the check-in booth attendant, daring to ask for their tickets and passports. Many a time, we found ourselves behind a car where the driver or passenger had to leap out and rummage through some bag or other stowed away in the boot.

You could almost see the driver's frantic scramble, accompanied by muttered exclamations of "Where on earth did I put that blasted ticket?" Meanwhile, the check-in attendant would wait patiently, often with a bemused smile, as the search continued.

But the most amusing of them all, by far, are the caravan owners. They roll up at the ferry port towing their portable holiday homes, many of which seem to weigh more than the cars pulling them. Unlike cars, they require no MOT or other legal tests to prove their roadworthiness. Yet out they come, stirred from their winter storage – often someone's driveway – and hooked up to be dragged behind a car for goodness knows how many miles through France and often beyond.

On one occasion, we witnessed a particularly clever sod in a large 4x4 towing what could only be described as a six-berth bungalow. Upon arriving at the port, he decided that queuing was for lesser mortals and drove past the line of fellow caravan enthusiasts into an empty check-in lane, oblivious to why it might be empty.

Regrettably, two problems arose from this act of insolence and bravado. Firstly, there was no one in the booth to check him in. And secondly, the lane he had so confidently chosen was a restricted height lane – hence the absence of other caravans. Yet this minor detail didn't deter our antihero from fuming at the world, as if the port authorities had neglected to provide special dispensation for this moron with a caravan. The result? He had to reverse his car and caravan out of the predicament, rejoining the now longer queue.

Typically, no one made eye contact with this buffoon. And being quintessentially English, the most we could muster in acknowledgment of his show of buffoonery was a shake of the head. Although I do recall that I actually tutted.

Back at the embarkation area, the caravan owners gather like participants in a grand parade, and if trailer envy was a contagion, then caravan envy is an outright epidemic. But with an added twist: a collective disdain for anyone driving a motorhome. This curious camaraderie among caravan owners is tinged with a hint of discrimination, as if motorhome drivers had committed some unspoken faux pas.

When it's time to board the ferry, on go the (not so) mandatory hazard lights. The caravan enthusiasts bid their club members a safe journey, exchanging knowing nods and waves, before driving up the ramp to join the pandemonium that is the herding of these mobile houses by the car deck crews.

Onboard the ferry, it would normally be breakfast time, so we, along with most others, would head to the galley. There are a couple of noteworthy observations here. First, and as previously mentioned, the French simply cannot cook an English breakfast to save their lives. It's as if they missed the memo on what constitutes a proper fry-up.

Second, more often than not, the English – typically the

older sorts again – steadfastly refuse to attempt speaking French. Even a polite "Bonjour" seems to be too much trouble for these closet colonials. They march up to the counter with an air of entitlement, as if expecting the world to accommodate their linguistic preferences.

Being hungry, and not quite understanding the allure of croissants, I would always order a full English breakfast – despite the chef's lack of ability – or as the French say, *"Petit déjeuner anglais."* One of the first things I insisted on learning with our French tutor – more about her delightful lessons later – was how to order a full English breakfast, but without tomatoes. I simply don't like fried tomatoes. So, my carefully practiced line was, *"Bonjour, Je voudrais un petit-déjeuner anglais, sans tomates."*

Despite my meticulous pronunciation and varying speeds of delivery, I always ended up with tomatoes on my plate.

As for the house purchase, it rolled on – or rather it didn't – much like the summer, slipping away with little progress. Consequently, my journal entries became fewer and far between. Not that I could ever claim to be a committed writer.

***

Journal entry from September 2014 – *Got back from Hong Kong yesterday so a bit lagged if I'm honest. While I've been away I haven't managed to keep up to date with this journal, although there hasn't been much to write home about. Clare has kept me abreast of what's going on in France. Which quite honestly isn't much at all.*

We've now told friends and family of our plans and will tell them more once there's something concrete to share. We got a mixed reaction. Ranging from, "I thought you hated France", to "now we've got somewhere new to go on holiday". We're still hopeful of getting the keys soon.

***

Imagine, if you will, being promised something you're then not allowed to have. Picture yourself sitting at a birthday party tea table, but being forbidden to tuck in – for months. Or being handed a tantalising Christmas present which you're not allowed to open. You get the point, I'm sure, but that's exactly how it was for us. The tantalising promise of our French home dangled before us like a forbidden fruit, always just out of reach.

It is said that all good things come to those who wait, but all we wanted was for the actual 'waiting time' to be a bit more specific. Instead, we were left in a perpetual state of suspense, each day stretching into the next with no end in sight. Our dreams of a tranquil life in Brittany were indefinitely deferred, hanging in limbo like some grand joke at our expense.

***

Journal entry from October 2014 – *It's been a few weeks since the last entry and reading back, I see that I was still hopeful of getting the keys to our place in Brittany, by the end of summer. Since the initial flush of excitement and activity it has all come to a grinding halt. Although we haven't been sitting on our thumbs because we've been over once or twice and I got to meet and shake the hand of the Notaire again. Once again I felt that this small deed on my part gave him some level of assurance that I wasn't leaving this entire business transaction in the hands of a woman! The good news is that he has received no offers for the house from the farming community meaning that he should be able to start to draw up the contracts imminently. Though imminently seems to have a different meaning in France than I've been used to back here in England. Remaining positive though: this means that Clare, already chomping at the bit, is somewhat closer to being able to go on a spending spree for kitchens, bathrooms and all manner of the other things, that a 3ʳᵈ world country such as France will be unable to provide for us.*

In the meantime, we've been discussing the obvious and impending language issue. And agreed that we can hardly continue to rely on Alan and Hélène when we're actually living there. It seems that shouting loud, and gesticulating will only get us so far. I reminded Clare how I seemed to have done alright in our hour of need during our French holidays, who, when it came to interacting with the locals, she and the rest of our family took a huge step back,. But she's right when she says "où sont les toilettes" will only get us so far. She's going off to seek out a proper French tutor, one that can come to our house.

***

It's a funny thing, you know, how the Brits can be quite dismissive of other people's languages. I recall a chap who worked for me briefly, having lived in Bordeaux for several years. Initially, I thought having a Brit resident in France would be perfect for liaising with local French building services providers. That was the plan, anyway. However, it turned out he spoke little, if any, French and had no intention of learning. Apparently, this is quite common.

Alan and Hélène often regaled us with tales of immigrant enclaves where groups of Brits gather for coffee and resolutely speak only English. But worse still, they demand that the local French people do the same! As if assimilation into their adopted country were a task for everyone else but them.

This rather unfortunate trait was something we, too, observed amongst the English abroad. During our time in France, we often encountered English immigrants and holidaymakers, predominantly of the baby boomer generation, who insisted on ordering food and conducting their affairs entirely in English. Some would even become irate when the waiting staff failed to understand their requests.

Ironically, these same individuals would likely be the first to complain back in England about immigrants who don't speak the language. You've probably heard the refrain as often as I have: "If they can't speak the language, they shouldn't be living here," or words to that effect.

Beyond my natural annoyance, I can't help but find it an amusing contradiction in the outlook of British expats (or immigrants) on life in their adopted country. Their linguistic stubbornness feels like a genuine quirk of human nature, one I've noticed wherever I've been, leading me to conclude that, no matter where you are, some things remain delightfully and absurdly consistent.

Determined not to be English dummies abroad, Clare and I took action. Clare put out feelers for a French tutor, hopefully one who could come to our house and spare us the embarrassment of butchering the French language in public. Meanwhile, we both signed up for an online app, which was a boon for me as I could practice on the move or while holed up in a hotel room.

***

Journal entry from October 2014 — *Still no sign of any keys and we're now getting towards the end of October. But the good news is that we have had final confirmation that no French farmer wanted the house. I'm not sure whether I should be pleased about that or not because I can't help thinking that if it is the bargain we think it is then why wasn't it snapped up? The other thing that occurred to us is that having paid our 10% deposit, if someone were to have come along from the farming community, would we have got it back? Alan and Hélène were unsure, although did their best to put our minds at rest. As for Maître Gonan, he was silent on the matter.*

***

Our French lessons had become a delightful fixture in our weekly routine. Every week, our French tutor, Judy, would arrive at our place, armed with endless patience and a cheerful demeanour, ready to teach two linguistically challenged Brits the art of speaking French.

For reasons unknown, I had developed this habit of slipping back into English with a French accent whenever I encountered a word or phrase I didn't know. One memorable session involved a bit of restaurant role play. I was supposed to ask, in perfect French, "Can I have a table for four people, please?" Ideally, this would have come out as, *"Puis-je avoir une table pour quatre personnes, s'il vous plaît?"* However, in my finest Franglais, I proudly said, *"Puis-je avoir a table for four people, s'il vous plaît?"* This, of course, sent us all into fits of laughter.

And don't get me started on nouns. The whole concept seemed to elude me entirely. I wasn't sure I'd ever graduate beyond Level 1 – English Dummy, but I was determined to persevere.

Judy's patience was truly commendable, though I began to suspect she continued our lessons more for the sheer entertainment value than any real hope of progress. Nevertheless, we soldiered on, each lesson peppered with humour and a fair share of misadventures, all part of our grand journey into the French language.

We finally received the call we'd been waiting for.

PART THREE

CLEAR FOR TAKE-OFF

After enduring what felt like an eternity, far surpassing the obligatory twelve weeks, it seemed as though we could finally move forward. Whether this would lead to completion or yet another hurdle remained to be seen. But our levels of expectation and excitement were at an all-time high. In no time at all, the ferry was booked for us to make the trip to the Notaire's office and sign on various dotted lines.

Picture us, brimming with excitement, clutching our ferry tickets – despite them being E-tickets – as if they were golden tickets to Willy Wonka's factory. The sense of relief and anticipation was palpable, and even the usual chaos of the ferry crossing seemed to take on a more magical quality.

Our minds raced with thoughts of the final steps, the signing of documents, and the realisation that this adventure might finally be entering its next chapter. With a touch of irony and a healthy dose of optimism, we embraced the journey ahead, ready to face whatever bureaucratic antics awaited us at the Notaire's office. After all, what's an adventure without a few twists and turns?

***

Whilst all of this was going on, our family remained surprisingly mute, even the kids. Despite us drip-feeding them information – strictly on a need-to-know basis, mind you – as things started to unfold, they (the kids) remained relatively unopinionated, which is rare for them.

Growing up, and virtually from the time they could talk, they found it easy (and necessary) to give us advice on pretty much everything and anything. As they got older, their day-to-day opinions extended to include what we were wearing, eating, drinking – particularly our alcohol intake – our political views (which were always contrary to theirs), and even what time we chose to go to bed.

Another thing I discovered as we got older – by older, I mean in our forties – was that sex was something we were no longer permitted to do. According to our kids, parents 'doing it' is disgusting.

But as far as the Brittany adventure was concerned, two of our three offspring were relatively detached from the whole affair, having flown the nest and set up their own lives elsewhere. When we sought their thoughts on our grand plans and progress, we were met with a patronising thumbs-up emoji from one and a nonchalant shrug from the other. It was as if they were saying, "Go ahead, ruin your lives if you must, but count us out."

The detached reactions of our children, their casual indifference to our grand adventure, and the subtle implication that we were embarking on a fool's errand are all testament to the quirks of our family dynamic. A gentle reminder that, no matter how grand we thought our plans, we needed to accept that the younger generation would often view them with a mix of bemusement and detachment.

As for our stay-at-home youngest, we became increasingly nervous about her continued apathy towards the move to Brittany. For the first time ever, we actually wanted her to explode, take a door off its hinges, call us both selfish, or at the very least, hate us. Anything to give us a clue as to how she felt. But there was nothing.

Unbeknown to us, her silence was not born out of indifference but rather from a cunning plan she was formulating, one that would reveal itself in due time.

Either way, the thought of us moving to Brittany didn't seem to excite the kids as much as it did us. Despite our youngest secretly hatching her own plan, we still believed that the actual move couldn't happen until she had finished her schooling.

To add to the chaos, we were informed that the inconsiderate owners of our rental wanted their house back. So, while trying to secure our dream home in Brittany, we also had to start searching for another temporary home in England.

So there we were, juggling the excitement of our impending adventure with the practicalities of finding a new rental, all the while navigating the indifferent reactions of our children.

But on this occasion, we decided to seize the opportunity and look for a place closer to the school, so our little angel wouldn't have to rely on us for rides every day. By a stroke of luck, we found a rental just outside the picturesque village of Iwerne Minster – bet you can't pronounce that one correctly either – which happened to share the same postcode as her school. From our garden, we could just make out the spire of the school chapel. So, no more school runs. Or at least, that was the plan.

As it turned out, throughout her remaining time at the school, our daughter walked there and back on exactly zero occasions. Each morning and each evening, one of us would make the three minute journey in the car to either drop her off or collect her. Insisting otherwise would risk an evening of door slamming – or worse. So, for the sake of a pint of petrol a month, a peaceful life, and not having to make regular repairs to the paintwork on door frames, we were happy to oblige.

Once or twice, we suggested that a walk to or from school could coincide with a dog walk. Jack, our border terrier, was beloved by us all, but none more so than our youngest daughter. A prime example of this was her attitude towards her brother Sam compared to Jack. If her brother even dared suggest that she share a plate or cup with him, she'd have none of it. Yet if she had an ice cream, she had no problem with Jack licking one side of the cone while she licked the other.

As it turned out, our dog walk suggestion wasn't met with an outright no, but rather a compromise. And so, on more than one occasion, I found myself chauffeuring both of them – our daughter in the backseat with her arms around Jack – as I drove the three minute journey to the school drop-off point.

The three minute chauffeur service, Maggie's doting affection for Jack, and her delightful resistance to walking to school still make me smile.

***

Journal entry from November 2014 – *We're in France staying with Alan and Hélène. Here to do some initial signing of documents and go through the contracts. The crossing was quite rough, which I'm not too fussed about, but Clare doesn't do rough (or smooth) ferry crossings very well. Always good to see my old friends though and looking forward to somehow repaying them one day for their help, which has been invaluable.*

***

Journal entry from November 2014 – *Well that was an experience. So there we were, Hélène, Clare and me, in the Notaire's office. Sitting in the same room, but at a polite distance from quite a few of the family members who we are buying the house from. In the middle, sitting behind a really grand desk was Maître Gonan. For the next hour or so we went through every page of the contract and at each turn he'd look to us to agree that we were happy, then we'd have to stand, walk to his desk and initial said page. It was quite a sombre affair until that is Maître Gonan noticed the name of the town we were living in – Mere. Which in French means mother. So according to him we live in mother. At least it gave the other lot a laugh, albeit for just a short while. I didn't like to tell him that we no longer lived in Mere for fear of it tilting things. Plus explaining that Iwerne Minster is pronounced yewwern Minster was something I wasn't prepared to get into.*

With neither of us having little or no idea as to what was being said, Hélène translated as best she could. And with each page giving rise to a mumbled discussion within the group across the room from us, the time really dragged. These discussions within the other party were concluded by a unanimous nod of heads. At which point their nominated signer would stand, walk to the desk and do the deed. As the house was to be in both our names, both me and Clare had to repeat the same action from our side of the room. Goodness knows how many steps we'd done by the time we got out of there, but I was left wondering why the chairs couldn't have been a bit closer to the desk.

Unfortunately we didn't quite make it to the end of the contract because it seems as though there's some discrepancy or other with the boundary. Looks like our soon to be farmer neighbour has moved a marker pole in his favour. In other words stealing a bit of land. Not unusual by all accounts.

Looks like the family have to pay some money to get a surveyor to visit the house and then have the plans redrawn, which they weren't happy about.

Even with my limited French I was able to pick up on that.

They also had a moan, although not sure as to the extent of it, because they're going to have to pay inheritance tax which is quite severe in France by all accounts. We're assured that the discrepancy won't take too long to sort out and the next time we see one another, again all in the same room, it will be to complete the deal and collect keys.

At least we had some time for another walk around our soon to be purchase without the Notaire in attendance. I have to say that the amount of work to be done is quite overwhelming. And not just in the house but everywhere. The rose-tinted glasses have well and truly slipped. But I'm still smiling because I've finally managed to convince Clare that I'm definitely going to need that tractor I've been talking about (constantly), with attachments, yet to be determined and a sit on lawn mower. Alan's also backed me up for the need for a chainsaw – definitely his spare one, for just a few Euros. As he once more felt it necessary to tell me how wood is like currency in Brittany and a man is measured by not only the size of his woodpile but how well it has been put together. He's told me the same thing a few times now, in case I'd forgotten I guess. Though apparently there's a specific architecture, which he was keen to point out to me on our journey back to theirs. I really never realised before now. To me they were piles of neatly stacked logs. Seems as though I have some learning to do.

The subject of the septic tank, or fosse septique as it's called here, came up again yesterday evening. It was mentioned in passing a few weeks ago but it went over my head. It was the €10,000 that grabbed my attention over dinner. Hélène has done some digging and it would seem that if our existing one is over so many years old then we need to have a completely new installation. I have a bad feeling about this, despite Hélène telling us that she read somewhere that grants are available in special circumstances. In the past my luck or personal situation has rarely qualified me for any special help or handout. So I won't hold my breath. But we nonetheless had plenty to celebrate and remain hopeful of getting the keys to our new adventure before Christmas.

Nothing more to say for now as I look out from the back of the ferry from St Malo watching the sun slowly sinking to our right. Clare's down in the cabin probably trying her utmost not to be sick.

***

Journal entry from November 2014 – *The big news is that we're now all good to go. The plans have been redrawn which we've seen and agreed that we're happy with. So we emptied our English savings account and transferred it all into our new French account. At some point we have to then transfer the money for the house to the Notaire who sits on it for a few days before completion. So back to France next week for the official handover of the keys (I hope). What all of this means is that I need to find some time to go hunt down a tractor. Not a big one just one that I can attach a topper to, a bucket and small plough. 'Topper' – hark at me. I didn't even know what that was until a few weeks ago. As for a chainsaw me and Alan have done a deal for his spare. In the meantime I need to buckle down to work because I have feeling that I'm going to need to get some money behind us.*

***

It took roughly two weeks to sort out the boundary issues. Once it was resolved, we found ourselves back on the ferry once more. My usual refrain of *"Bonjour, Je voudrais un petit-déjeuner anglais, sans tomates"* was met with the same result as previous journeys – tomatoes on my plate. It seemed that my endless battle against unwanted tomatoes was set to continue.

Meanwhile, Clare was tucked away in the cabin, dealing with her queasy stomach in preparation for the day's adventure. The familiar routine of ferry crossings had become a staple of our lives. For how much longer though? That was the question.

IT'S ALL OURS

A monumental day for us. After so much waiting our day had come – or maybe it's our time that has come?

***

Journal entry from November 21st, 2014 – We are the proud owners of our very own Bretagne money pit in the very small hamlet of Saint-Barthélémy. And we were like jabbering kids having spent all of our money on a really big broken toy that we nonetheless love. We're brimming with confidence that we can and will make this neglected property beautiful once again. Our own magic cottage. Alan and Hélène left us to have the moment together and we agreed to meet up later in the day. This is a moment that I know will live with me forever. I am genuinely happy, and for the first time in what seems like a lifetime I haven't given any thought to work. Although I need to because this place is going to need all the financial help we can give it – and some.

Clare making a welcome speech of sorts to an audience of one – me.

***

Journal entry – Continuing our Day 1. *Capturing this moment as we're both sitting in one each of those cheap fold up fishing chairs. We picked them up years ago at the pound shop for a tenner – not sure how that works. I dragged an old board table I'd found, out from the barn, which I need to add to my list of things to repair.*

Anyway here we are eating bread and cheese and ham in the very late autumn sunshine. Our first lunch in our new old house. There's still a bit of warmth in the sun as we sit in silence with the long grass around our ears and it's deafening. My wife is a notorious chatterbox but not today. This is undoubtedly a special moment and whatever the future throws at us we will always have this memory to look back on. Spent some time with Alan and Hélène making a list of the big-ticket items as we saw them. I'm sure there are plenty of others that we can't see yet. Oh and another milestone. We used the toilet.

Our first use of the toilet revealed that the existing fosse septique is full. As our doings came back at us. Alans rigorous plunging did have some effect in moving stuff down the pan but then we saw a steady stream of water coming out of the ground to the side of the house. Add that to the list.

The light is going now, as is the battery on my laptop, so we need to head back to Alan and Hélène's. We won't be sleeping in our own house for a while yet. But what an afternoon we've had. We've even met some of our soon to be neighbours. There was Beryl who as the name suggests is as English as we are – I've a feeling that we're going to see a lot of her. She in turn introduced us to our immediate next-door neighbour – Bertrand and his wife, whose name I instantly forgot. Beryl can obviously speak decent French having told us she's been here for a few years. But amusingly she speaks the words with a Kent / London accent. Not sure which but most definitely not like a native. As for Bertrand he seemed none too pleased to have English both sides of his place, deduced by the grunt – which is the same sound in French as it is English. When we were introduced he asked me if I spoke Breton.

Our meeting resulted in my first and probably not my last language cock up. Note to self: Need to remember that Clare is my wife not my husband as I have just told Bertrand.

***

'...cheap fold up fishing chairs. We picked them up years ago at the pound shop for a tenner – not sure how that works. ...I dragged an old board table, that I'd found, out from the barn...'

***

In describing times like those, I often wish my writing could capture the eloquence and vivid imagery of *Laurie Lee*. If you've read *'Cider with Rosie,'* you'll know the kind of poetic charm and nostalgic warmth I'm aiming for.

Over time, our relationship with our neighbour Bertrand did soften, and although we never became friends, he was always cordial when we met. In fact, he spoke to us far more genially than he did to his own wife – whose name, regrettably, I still can't remember. For the sake of this tale, let's call her Marie. She was a pleasant enough lady, short and sturdy, much like a pit pony, with a face that perpetually seemed to be trying to spit out a wasp.

Bertrand, on the other hand, was a man who clearly had no time for elegance. He dressed and sounded as inelegant as anyone I had ever met. His farmhand style, practical clothing served no other purpose than to cover his body, giving no clue as to his actual shape. Atop this ensemble was a sizably round, balding head, adorned with a weather beaten face that bore the marks of a thousand rugby scrums. From this face, a cigarette perpetually protruded, defying gravity and common-sense.

His asymmetrical gait gave him the look of someone forever on the brink of falling down, yet somehow never quite managing it. Bertrand was a character, to say the least, and our interactions with him, while not exactly warm, were always memorable.

It was quite usual to hear Bertrand calling out for Marie. Whether she purposefully ignored his numerous summonses or not, she never responded to his first call. His initial call would be in a conversational tone, growing progressively louder as he received no response. This predictably culminated in him nearly bent double, coughing up at least one lung, whilst still trying to get her attention. Then, as if by magic, she would appear, admonish Bertrand for shouting, and promptly walk away again. This seemed to be their routine – him shouting, her ignoring, until he was at death's door. Yet, watching them together, you'd quickly realise how much they cared for one another.

But on the day of our introduction, Bertrand's manner was anything but sweet. The first thing he asked me was whether I spoke Breton – not French, mind you, but the local language. Of course, I didn't, so that was that. Conversation over before it had a chance to begin. Beryl explained that he was an obstreperous old bugger, but assured us he'd come around eventually. She advised us never to attempt speaking English with him, as he would refuse. However, he might deign to speak French from time to time.

Later that day, I encountered Bertrand again, and let's just say it didn't go much better.

With a few French lessons under our belt, I was now confidently able to order my breakfast on the ferry – albeit still served with tomatoes. Feeling quite self-assured, I decided to introduce him to my wife. I took a deep breath and, with all the confidence of a newly minted linguist, said, *"Puis-je vous présenter mon mari."* Bertrand shook his head, turned, and walked away.

It was at this point that Clare tapped me on the shoulder and gently informed me that I had just introduced her to Bertrand as 'my husband'.

My enthusiastic yet misguided attempt at French, Bertrand's bemused reaction, and Clare's amused correction are all examples of how even the best intentions can go awry, which they often did – read on.

***

As for Beryl, she became someone with whom we had quite a bit of interaction. Not quite a friend, but a good neighbour nonetheless. A rotund lady in her seventies with a pleasant demeanour, she lived alone in a small house just down the lane from ours. She often mentioned her former partner, Patrick (at least I think that was his name), who had decided to move out soon after they arrived in Brittany years ago. Oddly enough, he was ever-present at her house, doing odd jobs and staying for meals, that sort of thing.

Speaking of meals, Beryl prided herself on being a convivial host, which she certainly was. Clare and I enjoyed her company and conversation on many occasions – though not necessarily her cooking. After a cordial evening otherwise spoiled by the cuisine, Clare and I would often lay in bed, marvelling at how someone could have such a natural talent for making ingredients utterly unrecognisable from their original form. These conversations often went well into the small hours, less due to the subject matter and more because our bodies needed time to come to terms with what we'd been subjected to. Digestive distress on a scale that neither of us had experienced before.

***

As I strolled through the grounds of our newly acquired property, with dew drenched grass soaking my feet and everything up to my waist, I found myself grinning like a Cheshire cat. My wife had made a brilliant choice, and I felt incredibly fortunate on so many levels. On that day, it seemed as if all my Christmases had come at once. "So this is what perfection looks like," I mused. And I wasn't just referring to the house and everything that came with it – those details could wait. It was the sense of belonging that truly resonated with me, and I most definitely felt like I belonged there.

But, like all Christmases, they end far too soon. You spend months planning for them, and the time leading up to the big day, especially when you're a kid, seems to drag on interminably. Then the day itself whizzes by in a blur of excitement, and before you know it, you're waking up on

Boxing Day. Our Christmas day had come to an abrupt end as we locked the place up, said our farewells – not before handing a set of keys to Alan and Hélène – and setting off for St. Malo that very evening, to catch the ferry back to Portsmouth.

I distinctly remember the silence that enveloped us both in the car and onboard the ferry – thank goodness it was an overnight sailing. Conversation felt unnecessary, as we were both likely experiencing a sense of coming down from the incredible high of the past couple of days. After all the anticipation of acquiring our house, which officially marked the beginning of our new adventure, it felt as though it was being snatched away from us once more, or at the very least, put on hold. But we knew we would be back in the new year, ready to embark on our grand adventure afresh.

'On that day, it seemed as if all my Christmases had come at once. "So this is what perfection looks like," ...'

PART FOUR

A Balancing act

The following year, 2015, was a year full of competing priorities. Our new adventure took up most of our thinking time, which was expected. But then there was my work – something that ended up requiring more time than we initially planned, mainly because of the number of major projects (on our new home) needing significant funding. Add to that our daughter's ongoing education and the everyday demands of life.

If the logistics we faced during the buying process were challenging, then turning a house in Brittany into a liveable space, while still living and working from England, was even more complex. I also became quite lax in keeping my journal up to date. I was so engrossed in everything else that I didn't write as often as I should have, and I'm annoyed at myself for that. While my memories of these times are still quite vivid, I do wish I had documented them better.

Anyway, enough of the introspection – here's what happened next.

The year was a curious blend of brief and lengthy sojourns to our house, juggling all the previously mentioned priorities.

These visits generally left us utterly knackered, as each one involved rolling up our sleeves and diving into hard graft from dawn till dusk. But in no time, we found ourselves falling into a routine that felt almost normal.

We were always eager to arrive and invariably saddened when it was time to depart.

On the more extended visits, we took Jack – arguably my best mate. This, of course, introduced its own set of challenges. Jack had to undergo injections, worming medication, and carry all the necessary documentation to prove he was fit as a fiddle, or rather, fit as a dog with two tails. Ensuring he wouldn't either catch or spread anything among his fellow creatures while we were there.

Then there was the small matter of his travel anxiety. Jack loathed car journeys, panting every mile of the way and stubbornly refusing any offers of water. The sole exception was our seaside excursions. On these rare occasions, he would attempt to drink the entire English Channel, only to promptly throw it all up, along with whatever else he'd recently ingested.

As you might imagine, trips involving a car, a ferry, and then a car again, were less than idyllic. By the time we finally rolled into Saint-Barthélémy, Jack was more than ready for a long drink of water and an even longer nap under one of the many shady trees.

'By the time we finally rolled into Saint-Barthélémy, Jack was more than ready for a long drink of water and an even longer nap under one of the many shady trees.'

***

Before I move on, it struck me that while you've been introduced to our friends, our dog, and us, the offspring have yet to take their bows. So, let's have a drumroll for our eldest, Jamie Ann. Her affection for all things Peter Pan, an insatiable appetite for books (which puts even the most industrious librarian to shame), and like me, able to find hilarity in life's quirks – though, regrettably, not in her father's well-intentioned but frequently ill-fated jokes – have made her company an absolute delight. Where every moment is punctuated by a chuckle at some shared joke, often undecipherable by casual bystanders.

Next in the lineup, often feeling the squeeze of being the middle child, is our son Sam, the sharpest mind in the family and my most reliable pub buddy. A man of few but potent words, Sam operates on a principle of verbal efficiency that would leave rambling philosophers bewildered. He does not dispense idle chatter; rather, every utterance carries purpose. You will never catch him contributing to the epidemic of meaningless small talk – no weather reflections, no unsolicited commentary on the price of milk. Instead, he wields silence as both shield and weapon, letting others flounder in the unbearable void while he remains comfortably composed. It's a rare and dignified art, and one worthy of admiration.

And finally, our youngest, Maggie, who you already know – to a point that is.

For example, you should never let her prim, privately educated exterior fool you. Beneath it lies a little imp whose favourite pastime is to break wind with an enthusiasm that would make even a brass band proud. This delightful habit, much to our amusement, is usually performed in the presence of one of the most particular people on the planet – my mother-in-law.

All three children will make appearances throughout the unfolding saga of our time in Brittany – some more than others – Enjoy!

GETTING SOME OF THE BASICS SORTED

Eager as we were to return to our 'wreck with potential,' we were wise enough to realise that there was little we could accomplish until some essential remedial work had been completed. Top of the list was ensuring the toilet did its job of flushing away and that the electrics were sorted out, allowing us to switch on lights without the risk of an impromptu shock therapy session. And let's not forget the small matter of heating and hot water.

The boiler – if you could still call it that – was a relic of its former self. Its innards had given up the ghost and rested in a forlorn heap of rust on the boiler room floor.

Sorry to digress, but circling back on electrics brings to mind an event during one of our house hunting escapades…

Arriving ahead of schedule for one of our numerous *'à Vendre'* house viewings in northern Brittany, we were greeted by the owners, an English couple who seemed plucked straight from a quaint countryside novel. They introduced themselves warmly and invited us in to wait for the ever elusive estate agent – or *Agent Immobilier.*

The gentleman, brimming with enthusiasm, suggested that they could begin the tour themselves – no doubt confident that their intimate knowledge of the house would outshine anything the agent might offer. With a shrug and a smile, we agreed to their proposition, ready for whatever quirks and charms lay ahead.

Long story short, this English couple, in the five years they had owned the place, had somehow – how remains a mystery – turned a beautiful seventeenth-century mill house into what could easily pass for a twenty-first-century English box, complete with those ubiquitous magnolia coloured walls. It could have been plucked straight from any new housing estate across England.

They regaled us with tales of how they had stripped out all the old flagstone flooring because it was too cold in the winter, the old oak doors because they were, well, old, and the ornate windows because they weren't double-glazed. Everything that could have been considered quaint or historically elegant was replaced with modern (read: cheap) fixtures, flooring, and fittings – all purchased from that popular DIY store in the UK and subsequently imported to France.

As if that wasn't bad enough, the chap proudly informed us that he had rewired the entire place to full English specifications. "So you won't have to worry about changing the plugs on all your appliances," he boasted. Square three-pin sockets throughout, bayonet cap light fittings, all knitted together with good old-fashioned UK-spec cable. Not only was this illegal in France, but as the agent later confided – well out of earshot of our hosts – any insurance they might have had on the place would be null and void in the event of any mishaps.

But they were either too thick-skinned or just plain thick to acknowledge this. Plus, they'd have a devil of a time selling the place in such an illegal state. This, unfortunately, wasn't an isolated incident during our house hunt. We saw many examples of British folks doing all the wrong, often illegal things to their houses. Stripping out the charm and replacing it with the character and personality of themselves – dull, and devoid of imagination or style.

***

So, for those mid-winter months, at least, we stayed put in England. I focused on my paying job, Maggie grudgingly returned to school (occasionally), and Clare launched herself into full-blown planning mode.

One particularly bleak Tuesday evening, with Clare

insisting we sift through her mountain of brochures – thank heavens she never mastered PowerPoint – I found myself in a losing battle with sleep. Just as my eyelids were on the verge of surrender, the phone rang. It was Alan. Not an unusual occurrence, as we communicated quite regularly, especially with our impending status as near neighbours.

***

Journal entry from January 2015 *– Had a call with Alan and Hélène a couple of days ago. To be honest I wasn't surprised and was half expecting it if I'm honest. Lying in bed on Monday listening to the wind and rain beating down on our rental, had me thinking what the weather was like in Brittany. The call from Alan on Tuesday confirmed my suspicions that it wasn't good. The barn roof, already on the verge of collapse, took a battering with much of it now spread about the place. We also lost a couple of large trees. Luckily, neither of them fell in the direction of any of the buildings we wanted to keep. He's already mobilised Christian, a local roofer, with some works being carried out by way of a temporary repair on the barn roof. It wouldn't have been so much of an urgency, had it not been for the fact that the electricity supply for whole farm is housed in that barn. He tells me that wide areas of the region were without power because of the storm. I asked whether that was also to do with our barn roof as well? But he said no, the two issues are not connected. As for the fallen trees they're not going anywhere, so we can deal with them when we're next over. The good news is that Alan managed to do a rough cut, with his large tractor and topper, meaning that most of the grass around the place is much shorter, despite it being so wet. I'm not sure my tractor, when I get it, will be a big bugger, but I'll definitely need something. A Flymo ain't going to cut it – literally.*

Footnote: *I couldn't help noticing how animated and*

excited Alan was on the phone, at our misfortune of losing two trees to the storm. No doubt seeing a logging opportunity.

'The barn roof, already on the verge of collapse, took a battering with much of it now spread about the place.'

***

Alan was, and still is, utterly obsessed with the weather (*la météo*). In his household, the world comes to a halt while he devours the early evening forecast on his venerable twenty-year-old telly. Regarding the power cuts – while a nuisance to most people in the region – they're a regular occurrence, regardless of the weather.

As for those fallen trees... The way Alan described them, you'd think we'd received a divine gift rather than faced a minor catastrophe. It didn't matter who or what the trees had landed on; to him, they were a bounty from the gods. He enthusiastically explained that these fallen trees would now provide us with enough firewood to last for years. Of course, this would require logging – undoubtedly with the chainsaw Alan was keen to sell me – and dry stored for a couple of years.

As for Christian, the local roofing chap – whom I'll tell you more about later – it was a stroke of sheer luck that he was on hand with his very large roll of black polythene. He made some temporary repairs that, knowing our luck, would likely remain 'temporary' for a couple of years. Later that evening, some photographs arrived, and for the first time ever, Alan wasn't exaggerating. We were now the not so proud owners of a seventeenth-century stone barn, boasting a twenty-first-century black bin liner roof.

In other news, one thing I could cross off my to-do list was the demolition of an old outbuilding I had already earmarked for destruction. One of the fallen trees had taken care of that job for me by crashing right through it.

And so, the cost of our adventure continued to spiral, even though we weren't even living there yet.

'We were now the not so proud owners of a seventeenth-century stone barn, boasting a twenty-first-century black bin liner roof.'

***

Journal entry from February 2015 – It's now February and proper cold here in England. I tend not to have the central heating on when I'm working at home. No point in heating up the whole house for the sake of my small office space. So I have, what is called, an electric space heater. To my mind it does indeed do exactly what it says on the box, but the space it heats only covers my feet and shin bones. So the rest of me is freezing.

We've had numerous telephone conversations with Alan and Hélène about the initial works on the house. We've agreed to use a local contractor – Stephane something or other – who has done work on their house over a number of years. Although I'm not expecting mates' rates. It's not something they seem to understand over there. Having agreed in principle to spend numerous thousands of Euros with Stephane – new boiler, bathroom, rewire etc etc – I made an error in suggesting that for that amount of work surely there must be some kind of discount. Apparently not. They send us a Devi – an estimate / quotation – we sign it and send it back and that's it. The other error I made was asking them – Stephane's lot – if he will be able to organise the associated building work. I received a resounding, Non! Lines of demarcation seem very important to the French and must be adhered to at all times. However he does know someone that can do general building work and he's given us a telephone number. Alan and Hélène are going to speak to this other bloke. They've also told us they know someone who can do plastering / tiling that type of thing. My question to them, which I thought reasonable; if we don't know when Stephane is going to start his works, then what are we going to give the building chap as a start date? However despite my reservations I'm assured by Alan that the system works, and they do tend to play nicely together, but in doing so *acknowledge, and play, within those all-important boundary lines. Oh and if we want them – Stephane's lot – to start work in the kitchen then he can only do it at the end of February. By which time the room needs to be cleared out completely. And of course this being another red line they won't cross. We were going to replace the kitchen anyway hence the hours we'd spent this week at the kitchen showroom in Poole, but I wasn't expecting to do anything just yet. I was hoping to keep some of the existing kitchen for a short while, so that we had something to use when we go there. Anyway the ferry is booked and apparently Maggie is coming with us. Clare's mum and dad will have Jack and the cat will go to the cat hotel. In the meantime I've got my budget and business plan for the coming year to finish off, for a (not) understanding client.*

Question: why is a cat hotel called a cattery and a dog hotel not called a doggery?

***

I was to learn a great many things about dealing with tradespeople in France. Although I was more than willing to respect their lines of demarcation, I found their lack of commitment to any start date and their inflexibility rather trying. Turning up unannounced seemed perfectly acceptable to them. I also discovered that there is no such thing as an urgent job – or at least, jobs that *we* deemed as urgent.

Despite these quirks, we were quite pleased with the quality of their work, especially their meticulous attention to detail.

And so it was, back on the ferry we went, for one of only a few times we dared to cross the Channel in midwinter.

***

Journal entry from February 2015 – Our first of many trips back to France I'm sure but the first for this year. No need for the trailer just demolition tools on this occasion. The crossing over was gale force. We had an overnight cabin for the three of us, Clare, Maggie and me, and the journey was grim for two out of three of our party. I slept like a log – or at least I tried to – whilst the other two heaved and moaned all night. I'm pretty sure that at some point, in the small hours, Maggie hated the whole Brittany thing even more than she did already, and sure even Clare was having second thoughts, but she never said as much. Over the course of the last few weeks we've signed off numerous Devis for Stephane and still not much, if anything, has been done. Nor any indication given as to when things might start. My thought is that once we were there we could chivvy things along a bit. It's not that we're in any hurry but having committed to spend a French king's ransom with this fella I thought we deserved something in return.

***

Journal entry from February 2015 – With no heating at the house the place was freezing. That was something else we learned. The winters in Brittany can be as bleak as England, although not so snowy and cold. It was nonetheless really damp and cold enough I can tell you. Frosty mornings gave way to a cold mist that seemed to seep right into my bones. There is a fire in the place which I had going from the moment we arrived. I even manged to scrape together a few logs left by the previous owners. Or rather overlooked by the pilferers that had no doubt taken advantage of an empty plot. However with zero ventilation, coupled with a poor draw in the chimney, the room soon filled with smoke. This meant that the windows had to be opened slightly. All of which gave Maggie plenty of opportunity to moan – constantly. Luckily we have Alan and Hélène's place to fall back on, for board *and lodgings, at the end of each day. We're only here for what amounts to little more than a long weekend, but we still intend to cover a lot of ground. Including what will amount to our 'first demolition'.*

***

Despite the lingering chill, we were happy to be there. Alan and Hélène owned a delightful little house not far from the Blavet – a charming spot they rented out in the summer to bolster their non-existent pension. With no bookings expected until spring, we were allowed to use it as a bolt hole, which ended up being nearly a week's stay despite our initial plan for just a few days.

I deftly manipulated my diary to conduct my business remotely and Maggie, being in the sixth form, managed to wangle a series of free study periods for herself. Though, truth be told, I witnessed more moaning than any serious studying.

Regarding my work, I set up a number of conference calls with colleagues around the globe. Thanks to the marvels of technology, I could mask the fact that I was actually in Alan and Hélène's house in Brittany – or more precisely, a small attic room at the very top of the Moulin (mill), the only spot with a decent internet and phone connection.

Everything was splendid until I, or a team member, attempted to share a document. At that point, the entire call screeched to a halt. Eight or nine colleagues stared at me with fixed expressions as my sluggish connection struggled to keep up. It was then I learned that the one and only provider in Brittany, Orange, offered three speeds of internet in Morbihan: slow, super slow – the package Alan and Hélène had clearly opted for – and ultra slow, which was only marginally faster than the old dial-up modem. You youngsters may have to Google that. A barrage of messages filled the screen, each inquiring about my well-being. It seemed I had frozen, my visage resembling someone in the throes of a stroke, hence their concern.

According to my brief journal entry, one of the principal reasons for our visit – besides an intense longing – was to carry out some preparatory work so that the electrician could eventually work his magic. At some indeterminate time in the future, of course. The tasks at hand involved replacing the kitchen electrics and installing a new fuseboard.

The reason for this urgent work? The existing fuseboard was inexplicably located under the kitchen sink. The local electrician, with Alan nodding sagely by his side, explained this to me very slowly in French: *"...le – fait – d'être – dans un – tel endroit – signifiait – qu'il – pouvait – entrer en – contact – avec – l'eau."* · Which kind of means: "Being where it is meant that it could come into contact with the water."

No kidding!

But I decided to keep my English irony and sarcasm in check, given that my relationship with the local tradespeople was still in its infancy. Now something for all you aspiring French adventurers, house renovators, or house demolishers, here's a little nugget of wisdom. If you plan to hire a skip (*Benne*) from the local skip hire company to dump the rubbish, as we do in England, you can. However, don't expect to throw all your rubbish into one general skip. Oh no, you'll need a separate skip for each type of material you're disposing of. This means that if I had opted for the skip route to manage the burgeoning and predictably massive amounts of rubbish from the house and beyond, I'd have needed multiple skips. Needless to say, this would be quite expensive and take up a considerable amount of space.

I was also unable to take stuff to the local tip, or *Déchetterie*, because I wasn't yet a bona fide resident. So, for those early – and some of the later – demolition works, I had to squirrel the rubbish away in many various nooks and crannies of our land. Good thing we had over an acre to play with.

With all these regulations in place, you'd be forgiven for thinking that 'fly tipping' must be a real problem in France, just like in England. And you'd be dead right. Just take a drive into the countryside and you'll find many a large hole in the ground, either as a natural phenomenon or purposefully dug by some obliging farmer. Each one filled with old cars, domestic appliances, rusting drums of goodness knows what, and all manner of other detritus – especially asbestos sheeting.

So, on that first of many trips, having been unequivocally informed that a fuse-box under the sink was hardly ideal, our main mission was to remove the existing kitchen and stash it somewhere around the farm. We also set about demolishing the wall between the kitchen and dining room – because Clare decreed it – and then we went shopping. Many, many times.

'Alan and Hélène owned a delightful little house not far from the Blavet. Which we were allowed to use it as a bolt hole.'

***

Journal entry from February 2015 (final day of our first proper work visit) – *Maggie helped out, and although I won't dare to suggest it, I reckon she quite enjoyed herself – big hammer, bigger hammer, venting anger that type of thing. Or perhaps she was just happy to be a bit warmer. We also knocked down quite a bit more than we initially intended. Some intentional some not, largely due to our teenage daughter wanting to raze the whole place. It was always our plan to have an open kitchen diner but never thought we'd do it within a couple of months of getting the place – hey ho! Or indeed within just a few hours of entering the building. The same can't be said for the clearing up mind. What a mess. Having spent this morning constantly moving rubble and kitchen cupboards to the farthest corners of our plot, I'm thankful for the opportunity of writing this entry having set myself up in front of the fire on one of those folding fishing chairs. If it wasn't for the smoke making my eyes water, and Maggie continually asking, "can we go now," I could quite easily have dozed off. Looks like the fallen trees are going to have stay where they are for a while. Alan's busy dealing with other people's fallen trees. I understand that timber is money for him - once its logged and seasoned that is.*

'We also set about demolishing the wall between the kitchen and dining room – because Clare decreed it...'

***

Journal entry from February 2015 – *Back on the Ferry, and in the bar, heading for home – wonder how much longer I'll be saying that? The other two are in the cabin probably being ill, although the sea is quite calm compared to our outward journey. I really don't know what to make of the last four or five days. I lost count as to how many wheelbarrows full of rubble I took out of the house, but my back is proper aching. Looks like we now have a designated dumping ground around the back of the barn. There's undoubtedly going to be a lot of hard labour in the future so I'm thinking that I'm going to have to get a bit fitter. I'm a bit overwhelmed if I'm perfectly honest, tired and looking forward to sleeping in my own bed.*

Had the pleasure of meeting Stephane before we left. He paid us a courtesy call, I'm thinking to make sure that I'd cleared the kitchen as per his needs. He of course wasn't to know that I would have a pretty good understanding of what 'take out all the kitchen from the house' means. Or was his visit to simply have a look at the family who'll be funding his next few holidays, cars and children's education?

Although without Alan and Hélène being in attendance it was hard going language wise. He seemed pleased with our progress and I managed to deduce that the new boiler is on order and should be with us in time for the summer. At least that's what I think he said.

I never realised how much bigger trees look when they're on the ground as opposed to being upright. Good to know that I'll have my own supply of logs soon.

***

A TIME FOR SPRING, A TIME FOR WORK

Journal entry from March 2015 – *It's been at least a couple of weeks since my last entry. Although to be honest as far as our adventure is concerned there's nothing much happening. Shouldn't be too surprised I guess given that winter isn't quite over yet. I understand though that works have started on the bathroom, and I've provided drawings for the kitchen layout so that power points and plumbing can be put where we want them. Didn't receive any acknowledgement so assume all's well. I'll find out when we go there in a couple of weeks' time. By all accounts the weather's warming up so that'll be nice. Between now and then I have another trip to Seattle to contend with. In the meantime our French lessons continue although I've missed a few due to work commitments but Clare's cracking on. The feminine and masculine words are still a mystery to me and as recently as Friday Judy left us to learn all about the verb Aller, which is, by all accounts, very important. I literally don't know whether I'm coming or going. In either a masculine or feminine way.*

***

As Spring arrived, the pace at the house began to pick up. With no business trips on the horizon – meaning I was working from home most of the time – we mulled over the idea of me working online from Brittany. This involved attending conference calls, emailing, and the occasional interactive planning meeting. In other words, at least giving the impression that I was working, while in reality, my focus was entirely on our house.

The fly in the ointment was the lack of Wi-Fi or indeed a phone line of any kind at our place. These basics were crucial because, as I've mentioned, many of my team members were scattered around the globe, and given the nature of our work, we all needed access to the same planning and design documents in real time. So, a reliable and relatively fast connection was a must. Definitely not the super slow connection available at Alan and Hélène's place. Writing this, I feel a bit ungrateful. Though I don't mean to be, it was pretty useless and an experience I wanted to avoid.

It was, therefore, with some relief that our dear friends readily accepted our need to stand on our own two feet.

As I've mentioned before, the provider of choice in France was Orange. Scratch that – 'the only provider in France was Orange,' or at least it was for us. Whether that's changed now, I have no idea. Regarding the logistics of making it all happen, we were initially reassured. After a brief conversation with Hélène, we were brimming with confidence. She mentioned that getting a line installed was relatively straightforward. Fantastic, I thought, and promptly told her I'd hop onto the Orange website to set things in motion. However, we soon discovered, this was merely one of many things in France that are clunky, overly complicated, and positively archaic compared to the UK. Solving this online was out of the question. No, you had to visit your local Orange shop.

Which, dutifully, we did.

Hélène suggested we head out one afternoon straight after lunch, because, apparently, we needed to get there early. Preferably before they even opened, as it tends to get quite busy. Our local Orange shop was in Pontivy – formerly known as Napoléonville, by the way – a mere twenty-minute drive away. We were advised to arrive at least fifteen minutes before opening time. Obediently, we did just that, only to find ourselves joining an already sizable queue snaking down the street. By the time the shop opened, the queue had doubled in length. A young man emerged from the shop and proceeded to divide the single queue into two: one for mobile phone business and the other for landline and internet.

Thankfully, our queue – landline and internet – was considerably shorter, though still quite substantial. As we inched closer to the building, we were required to take a numbered ticket, which would be called when it was our turn to be served. Although the queue moved at a reasonable pace, it took over an hour before our number was called.

Finally, we were seated in front of the same young man I'd seen before. Hélène proceeded to explain our needs. I must say, he was extremely polite and efficient and spoke remarkably good English, which he was more than willing to do for our benefit. On one hand, I was grateful, but on the other, I was acutely aware of how much work I still needed to do to learn their language. I felt very much the English dummy, which left me feeling vulnerable and, if I'm honest, a bit embarrassed.

The young man seemed eager to engage us in small talk – likely to polish his own English skills. So I asked him about the queue outside. "Did we come on a particularly busy day, or is it always like this?" I inquired.

With a congenial smile, he replied that it was always like this. "Have you never considered opening a larger shop or perhaps employing more people to handle the obvious demand?" I suggested.

To his credit, he did ponder the notion – likely out of politeness – before giving me a pleasant "Non" and a shrug. Both of which I was becoming increasingly accustomed to.

Within mere minutes, we'd ordered a landline complete with an internet package, all of which seemed very reasonably priced. However, it wasn't until we were well into the transaction that it occurred to me to inquire about Wi-Fi speeds. And that's when it all started to unravel.

The young man, armed with our postcode, took a quick glance at his screen and informed us – in English terms – that we had three speed options: Slow, Very Slow, or Really Slow, with none of them guaranteed. Those weren't the technical terms, mind you, but rather my interpretation of his explanation. Needing internet, we opted for the 'slow' speed, which was marginally faster than the other options on the table – and the best we were going to get anyway.

But it wasn't all bad news. As part of the deal, we qualified for a free mobile handset – a Nokia 3310 or something very similar if memory serves. Even in 2015, it wouldn't have been anyone's phone of choice. In fact I was surprised Nokia still produced such a thing. It was as unsmart as you could possibly get, but it was bulletproof and, as it turned out, perfect for having in – and falling out of – my pocket while doing all manner of jobs around the farm.

We left the shop with our handsets for the house and the promise of an engineer's visit the following week.

***

Journal entry from March 2015 *– Still not able to live in our own house yet but the works are looking good and the new boiler, which was a nice surprise, is giving us hot water when we're there. Poo still not going away though and no word yet on the new fosse, though everyone agrees that we need one. The good news is that Our Wi-Fi went live today. The Orange bloke never said a word and apart from having to stop him from clipping the cable across the dining room ceiling it all went well. So we're online. I've got my first call with the team on Friday let's see how it holds up – finger crossed. Though Maggie has already gone online and given the connection speed a resounding "rubbish" 'no star' review.*

And though the bathroom is well underway we won't be using it any time soon. But good to have a basin to wash our hands in and with hot water at that!

'And though the bathroom is well underway we won't be using it any time soon.'

***

But I bet you're dying to know: How did your first conference call go, from within your own house? Well, let me tell you, for all you doom-mongers out there.

I actually bottled it. In other words, for those not acquainted with such English idioms, I lost my nerve. Instead, I sent an email asking my team to send me all of their updates by return. But there was no rush. I would review each one and, if needed, arrange a call sometime during the following week – when I was back in England, though they weren't to know that.

A classic case of kicking the ball into the long grass.

***

We made multiple return journeys throughout the month, right through the spring and into early summer, taking full advantage of Alan and Hélène's little house. Despite the installation of a new bathroom and, a couple of months later, some of a new kitchen, our ongoing fosse problem meant we couldn't live there for any length of time – just a few overnight stays at best. Also, with work commitments on the home front, our stays remained relatively short. It would, in fact, be almost a year later before I could declare to the world that I was a retired man, though I had been on an increasingly 'go slow' for quite a few months leading up to it.

With the kitchen rewired and the rest of the house deemed electrically safe, our stays became progressively more comfortable. However, we still had no real means to cook food during the day or keep even the simplest of foodstuffs, such as milk, from spoiling. So our attention turned to solving the problem of cooking our own food during our days at the house. Armed with a decent idea of what we wanted – no, that's not quite right – we were armed with a decent idea of what Clare said we wanted, we set off to the local appliance shop in Baud.

***

Journal entry from March 2015 – *We went to the local showroom and bought our first French electrical appliances. With our French language skills still on the shaky side I was slightly nervous as to how it might go. We knew what we (Clare) wanted and hoped that would be exactly what we'd end up leaving the shop with. Item one a fridge or frigo or even réfrigérateur as the French say – pretty much same word as in English but said with a French accent. There's a few of those. The real challenge though was the cooker. Clare was very specific on her requirements. A 1000mm electric range cooker. Fan oven, induction hob. She even had it all spelled out on a piece of paper – "Je voudrais acheter une cuisinière de 1000 mm s'il vous plait." The young lady serving us seemed delighted, going on to tell us that they had quite a few 'pianos' in the store. How what Clare had said – which I though was pretty good – could have somehow been interpreted as us wanting a musical instrument? So Clare repeated the same line to the young smiling sales assistant. She even offered her the piece of paper with the words written on it, just in case. Which the young lady obligingly took. "Oui madame un piano." And then beckoning for us to follow her. Long story short. A range style cooker in France* *or 'grande cuisinière' is commonly referred to as a 'piano'. Lesson learned. It's being delivered tomorrow and they will even connect it up for us. Happy days on so many levels. For one, it's the first time anyone in France has ever committed to doing something on a specific date and at a specific time of the day. Even the wi-fi guy turned up out of the blue, a day earlier than we were originally told.*

"Oui madame un piano."

***

Remember me telling you about those folks on the ferry, with cars and trailers loaded with all sorts of paints and DIY paraphernalia? That was us for the better part of the coming year – and quite some time thereafter. Like many intrepid expats and immigrants before us, we soon discovered the vast difference in both cost and choice between the UK and France when it came to DIY supplies. Doing It Yourself wasn't as deeply embedded in the French psyche as it is in ours.

When it came to paint however, I did make a spirited

attempt to avoid lugging it across the Channel. After all, I'd seen French properties adorned in a delightful array of colours. Sadly, that argument didn't get past first base. My wife, with a tone of mild condescension, admitted that I was right – some French houses do look colourful. However, they don't have Farrow & Ball. Which wasn't entirely true, but in the grand scheme of things, you have to pick your battles. In marriage, it's even more important.

We never used posh paint everywhere in our house, but neither did we buy the not so posh stuff from a French shop either. It was all imported, having no doubt been imported into the UK – though not necessarily from France – in the first place. Apart from decorating materials our trailer, and roof rack, was to be loaded up with all manner of equipment and household adornments. Most surprising, though essential, was a petrol motored electrical generator – courtesy of a friends mother. Remembering Alan's wise words of how essential it was to have a standby generator. With power cuts being a common occurrence in rural Brittany and not necessarily as a result of extreme weather.

Spring Turns to Summer

An extremely busy period at work kept us in the UK for most of this time. Plus, it was examination season for Maggie, which meant we managed just one or two short trips, primarily to inspect the work Stephane and Co had been doing. I must say, the quality of their workmanship remained exemplary, with the only minor mishap being the inability to close the bathroom door due to the washbasin being in the way. A mere irritation, quickly rectified to suit their convenience.

Back in England, Clare was still deep in planning mode. My only involvement was to accompany her to various shops, whenever time allowed, to rubber-stamp the selections she had already decided upon.

**

Journal entry from May 2015 – *Today I bought my very first and very own ride on mower. Alan helped me with the negotiations at the Bricomarché in Baud but he wasn't around for the delivery a couple of hours later. Between me and this journal I have an admission to make. I had absolutely no idea what the delivery bloke was saying as he set about telling me how to operate it and all of the machine's features. And I think he knew it too. I tried nodding sagely, but saying 'oui' when I know from his body language my response should have been a 'non', kind of gave the game away. With the shop fella finally leaving me to my own devices. And with Clare and Maggie out shopping, I was able to freestyle around the place unhindered and without judgement. Though the first proper noisy toy of my retirement won't see much action for a while because the grass is too long. Looking forward to Alan making an appearance tomorrow with his tractor and topper. We also* *started laying out the potager, which didn't go off without incident. I wonder what any onlookers would have made of us running across the field, with flailing arms, chasing down the sheet of weed prevention membrane, that we'd failed to nail down. Our first cross words in France. Apparently it was my fault that it had blown away, despite the fact I was away collecting rocks at the time, to stop it doing just that.*

***

The subject of grass cutting seemed to be a recurring theme during our ad hoc visits. Each and every return saw our (my) time devoted to cutting the grass back to somewhere near the height we'd left it only a few weeks before. After speaking with many others, mainly at the ferry port, it turned out this wasn't just an 'us' problem. It was something everyone had to contend with.

Some good friends of ours had a place further south in the Poitou-Charentes region. They use it exclusively as a holiday home. The problem is, they spend at least the first week of their holiday wrestling with the garden.

'Each and every return saw our (my) time devoted to cutting the grass back to somewhere near the height we'd left it only a few weeks before'

However, I had an enthusiastic volunteer in the form of Maggie. She swiftly mastered the workings of the mower, freeing me to tackle multiple other tasks she had no interest in – which was, quite frankly, anything besides cutting grass. The only hitch was her youthful exuberance and complete disregard for instructions. She attempted to finish the job in record time, blatantly ignoring my advice to take it slowly, do a high cut in the orchard, and a lower cut elsewhere.

The poor sit-on mower was less broken in and more raced in. Maggie set it to 'shaving the ground' mode and zoomed around the plot at full throttle, bouncing up and down on the seat as she hit every hole. Predictably, it ended in tears. The blade caught a hidden pile of rocks, causing the motor to stall. The tears were real; Maggie genuinely thought she'd wrecked the mower on her maiden voyage. It hadn't, of course, but I seized the opportunity. Instead of scolding her, I did something far more effective: I walked away, tutting and shaking my head, leaving her to stew in her own guilt. Maggie was allowed to cut the grass again, and I'd like to believe she learned a lesson or two. Absolutely not.

***

With lofty dreams of growing our own produce, we laid out some weed prevention membrane stuff. According to the packaging, if you lay it on the ground, the weeds underneath will compost naturally and inhibit the growth of new ones. This wasn't part of any grand scheme to become self-sufficient in vegetables or launch a greengrocer business; it was just a little project we fancied.

Given the amount of land previously devoted to the family potager, we could quite easily have gone into business. While Clare had visions of grandeur, my ambitions were far more modest: I aimed to grow a cauliflower. Not just any old vegetable, but the magnificent cauliflower – something I had never grown before. So, why not?

Like most jobs, this one turned out to be far less straightforward than we initially thought. Much of the problem stemmed from our complete lack of communication. One-metre-wide by twenty-metre-long runs of membrane definitely required a few rocks to hold them down. So, having agreed it was a good idea, off I went with one of my inherited wheelbarrows – the previous owners were kind enough to leave all manner of items, including a number of old wooden wheelbarrows – to collect rocks from around the farm. Head down and busily searching, I noticed a presence behind me. It was Clare.

"So who's holding the membrane down?" I asked. She looked puzzled until the penny dropped. She turned and sprinted back to the soon to be potager, which was now completely devoid of any membrane. The wind had carried it into an adjacent field and from where we were standing, it clearly had no intention of coming to rest. The membrane was being picked up, moved a few metres, and put down again, steadily heading toward the horizon.

We briefly exchanged glances before setting off in what can only be described as an enthusiastic stumble across the field to retrieve our fleeing weed prevention membrane. Dragging it back to the potager, we spent the time blaming one another. Though it was undoubtedly my fault for not making it clear that she needed to be on point to stop it blowing away, despite the wind working against us in the first place.

I'm sure if Clare were writing this, her account would be markedly different. But she's not, so there you have it.

***

Journal entry from May 2015 – *Just having breakfast on the Poole to Cherbourg ferry. Faster crossing but a longer drive the other end. Ordered my usual. "Petit déjeuner anglaise, mais sans tomates." Full English – despite the French ferry* *cook still being unable to do a proper full English – without tomatoes. And once again served up with a smile and tomatoes! A full trailer load of oak flooring down below and plenty of other stuff on the roof rack too. Good job there isn't a weighbridge, or at least I hope not, on their side. Also thank goodness for our Landy. Slow, cramped and noisy it might be, but it pulls and carries weight effortlessly. Looking across the table at my wife as she tucks into a sorry looking croissant. Looks like the French kitchen can't even get that right.*

***

The trip from Cherbourg to our house in the hamlet of Saint-Barthélémy was a good four-hour jaunt – traffic around Rennes permitting, of course. Naturally, this necessitated at least one pit stop for a pee and a coffee, lest we risked turning into full bladdered, caffeine deprived, zombies en route.

Still a bit green in the trailering department, I recall a previous escapade where I pulled into some services on the E3 and parked in a regular car space. Completely oblivious to the fact that I had the trailer on the back, which was now causing a vehicular gridlock. As if that wasn't shameful enough, I then had to endure the silent scorn of the seasoned caravaners and trailer brigade, as I nervously attempted to reverse car and trailer out of the space.

Fast forward a few years, and I'm pleased to report that reversing a trailer is no longer the nerve-wracking ordeal it once was, especially on that fateful day. Turning the steering wheel in the opposite direction to where you want the trailer to go was still counterintuitive. I inevitably ended up turning the wheel first one way, then the other, as I waited for my brain to catch up with the process. I'm fairly certain those seasoned trailering onlookers had been in my shoes once upon a time, but you'd never have guessed it, as they shook their heads at my efforts.

Having survived my own baptism of ridicule, I now feel I've earned the right to shake my head when I see a rookie making a pig's ear out of reversing their trailer or caravan. And when the opportunity presents itself, I exercise that right with relish, I assure you.

Arriving at our house, we unloaded our cargo – the oak flooring, which, by all accounts, needed to acclimatise for a few weeks before being laid. We then set about cutting the grass for the next couple of days. Maggie stayed back in England to spend some time with her brother, who was home from university. Alan and Hélène would always arrive a bit later, and after helping us to open the house up properly, we'd head over to theirs for apéritifs, supper, and conversation. This was our chance to regale Alan, in particular, with the latest news from England. Despite being very much a resident of France, he still relished hearing the latest from the land of his birth.

And that was pretty much the routine of our lives in the months leading up to my retirement and our grand move to France for good. And yes, I know I made the point – and so did Alan, on multiple occasions – of saying it wasn't France, it was Brittany. But at the end of the day, it is a region of France, and some people – particularly the Bretons – need to get over it. As indeed do the Cornish.

AN EVENTFUL MONTH UNFOLDS

With July providing us with a summer break from work, and Maggie's from school, meant we could relish a longer stay at our soon to be home in Brittany – weeks, in fact. We even devised a cunning workaround for the fosse problem. Or rather, the sluggish water and waste run-off from the bathroom problem. Our solution? Rigorous plunging of the toilet pan before use. This created a sort of vacuum in the system, enough to send the flushed contents down and out, to goodness knows where. Somewhere underground in the farmyard, we assumed.

There's another thing I forgot to mention. The reason for the delay in getting our fosse completely upgraded was because the local authority surveyors had been unable to locate the exact whereabouts of our existing septic tank (*fosse septique*). They had evidently found the pipework but couldn't determine where it was going or where it terminated. Alan informed us that, in our absence, the local authority (*Baud Communaute*) even employed the services of a water diviner, but to no avail. I did suggest that, as we weren't living there, we would be happy for them to dig up as much of our ground as they needed to in order to trace the pipework. But as we hadn't yet signed a Devi for the whole, yet to be determined project, it was out of the question.

As good humans do, we fell into a routine. I was employed as chief plunger – no you won't find that on my CV – meaning that no matter where I happened to be – day or night – I was summoned to rigorously plunge the toilet bowl before use. If said plunging failed to work, in other words, if after flushing or showering waste still remained in the bowl or shower tray, then I would be once more called upon to deal with it. What that entailed you don't really need to know, but it involved mops, buckets, and multiple trips across the farmyard.

Jack accompanied us on our extended visit, and although he loathed the journey and struggled with the heat, he nonetheless revelled in the freedoms that a farmyard, orchard, and small paddock provided. Being a terrier, we assumed he would be in his element, keeping the place clear of the usual farmyard pests – meaning rats, of course. The thing is, our Jack may have been a terrier by name, but he was nothing like one by nature. When it came to managing those farmyard pests, it was as though he had struck a deal: he would do less in the way of hunting if they kept away from anywhere he and us humans lived. When in residence, we never caught sight of a single rat in or around the perimeter of our house. In most other areas, they had the run of the place.

When our cat Nettle took up residence however, there were no such agreements, and never likely to be. Unequivocally Maggie's cat, possessing a dismissive manner and a total disregard for anything she deemed unworthy of her attention, Nettle was a voracious and hugely successful hunter. So our pests, Jack's frenemies, were on borrowed time.

***

Journal entry from July 2015 – *This place just keeps on giving. Took a break from laying the oak flooring today. Too hot and my knees are killing me. Went out and did some clearing behind the barn. First time I've used the brush cutter attachment on the strimmer so a bit nervous. Not that Clare needs to know that. And I found a toilet! Or a thunder box as the old folks used to say. I remember seeing a small roof of sorts a while ago and curiosity just got the better of me today. Strange the things that make us smile. I showed Clare what I'd found and in doing so suggested that we now have alternative facilities, some that might not need* *plunging, she didn't seem at all enthusiastic.*

Note to self: Don't wear shorts when your strimming, or worse still, brush cutting.

'And I found a toilet! Or a thunder box as the old folks used to say.'

July 14th – Bastille Day

Journal entry from July 2015 – Bastille day tomorrow apparently. Which I acknowledged with a shrug when Alan told me. I have no real idea what the day and subsequent evenings celebrations are all about. But according to Alan (and Beryl) we should definitely make the effort to join in the fete (la fête) down at the Blavet. It's a bit of a 'do' by all accounts with drinking and fireworks. Two of my most favourite things as it happens. Funny thing though. When I shared my understanding of Bastille day; which was that it is very much a French thing, or rather a Paris thing – apparently the Parisians have a very distinct 'better than you' attitude to anyone living outside of Paris, according to Alan – in doing so going on to ask; why is it that the Bretons make such a big deal about it as well? Only to be met with a shake of the head and being told I still have so much to learn. Which is true. But I nonetheless pressed the point to which Alan replied – but not before a weary sigh – with a question of his own. "Do the Cornish celebrate Guy Fawkes night?" To which – I think – the answer is yes. And told him as much. He merely gave me a 'there you have it' kind of gesture and walked to his car, waving and telling us they'd see us down at the Blavet tomorrow.

***

So, Bastille Day, a jubilant cornerstone of French festivity, where it would seem that the whole of France, Brittany included, transforms into an energetic spectacle of merry chaos. Where, eating, drinking, and fireworks reign supreme, stretching from the early hours of dawn until the last reveller finally surrenders to the call of their bed or in some cases the call of wherever they happen to find themselves at the time.

Bastille Day vs. Guy Fawkes Night: A Templeman Perspective.

Each year on the 5th of November, we, the British partake in the annual ritual of commemorating a failed coup with bonfires, fireworks, and effigies of poor old Guy Fawkes. A celebration of failure some might say, "We may not have succeeded in toppling the government, but at least we can still have a jolly good time!"

In contrast, the French insurgents, with their grand aspirations of liberty and justice, managed to free a grand total of seven prisoners from the Bastille. Seven! Hardly the makings of a blockbuster prison break. Yet, in true French fashion, they've turned it into a national celebration of revolutionary fervour, with none of the awkward "better luck next time" undertone that characterises our own Guy Fawkes Night.

As fireworks light up the night sky, the French raise their glasses, toasting to the spirit of liberté, égalité, fraternité, while we Brits gather around our bonfires, chuckling at the irony of celebrating a plot that went gloriously awry. In the end, both Bastille Day and Guy Fawkes Night remind us that sometimes, it's the grand gestures, the spirited attempts, and the sheer audacity of rebellion that make for the most memorable celebrations – even if they don't quite go according to plan.

***

Anyway, back in our little commune, the locals had their very own Bastille Day committee. As indeed do communes right across France. Their mission? To organise and coordinate the festivities with meticulous precision, culminating in a grand fireworks display down at Saint Nicolas des Eaux. A commune of Pluméliau, Saint Nicolas des Eaux is a charming hamlet on the Blavet, bursting with a vibrant expat / immigrant community. One of those communities that revel in their Englishness at every opportunity. Fish and chips in the heart of France? Naturally. But not on Bastille Day, oh no. This is strictly a French celebration for the French, and the rest of us are gracious invitees.

***

But before I continue telling you about the events of this particular day – trust me it's worth sticking around for – let me share a story, as I remember it. One that happened within a little bar, tabac, creperie in our quaint little hamlet of Saint Nicolas des Eaux.

Once we'd become bona fide immigrants in Brittany, our little haven quickly became a magnet for visits from family and friends. One memorable occasion saw the arrival of our much loved friends, Julie and Stuart, who decided to bring along Stuart's dear old mum. Well into her eighties and a little unsteady on her feet, we thought a gentle drive down to Saint Nicolas des Eaux for a leisurely walk and perhaps a tipple would be just the ticket.

Arriving at the charming hamlet, the only establishment open was an ancient bar-tabac-crêperie. Built of sturdy local grey stone some two hundred years ago, it stood as a testament to the timeless architecture of old French houses. This one, with its double fronted classic design and central entrance, sported identical green framed windows – unchanged through the decades, as if in defiance of trendiness.

The bar's location was idyllic, offering an uninterrupted view of the Blavet, set back slightly from the canal path (now a road), allowing for a few small tables and chairs to be positioned outside. It was a scene that seemed plucked from a vintage postcard.

As we stepped inside, it was as though we had been transported back to the late 1930s. The interior, decorated and furnished with a charming blend of nostalgia and neglect, retaining an antique allure. The worn wooden beams, faded wallpaper, and an assortment of mismatched furniture told stories of generations past.

Adding to the ambience, was the familiar sight of a few bar flies already in residence. Some stood at the bar, others sat at the few available old wooden round tables with mismatched chairs. Most were sipping wine, while others enjoyed beer or cider in small straight tumblers – each drink a small celebration of local tradition.

Behind the bar stood a small-framed, elderly, fierce, no-nonsense looking lady, her eyes sharp as a hawk's. Beside her was a younger man – though still quite old – whom I instinctively took to be her son. Perhaps it was something in the eyes, or maybe I was simply concocting stories in my head. Stuart's mum, bless her, immediately made a beeline for the nearest chair, settling in with the air of someone who had just rediscovered a long lost treasure. Clare, Julie and I surveyed the surroundings with a mix of admiration and amusement, while Stuart, ever the pack leader, headed to the bar to buy some welcome drinks. Whereupon the elderly lady gestured for him to take a seat, indicating that someone would come over to take our order. Moments later, the younger, older man arrived at our table, asking what we would like to drink. Though unsmiling, he was not sullen, and he effortlessly committed our order to memory, showing remarkable patience with our pidgin French.

Stuart's mother, eager to impress with her language skills, insisted on ordering her own drink. Stuart, with a hint of apprehension, questioned this decision, but she waved him off with the confidence of a seasoned polyglot. Leaning forward, she addressed the barman with a determined expression and said, "Bitte kann ich ein Glas Rotwein trinken?"

A horrified Stuart leaned across to his mum, his eyes wide

with disbelief. "Mum, what are you doing? You've just ordered your drink in German!"

Unphased by her son's rebuke, she replied with serene confidence, "Yes, I know. But I don't know any French." Her order was taken nonetheless, and after the initial shock of hearing German in what is a very traditional old Bretagne bar, conversations resumed around us. The bar flies, now suitably entertained by our linguistic escapades, exchanged knowing glances and continued their own chatter, perhaps thinking on the eccentricities of their English visitors.

The younger, older man returned with our drinks, placing Stuart's mum's glass of red wine before her with a courteous nod. "Merci, madame," he said, his eyes twinkling with amusement. Stuart's mum, undeterred by the language barrier, raised her glass and responded cheerfully, "Danke schön!" – drawing a few more raised eyebrows and shaking heads from the patrons. We in turn raised our glasses in a toast to this delightful little farce. Stuart's mother beamed with pride, convinced she had flawlessly navigated the linguistic waters, while the rest of us savoured the charm of this timeless, unchanging bar-tabac-crêperie.

Despite Stuart's mum's linguistic antics, if the owner of the place was offended, she certainly never let it show. We had a thoroughly pleasant evening, even chuckling to ourselves at how the locals were circumventing the recently introduced 'no smoking in public places' regulations. They continued lighting up in the bar, as they had for centuries, but with a twist – waving the smoke up the chimney. Priceless!

'...an ancient bar-tabac-crêperie... unchanged through the decades, as if in defiance of trendiness.'

***Photograph courtesy of the Internet.*

***

Anyway, back to Bastille Day. We were informed that Christian – the heroic saviour of much of our barn roof during the February storm, and hopefully the one to replace it – had been appointed as the firework display team leader, ably assisted by three other valiant souls. As the evening progressed, the number of revellers swelled to the point where the hamlet was nearly bursting at the seams. But the merriment, though becoming increasingly boisterous, retained a gentle, joyous spirit. Laughter echoed through the air, and there wasn't a hint of any aggressive or drunken behaviour to be seen.

The smell of crêpes and a variety of other enjoyable foods filled the air, turned out at an impressive rate, each aroma more pleasant than the last. Unlike the events I had attended in England, where the dominant smell always seemed to be over-fried onions, this celebration was a feast for the senses. Even with wine and beer flowing freely, the whole party remained wonderfully cordial, though there was an undeniable hint of mischief in the air.

As the anticipation built, a shout went up, calling for everyone to make their way to the bank of the Blavet, for the fireworks were about to commence. The excitement was palpable, and we joined the throng, eager to witness the grand finale of this enchanting day.

Having come from a country where health and safety regulation has made it its mission to water down or eradicate any form of risky revelry, I'm pleased to report that the French, or rather the Saint Nicolas des Eaux Bastille Day committee, were the complete opposite. In England, the mere thought of a firework display would summon an army of clipboard wielding officials, each armed with a plethora of forms and dire warnings about the dangers of merrymaking. But here in Saint Nicolas des Eaux, the committee embraced a rather more laissez-faire approach.

The festivities were a joyous blend of organised chaos and spirited spontaneity. As revellers gathered on the banks of the Blavet, the air was thick with anticipation for the impending pyrotechnics. Christian and his team of amateur arsonists – I mean, firework enthusiasts – buzzed about, setting up their explosive delights with the carefree abandon of children. No fluorescent vests or safety barriers here; just a motley crew armed with lighted tapers, a hearty dose of enthusiasm, and possibly a bottle or two of the local cider. The only nod to health and safety was a half-hearted announcement, muffled through a temperamental megaphone, advising everyone to *"Gardez une distance de sécurité"* before the speaker promptly gave up.

In that moment, the rigid regulations of England felt a million miles away as we stood by the Blavet, watching Christian and his intrepid team rowing out to a pontoon in the middle of the canal, their small boat laden with large crates of fireworks. But these weren't just any fireworks – no, not the kind you might timidly ignite in your back garden. These were the kind that make you stand back in awe, the ones that transform the night sky into a dazzling tapestry of light and sound during a grand public display.

Having caught Christian just before he set off, I inquired about his plans for protection against the inevitable fire and burn risks. With a quizzical but amused expression, he placed one hand on my shoulder and the other pointed to his head. *"Vous n'avez pas à vous inquiéter parce que j'ai un chapeau,"* he said. Meaning: "You don't need to worry because I have a hat."

The hat in question was a wide-brimmed rattan affair, typically worn to keep the sun off one's head. Perhaps Christian thought that if the sun couldn't set it alight, then what chance would a few fireworks have? Regardless, any concerns for their personal safety were soon forgotten as the firework display began.

Watching the firework team's slick but hardly skilled choreography, I was convinced that at any moment one or all of them might go up in flames. Team member number one would pass a firework from a crate to member number two. Number two would then place the firework onto the designated launch pad, waiting for Christian, the team leader, to light the taper at what he deemed the perfect moment. Up went the firework, accompanied by applause from the crowd and the usual firework noises, as it exploded in a riot of light and near-deafening sound.

Back on the pontoon, team member number four, gloved hands at the ready, was busily patting down his teammates' clothing and hair, which were being liberally showered with debris and sparks from the sky-bound fireworks. His responsibilities also extended to stamping on any sparks that had landed on the pontoon, particularly those near the crates of fireworks – the lid of which served as a dry seat for Christian throughout the entire show.

Thankfully, no one died nor was there any serious injury to speak of, either this year or in subsequent ones. Just a few minor burns to skin, clothes, and, of course, Christian's trusty hat.

***

Journal entry from July 16th 2015 *– My ears are still ringing from those fireworks the other night. And as I was sitting replaying the evening in my mind Alan and Christian turned up. As seems to be the way in these parts, where there appears no need for an appointment, people just turn up when it suits them. The funny thing is we always seem to be here when they do. It turned out that the purpose of their visit was for Christian to give our barn roof a thorough look over in order to determine the extent of the repairs. As for Alan, from what I could make out, he was here to act as interpreter in the event that the massive job and devi wouldn't be understood. I also suspect he was ready for an ale. One from my stock of English ales no doubt. As for his interpreting services they weren't really required. From Christians frequent shake of the head and long exhaling – complete with whistling – I was able to figure out for myself that the job was a big one. As it turns out it's going to be a twenty thousand euros one. Which he kindly wrote on a piece of paper in case we'd misheard both him and Alan saying the same number in French and English. To be honest we weren't surprised, knowing already that most of the timbers holding up what was left of the slates had come to the end of their life. "But look on the bright side," announced Alan.*

"Think of all the firewood you'll have." He was right of course.

Needing to get the roof done, hopefully before the winter, I made the mistake of asking Christian when he might make a start. And true to French form, when it comes to arranging to have anything done that is, all I received for my trouble was a shrug. Though he did say it was very important that we get it done. We all agreed on that and had an ale. Need to get back to the vets tomorrow to get Jack's medical card and so on stamped for our return journey.

Introducing Gérard

There were quite a few highlights during this visit, all of which reaffirmed our decision to make Brittany our home – a choice that felt increasingly informed with each passing day. But before we head back to England, let me regale you with the tale of our first meeting with Gérard. – a memory as solid and vivid as they come.

Throughout my life, I reckon I've had thousands of introductions, most of which have faded into the mists of time. Yet this one stands out, crystal clear, as if it happened just yesterday.

It was towards the back end of our extended visit in July when we were first introduced to Gérard. He was one of those 'must meet' neighbours, according to Beryl. Since our arrival for the summer break, she had suggested on more than one occasion that Gérard was someone we absolutely needed to meet. Though she never divulged the reason, we soon discovered why. And even now, I have no clue why she insisted so fervently, but we were eternally grateful for her persistence. Because Gérard, quite simply, was superb!

Meeting Gérard was not just a highlight of that visit; it was one of the highlights of our entire Brittany adventure. His warmth, playfulness and exuberance left an indelible mark on us both, confirming that our decision to live in this corner of France was, indeed, a sound one.

He was such a principal character – probably second only to Alan and Hélène – in our daily lives, that you'll see him pop up time and again throughout this tale. This crazy, wonderful, endearing personality deserves all the exposure I can give it. These days people talk much about 'influencers'. Well, Gérard was our influencer, but you won't find him on any YouTube channel or social media platform. Not least of all because the most technological gadget in his possession was an electric razor, apparently gifted by some lady friend or other.

Gérard was a small-built chap of about five feet six, anywhere between seventy and eighty years of age, with a sprinkling of hair on his head. He looked as if, at some point in his life, he'd been in too much of a rush to waste time in the barber's chair and had decided to leave partway through the procedure – and the look stuck. His clothes were practical, all of which appeared to have been made for a much larger man. His rough hands and leather-tanned skin being typical of someone who chose to spend much of his time outdoors.

But the real measure of the man was in his face. His eyes, along with his ever present smile, spoke of someone who took joy from life in such an infectious way that you couldn't help but be drawn in. He was also – attested to by Beryl, often with rolling eyes – very popular with the ladies, particularly those of a certain age and type. Typically genteel ladies of wealth, many of whom would travel from as far as Paris to spend time and a night or two in Gérard's tiny, almost off-grid house with whatever allure he could muster.

He once told me that if his garden gate was closed, then we were not permitted to visit, as he would be entertaining. If his gate was open, then we could visit him anytime.

Beryl introduced him to us one sunny afternoon, just after our mandatory two-hour French lunch. I was preparing to give the grass in the orchard a particularly short cut – part of our usual routine for shutting the house up before returning to England the next day – when Beryl and Gérard meandered onto our drive.

"Woo hoo!" Beryl's enthusiastic greeting, accompanied by vigorous waving, was her signature arrival announcement, regardless of whether we'd already spotted her approach.

And on this occasion, we had. Nevertheless, she carried on with her routine right to the end. Either to support Beryl or perhaps thinking this was an English custom, Gérard also joined in with some frantic waving of his own, though he prudently opted out of the 'woo hooing'.

With his ever-present smile and mischievous twinkle in his eye, he stood beside Beryl, adding a touch of his unique charm to the already lively scene. His presence was like a breath of fresh air, and we immediately sensed that meeting him was going to be one of those cherished moments.

As we exchanged pleasantries, Gérard's infectious joy for life shone through, and it quickly became apparent why Beryl had insisted we meet him. His warmth and charisma were undeniable.

"Bonjour, ça va?" I called down the drive, embracing the French custom.

"I've brought Gérard to meet you," announced Beryl, making no effort to speak French for the benefit of our guest. Then, in perfect though charmingly accented English, Gérard said, "You must be Colin and Clare. Barrel has told me so much about you. I am very pleased to meet you at last," extending his hand with a warm smile. This was Gérard.

"I hear that you speak French also?" he continued without waiting for a response. "Well done for at least trying," he added, a huge grin spreading across his weather-beaten face.

"Ah yes, you picked up on my poor efforts at your language. Your English, by the way, is very good," I replied, accepting his proffered hand and delivering a manly grasp and shake. Remembering my father's sage advice: "The way you shake a man's hand is a first and lasting impression. Use the moment well. Always grasp firmly, look the other man squarely in the eyes, shake his hand up and down, no more than four times, and release."

Apparently, things to avoid included a limp grasp –

demonstrating uncertainty and probable weakness in character – and looking anywhere other than into the other man's eyes, was downright rude. Gérard's gaze and handshake were spot on, with an added mischievous smile for good measure. I instantly liked the man, and something told me we would be friends. It was also the first time I heard him refer to Beryl as "Barrel," enjoying the moment a little too much by rolling the r's for dramatic effect.

He then turned his attention to Clare. "Madam, my door will always be open for you. You must come visit, and if you wish, you can bring Colin too. But do not feel obliged to do so." Outrageous, and he knew it.

Then Maggie appeared, and Gérard's mischievousness went up a notch. "This is Maggie, our daughter," I said, as she emerged from the house, dressed and ready to don the mower and cut the grass.

"This is your daughter, really?" Gérard turned to Clare. "I can see immediately that your daughter gets none of her looks from her father." In response, Maggie gave Gérard one of those dismissive looks that only young ladies of a certain age are capable of and simply asked me where the keys to the mower were. Gérard simply laughed and patted me on the back. "She may not have your looks, monsieur, but she has your – how do you say in English – je ne sais quoi." The irony of him using a French language saying as being an English one, wasn't lost on me.

To break the moment and move the conversation along, I offered our guests a drink. Coffee, an iced soft drink – as it was quite hot – or even tea? After all, we were standing on English soil.

"Whisky!" announced Gérard with a grin.

For the remainder of the afternoon and well into the early evening, we found ourselves gathered around the makeshift table I had cobbled together from an old door and a collection of mismatched chairs left behind by the previous owners. There we sat – Clare, Gérard, Beryl, and I – drinking anything but tea or coffee. The harmonious sounds of laughter and our sit-on mower permeated our otherwise idyllic slice of Brittany.

As the afternoon wore on, Gérard became increasingly imbibed, and his English deteriorated into an unintelligible blend of Franglais. Amidst the revelry, we learned that he had spent a considerable part of his youth on the Channel Islands, which explained his English prowess, and that he had once been the mayor of a town somewhere in Brittany. His accent, however, grew so thick that we never quite caught the name of the town. Clare, ever the gracious hostess, provided apéritifs at the designated time – though Gérard deemed Twiglets to be "shit," – and our little soirée continued until it was time for dinner. As we parted ways, Gérard insisted that during our next visit from England, we must come to his house and allow him to return the hospitality – provided his garden gate was open. If closed, it meant he was entertaining. One condition: when at his house, we spoke French; at ours, we spoke English.

As Clare cleared the table, I watched Gérard and Beryl make their way down the lane. Beryl continued to reprimand him for mispronouncing her name. "My name is Beryl. B-E-R-Y-L. Beryl!"

"But that is what I am saying, Barrel – complete with rolled r's – B-E-R-Y-L, Barrel!" Gérard insisted, grinning mischievously.

Reflections

Journal entry from July 2015 *– Looks as though we're all set to shut the place up ready to return to England. For how long I'm not sure. I'll spend the time on the ferry tomorrow reflecting on this, our latest, visit to what I hope will become our actual home sooner rather than later.*

We seem to have crammed a lot in these past few weeks. Good to have Maggie helping out and a real joy to see her driving the mower around – and with such confidence. Not too many teenage tantrums which is always a bonus. Clare looks healthy, though, like me, tired from all the exertions. But it's a good tired, an honest tired. Not the brain sapping tiredness I get from my job. And boy have we slept. That is after the nightly ritual of clearing the room of mosquitos. They always seem to attack just as you're settling in. We're laying there dropping off to sleep and then there's the familiar buzz close to the ear. Switch the light on and the bugger's nowhere to be seen. But that doesn't stop me leaping from the bed, naked, like some crazed thing, brandishing a flip flop – no I don't mean my penis – attempting to hunt down the despicable creature. Then when I do bring it down I get an earful from Clare because I've squashed it on the newly painted bedroom wall. Some you win, quite a few you lose I guess. We were introduced to Gérard today. Now there's someone who I reckon will make our time here quite entertaining. Did he struggle with Beryl's name or was he just winding her up? But we both found it funny, as he repeatedly referred to her as Barrel, and even rolling his r's as he did so – loved that. She was clearly not happy, though I get the feeling it's not the first time. Looks like my shift on mosquito watch is over, no sound from along the corridor from Maggie's room and Clare is soundo. Lights off for me too, early start tomorrow.

***

There was no denying that we'd covered a considerable amount of ground over those few weeks – and the previous months – it must be said. Equally undeniable was the increasing difficulty we faced each time we had to pack up and return to England. Each farewell became a bit more bittersweet, and the allure of our little slice of Brittany grew stronger with every visit.

***

Journal entry from July 2015 – *The end of our summer holiday; Sitting in my favourite spot, outside at the back of the ferry as we head to Portsmouth. Clare, Maggie and Jack are in the dog friendly cabin. With Jack no doubt shaking and panting, Clare no doubt feeling queasy and Maggie no doubt moaning.*

I'm in no rush to join that little gathering so I'll just sit next to my new best friend, an ice cold beer, and think on the last couple of weeks. Despite some misgivings about the French I have to say I'm warming to them. There's a gentle candidness and a real sense of humour that I'm growing to like. Entertainment and amusement is uncomplicated where even the simplest of things, like our time in the garden yesterday, was hugely enjoyable. There's also something about the language that I know people have often said, but I can now say is an actual truth. The more you use the language the more confident you become. I wouldn't dare to say I'm anywhere near fluent yet, but I was pretty pleased with myself for being able to order the fish for our paella the other night. So nearly seven or so months into the year and we have part of the new kitchen done, most of the oak floor in the kitchen / dining area is laid and we have a fully functioning piano. The bathroom's finished, new boiler and oil tank and I have the much talked about generator on standby in the barn, ready to go. Never had one before – like a lot of things I currently have and yet to have. Much like the life jacket under the seat on an aeroplane, I guess. I'm pleased it's there but hope I never have call to use it. We've even managed to tame some of the land, although I understand much of it will be messed up by the new fosse.

I've dared to open a few emails from work so I know I'm walking into a bit of a shit storm on Monday. But for now I'll try and shut that out. It was good to meet Gérard at last and have a feeling that we'll be seeing a lot more of the bloke. That'll do for now. Must remember to phone Alan when we get back to see if he's heard from Christian yet. 20K is a lot of money but I'm not sure we have any choice.

I reckon it must be about time to go tractor hunting when I get home.

'We've even managed to tame some of the land…'

'So nearly seven or so months into the year and we have part of the new kitchen done, most of the oak floor in the kitchen / dining area is laid and we have a fully functioning piano...'

A RELUCTANT RETURN TO ENGLAND – KIND OF

Returning to England and plunging back into the daily grind was like going from a gentle stroll to a hundred yard dash. My whole days were in stark contrast to those wonderful weeks basking in our sanctuary in Brittany. Clare, too, felt the pinch; despite her freedom from the confines of an office, she found the bustle and hum of England a tough act to get back into.

Yet, amidst the pandemonium, some perks did shine through. For instance, the internet in England; surprisingly swift despite our rural postcode. Nearly everyone was happy to conduct business online, and tradespeople, bless their inflated prices, did their best to show up on time. The banks, in particular, revelling in their aloofness, making in-branch visits a rare ordeal – a far cry from France, where having to visit our local branch and writing cheques remained all too common.

But the crowning glory, unmatched by any other place on earth in my opinion, awaited me back in England: a pint of proper English ale, served in a genuine English pub, accompanied by a hearty pork pie. There really is nothing like the simple pleasures of life!

***

The rest of that year, specifically the ongoing works to our Bretagne house, came in fits and starts. Small jobs, finishing off one or two of those bigger ones, that type of thing. Though there were still many half-finished projects – too many for my liking.

Our hopes were high though, as there was the distinct possibility that we would have a functioning septic tank system anytime soon. Works had started, though with us having little time to be there, Alan acted as our sentinel, armed with a mobile phone for daily updates and snapshots. It all seemed rather straightforward – until they (the local council workers) hit the small matter of locating the elusive existing tank.

Despite the local council's best efforts, including the water diviner – likely now either pursuing other mystical endeavours or drawing on his unemployment insurance – the tank remained concealed. Eventually, it was discovered that our so called septic system was, in reality, an enormous concrete container cunningly masquerading beneath the boiler house. And was indeed full to overflowing, with no apparent means of emptying its decades long contents. Enter the merry band of septic tank experts with a solution that I would describe as adventurous.

Alan, in his customary style, regaled us with the details: The team hammered a hole through and into the concrete bunker and inserted a hose, which they attached to a super sucker tanker lorry. Generations of waste disappeared into the gaping maw of *two* lorries – enough, according to Alan, to make even the most stoic among the council workers wince. With the tank nearly empty, save for some stubborn residue, required – he assumes – the apprentice (likely last seen making plans to quit) to descend into the abyss, shovel in hand. A thorough jet wash followed, but it was doubtful one bath would cleanse the poor lad.

The final act was diverting the waste pipework from the pit, sending it off to join the new system being installed in what used to be called a front garden. Now only fit to re-enact the battle of the Somme. Although we were assured that some making good would be done. The old pit was filled in, left to slumber for eternity, or until the next unfortunate soul stumbled upon it.

'Our hopes were high though, as there was the distinct possibility that we could have a functioning septic tank system anytime soon.'

'...used to be called a front garden. Now only fit to re-enact the battle of the Somme.'

***

Things were indeed progressing in our absence, albeit in a manner that wasn't conducive to a couple of eager types. The new barn roof was still a figment of our imagination, but that didn't deter EDF, the intrepid electrical authority, from upgrading the farm's incoming equipment. Compliance with the latest regulations was their mantra, even though the next rainstorm would likely transform it into an electrical disaster. As I once thought of telling the French electrician – though thought better of it, if you remember – Even I knew that water and electricity were hardly the best of bedfellows. Hey Ho!

Alan cheerfully informed us that our quotation for the new roof had ascended Christian's priority list from 'thinking about it' to 'really thinking about it,' yet still no action. Meanwhile, we had a new wood burner installed, complete with a flat cooking surface on top – a gem of a recommendation from Alan. His wise words of caution about potential power cuts in Brittany meant we could still whip up a meal whilst living in a post-apocalyptic state. Little did we know, a year or so later, we'd find ourselves dining by candlelight, sipping wine and devouring crepes during a two-day power cut, toasting our wise old friend. More on that escapade later.

We did manage to venture across the Channel couple more times that year, surveying the remnants left by the Baud Communaute and indulging in short breaks, ensuring no malaise crept into our grand adventure. Not that there was much risk of that – taking life for granted was never our style.

***

As the year limped towards its finale, I somehow found the time to embark on a tractor shopping spree. With as much knowledge of tractors as a goldfish would have about climbing trees, it had all the makings of a disastrous venture. Surprisingly, it wasn't a disaster; it was a brilliant day out! I not only ordered a tractor but also an assortment of implements – gadgets and gizmos galore – that I had grand ideas for, even if their actual use was a mystery to me.

During this period, my journal entries ground to an abrupt halt. In fact, my solitary entry, destined to be the year's final flourish, was penned in that odd lull between Christmas and New Year's. Whether I was nursing the aftereffects of seasonal overindulgence remains a mystery, but as you'll see from the excerpt below, my spirits were decidedly less than buoyant.

***

Journal entry from end of December 2015 – *Funny old Christmas that. My usual over enthusiasm for the holiday seemed to desert me this year. My mind is clearly on other things. Obviously the house and new life we've planned for ourselves in Brittany, but strangely enough it's the prospect of going into work next week and announcing my retirement. And in doing so committing to a clear date to exit from gainful and paid employment. A definite end of an era. And bearing in mind how old I am now, it's one that will never be repeated. Do you know what? I have been, continually employed, in some form or another, and for one Company or another – including our own Company – for over forty five years. Never have I had a need (or desire) to call on the State to pay my way, I've always found work. Though not always in a job I particularly enjoyed but needs must when there's bills to pay. I blame (or thank) my father for my attitude towards (not) holding my hand out to the State. For him, as it has been for me and my brothers, carries with it a stigma,* associated with that of failure. I remember dad telling us that if he had to go dig up potatoes for the local farmer, to put food on our table, then he would, rather that, than hold his hand out. The same intelligent, flawed man, who I remember choosing to be a painter and decorators assistant rather than draw what we used to term as the 'Dole'.

I wonder what he'd make of today's career scroungers, who'd rather draw benefits than find work?

Clare and I have spoken of this moment (me retiring) for some time now and as much as she is keen to get things going, she has been consistent in letting me know that the timing of our move will be when I feel I'm ready. Twelve months ago I was ready to throw the towel in. I'm thinking there was a lot of bravado in that attitude.

To anyone out there, reading this. First of all, why are you reading my private journal? And secondly, do not underestimate the difficulty of actually retiring when the time comes.

Nothing to report from France. Had a call with Alan and Hélène on Boxing Day. They also sent lots of photos of themselves and family clearly having a great time. Something to consider when we're there. They have their French Christmas dinner on Christmas Eve, as is the tradition over there, and then – for Alans benefit – they have an English Christmas feast on Christmas Day. Not sure we'll do the same when we're there, but then who knows.

PART FIVE

THE ANTICLIMAX OF A CLIMAX

They say life doesn't come with a manual, and we were living, breathing proof of that. This was another year destined to change the course of our lives forever. No matter the outcome, there was no doubting that our adventure would leave us with indelible memories. Now, I'm not suggesting we never had our ups and downs – not at all. But you'll have to keep reading to uncover the full story.

Even before the clocks chimed in 2016, we knew it would be a year laden with certainties. The first of which was my retirement date – end of February. However, between now and then, a mountain of preparations loomed, none of which involved our move to Brittany.

If there's one lesson business has taught me, it's that reputation is everything. It's a precious thing, harder to keep than a handful of sand, and more challenging to protect from those who'd see it tarnished. Over the years, many tried – and failed – to sully mine. After forty plus years of safeguarding it, I was determined not to falter at the final hurdle. Once I'm gone, of course, the tarnishers can run rampant, and, knowing them as I do, they probably will.

"Blame Colin," they'll say. "He's no longer here."

Fast forward to the end of February, and after two whirlwind jaunts to Seattle, two to Finland, and a fleeting visit to Hong Kong, the day of my grand departure finally dawned. It was an anticlimax rivalling that of my school-leaving days. I recall walking to the school office, announcing that I had just completed my final examination, only to be met with a nonchalant, "bye bye then." No prom for me, but I did indulge in a 'gap' weekend before diving into the world of work the following Monday. At sixteen, I harboured the delusion that I knew everything there was to know about, well, everything. Reality hit hard when I realised I knew bugger all about most things.

Decades later, my exit from the professional arena was equally unceremonious. I managed to toast with a few comrades I'd known over the years, but alas, there was no grand party, no gold watch, not a crumb of cake. Just some digital well-wishes and a curt reminder to return all the Company equipment in the prepaid box provided. The whole affair felt more like a lacklustre administrative task than the end of an era.

On February 29th – that rare leap year gift – I found myself tying up a few loose ends. By the next day, March 1st, my access to anything business related had simply vanished. Overnight, the gateway to my professional playground had been bolted shut – for good. Why I even attempted to log in to my now bygone life is beyond me, and why I was so astonished when access was denied is another mystery. Nevertheless, there I was, staring at the screen in disbelief. Username and password not recognised!

I rose from my home office chair, made the ceremonial trek to the kitchen, and put the kettle on. Thus, the inaugural act of my retirement was to brew a cup of tea. I'm not sure how this stacks up against the grander pursuits of other fledgling retirees, but in hindsight, it does seem a bit underwhelming.

On that first day, and a few following, I found myself adrift in a sea of purposelessness. No emails pinged into my inbox, nor were there any frantic requests for online meetings at ungodly hours. I was perilously close to becoming a 'used to be' – that familiar breed of pub and bus stop philosophers clinging to bygone glories. "So how do you know that?" "Well, I used to be [a so and so]."

I was determined not to join their ranks. Instead, I dodged any queries about my former profession, skilfully steering conversations to the present. "So, what did you do before you retired?"

"Oh, this and that. I'm thinking of getting a weather vane for the barn, what do you reckon?"

Moreover, I took great pains not to reveal my background in business management or computers – dear Lord, no. Ask anyone with a useful trade or skill, and they'll tell you the same: the moment you reveal your expertise, you become an agony aunt for everyone's grievances. In my case, it was often IT issues – not that I was any expert I just happened to have worked with these monsters since before they became a household object.

In those early days of my retirement, Clare adhered to her well-honed routines, Maggie floated through her ever changing school schedule, and even Jack, had a daily itinerary that was as consistent as the tides. I, on the other hand, found myself brewing tea at all hours and coaxing Jack into impromptu walks. Unfortunately he became averse to these excursions unless they involved a pub stop and some pork scratchings. Even then, he seemed to find it all rather peculiar.

I needed to embrace my retirement, or more accurately, I needed to get myself to Saint-Barthélemy.

***

Journal entry from April 2016 – *Good to be back in familiar surroundings with quite a few recognisable faces, referring of course to the staff, though I don't know any of them personally. The only ferry we could get in short order was this Poole to Cherbourg one. So a bit of a drive at the other end, but at least the crossing will be short. Which Clare, Maggie and Jack are no doubt pleased about. Just had my usual breakfast – Full English without tomatoes but of course served with tomatoes. I think they do it on purpose now. Fully loaded Land Rover but no trailer this time.*

It was the first time we've been pulled over at the port by the British authorities to have a look at what we're carrying.

The inspectors, two in fact, one woman and a bloke, older than me, were quite amiable. Seemed like this was more of a hobby than a real job to them – very chatty they were. One where they get to have interesting conversations with seafarers such as ourselves. Less of an inspection and more of a meet up really. The actual process included, the lady asking me to open the back of the car, allowing her to peer inside. She was unlikely to see much as she never had a torch and it was well before six in the morning, so still quite dark. And the old bloke, presenting me with an A4 list that included knives, axes, petrol cans, and the like, going on to ask whether we had any of theses dangerous things onboard. To which I simply replied in the negative, despite us having quite a few of the items on the list stowed away in the back of the Landy. But they quickly waved us through as a very new looking caravan behind us seemed to grab their interest.

Maggie is off school now, revision or something, so we get to spend quite a bit of time there. No doubt grass cutting will be on the cards, though Alan has already done the first cut of the year with his tractor. Which reminds me, my tractor and all its accessories is due to be delivered in the next week or so. Better check on the others.

***

Returning to our soon to be home in Saint-Barthélémy was, without a doubt, a really good feeling. I sensed the same sentiment in Clare as we parked on the newly laid gravel drive, courtesy of the Baud Communaute's enthusiastic fosse septique project. There we sat in the Land Rover, engine off, gazing at the polyethene roofed barn that, in that moment, was the epitome of rustic charm. In all honesty, it was as attractive as a warthog clothed in black polythene, but our joy knew no bounds. Our future landlocked island paradise awaited.

Maggie, on the other hand, was keen to make a hasty exit from the car. Jack, ever the poor traveller, was relieved the journey had concluded, albeit for reasons of his own. With the back of the vehicle crammed with household items, bedding, tools, and a smattering of groceries, his travel crate had been evicted. Thus, he endured the entire five-hour trek from Cherbourg in close proximity to Maggie. Close proximity being an understatement, as he panted and drooled his way through the trip, much to Maggie's irritation.

Leaving Maggie to her own devices to regain her composure, wash her face, and likely change into something considerably drier, Clare, Jack, and I decided to take a leisurely stroll up the farm. We meandered past the hangar, our relic of rustic instability, and entered the verger, now magnificent with blossoms in full bloom. The evening air had just begun its passage from the warmth of a splendid spring day to the coolness of dusk, but the air still buzzed with the activity of countless unseen insects, creating a sound of nature's own making.

We found ourselves standing amidst our lively verger, momentarily pausing to soak in the serenity of the scene around us. The mingling fragrances of various fruit blossoms drifted through the air, carried by the warm breeze of a soon to end spring day. The setting sun bathed everything in a golden hue, just before it dipped below the overgrown laurel hedge – a grand and sprawling example that stood as a natural windbreak for what had once been, and would be again, the potager.

I'm no poet, but the atmosphere was almost magical, a sensory delight that enveloped us completely. The verger, with its subtle colours and scents, felt like a hidden sanctuary – our sanctuary – of tranquillity amidst the bustle of our life on the other side of the Channel. Jack, seemed to revel in the newfound freedom, his tail wagging furiously as he trotted about, sniffing everything in sight before settling down at a suitable sleeping place of his choosing. Clare and I shared a knowing glance, a silent acknowledgment of the peace and contentment that this place brought us. It was a moment of unadulterated joy, a brief escape from the mundane realities of the life we had endured since the beginning of the year.

'... as we parked on the newly laid gravel drive, courtesy of the Baud Communaute's enthusiastic fosse septique project.'

Apart from that first magical moment, when we'd just bought the place, sitting in our pound shop chairs with grass so long and no view to be had – though we knew it was there – we had yet to fully experience our soon to be home, in all its splendour.

Returning now, it felt as though we were seeing the place anew. Gazing upon the expanse before us, we grasped the enormity of the work that awaited us, stretching out not just into the foreseeable future, but well beyond into an unknown tomorrow. So far, our focus had been on overcoming the wild patch that would become our garden and soon to be vegetable plot, sparing little thought for the legacy left behind by the former custodians of this land.

Surveying what was once a tangled and neglected but undeniably charming verger, I could now identify at least five or six different types of tree that, one day, we hoped would reward us with fruit – most of which Clare already had grand plans to bottle and bake. There were apples (*pommes*) of various kinds, pears (*poires*), plums (*prunes*) – yes, I know – a walnut (*noyer*) tree, three peach (*pêche*) trees, and a couple of damson (*quetsche*) trees. Despite its scruffy state, you could still sense the care and affection that had gone into planting it all those years ago.

The trees' sizes suggested that this iteration – there had probably been a verger in this spot for countless generations, with trees being replaced and so on – was likely fifteen to twenty years old. Though with one or two thick trunked apple trees looking like they might date back to the dawn of the farm itself. Whatever its age, the layout was impressive: neatly spaced rows of apple and pear trees, another row devoted entirely to plums, and then just beyond, in a sheltered spot, were the peach trees.

However, the patriarch of them all was a colossal walnut

tree. Its trunk must have been at least three metres in circumference, and its height dwarfed every other tree in the hamlet by a significant margin. If you've ever been fortunate enough to taste fresh walnuts, you'll know how different they are from the ones you buy in the shops. By the time the store bought ones reach your mouth, they've lost much of their natural moistness and flavour. I only know this because we had the delightful experience of eating freshly harvested walnuts from our very own tree. And there's no going back.

Aside from the romantic daydreams that had captured our imaginations, and despite the verger's valiant attempt at impressing us, it was glaringly obvious that an avalanche of work awaited us. At that moment, my knowledge of pruning fruit trees was virtually non-existent, limited to the fact that this time of year called for minimal intervention – just the bare essentials, or as I would soon need to learn, 'horticultural triage.'

As for Jack, he was blissfully snoozing in the verger while we trudged back to the house, ignoring the battlefield – courtesy of Baud Communaute – that had once been our front garden, and into the house. The house now boasted a shiny new kitchen atop a half-finished oak floor, a sparkling new bathroom with a fully functioning waste system, and last but not least, a teenager exuding unrivalled levels of grumpiness.

***

Over the past year or so, we had been gradually smuggling a few home comforts from England. This meant that we – well, Clare actually – managed to assemble beds for us all in rooms that had been thoroughly stripped, yet still craved for the touch of refurbishment. We also had an assortment of kitchenware and crockery, allowing our new piano to strut its stuff. But with the weather being superb, my attention was firmly fixated on the outdoor space – of which, you already know, there was a generous amount.

Where to begin was the burning question, and it seemed that at every turn, I encountered a fresh obstacle. One task inevitably led to another. Either I lacked the necessary equipment, or some other impediment presented itself. Take the Somme, for example – a relatively simple, though back-breaking, task. I knew precisely what needed to be done. The area, approximately thirty by fifty metres, was destined to be transformed into a lawn. First, it needed to be roughly raked, rocks and large stones – of which there was an embarrassment of riches – removed, grass seeds sown, and then watered – religiously.

I had a plethora of hand tools, a fleet of wheelbarrows, countless locations where rocks and rubble could be exiled, abundant water from the well, but I lacked a vital component – grass seed. However, this was a minor hiccup, as I was reasonably confident that somewhere in Brittany, a shop existed where I could procure a few sacks. The real conundrum arose when I ventured to figure out how to extract water from the well.

The well was located near the entrance of our property and adjacent to it, at the end of the house, was a small pump room. Inside was a water tank and an intricate array of valves, along with what I presumed to be the all-important pump. It turns out that this elaborate setup was designed to divert well water into the house for use in the washing machine, etc. Not that we would likely employ such an arrangement, largely because the pipework had been disconnected just as it entered the house. Discovering this led to my first, of many drenching's courtesy of the well.

I soon discovered that using a well in the manner described was a common practice among farming communities in France. Not for drinking water, of course, thanks to the rise of modern farming contaminants. This practice, while still not uncommon among the older stalwarts, was banned some years ago, which is why fresh water is now piped into farms. However, we could have taken a sample of our well water to the local pharmacist, who would have provided us with a report on its potability. Just one of the many extraordinary services pharmacists offer. Another being mushrooms. Yes, you heard right, mushrooms! Foraging, while a trendy activity for city folk in the UK looking to make some statement or other, is a regular pastime in rural France.

People regularly go out and forage, especially for mushrooms, often the rarer, more expensive ones like Chanterelles. If you've ever gone mushroom picking, you'll know that many look alike, and some might appear appetising, but could actually be quite toxic. In France, pharmacists offer a service where you can bring in your foraged haul, and they will inform you of what is safe to eat and what isn't.

Now, here's the rub: considerable prestige is attached to one's foraging prowess. So much so that relying on a pharmacist to assess your haul is rather frowned upon. It instantly brands you as either a novice or, even worse, a foreigner – neither of which are deemed worthy of the exalted title of '*Cueilleur.*'

'...abundant water from the well...'

Back in the pump room, I strutted in, confident of my innate blokeish prowess over this intricate plumbing jumble. The girls were out on one of their customary shopping binges, so I spared them the expected "watch and learn" lecture.

I rolled up my sleeves and switched on the electrical isolator for the pump, optimistically expecting a torrent of water. At first, the pump played dead, but a neat bypass of some trivial safety device soon had it roaring to life. Let me tell you, there's nothing quite like the sound of water surging from the bowels of the earth.

In my excited triumph, I overlooked a crucial detail: any mechanism to shut off the pump when the storage tank became full. Could it be, by any chance that pesky safety device I so cleverly bypassed? A vital cog in this operation it would seem. Still scratching my head and with a small amount of panic rising, the pressure release valve performed its duty with exuberant zeal, releasing a spectacular geyser. The aged, rusting pipework, no longer able to withstand such excitement, disintegrated, turning the pump room into a watery underworld.

So there I stood, drenched from head to toe, as the pump continued – at an impressive rate it should be said – to, transform the pump room, the size of a telephone box, into an impromptu water world.

Managing to switch off the pump at the isolator – an ill-advised manoeuvre considering the water chaos that had just unfolded – I sloshed out of the pump room, unleashing a mini deluge as the door swung open. Drenched but undeterred, I stepped into the sunshine to dry off and collect my thoughts. Instantly, I determined that the well would henceforth be consigned to garden watering and car washing duties.

Determined to create a basic irrigation and cleaning system, I rummaged through the barn and triumphantly unearthed a substantial coil of rubber hosing, at least seventy metres long. With visions of self-sustained hydrological prowess in my head, I dipped into the limitless options of the online marketplace. It seemed the world was teeming with fellow enthusiasts of garden and car maintenance, all on the quest for the perfect pump.

In true bloke fashion, I disregarded all sensible recommendations regarding well depth and water draw, opting instead for the next size up. Better safe than sorry, and all that. Forty-eight hours and a large express delivery fee later, an unexpectedly hefty box arrived on our driveway.

Wasting no time, I had everything rigged up and bled the pump motor with impressive efficiency. The moment of truth had arrived: would my improvised apparatus summon water from the bowels of the earth on the first try? As it happens, it did – exceeding all my expectations and then some.

With Maggie delightfully preoccupied with cutting some

early spring flowers about fifty metres or so away, she seemed like the perfect target for both range and accuracy. I figured a gentle sprinkling would suffice for my unscientific research, although I braced myself for a potential tantrum. Ready, aim, fire! Within seconds, poor Maggie was unceremoniously knocked off her feet, her basket of flowers soaring into the neighbouring field. Evidently, I had inadvertently purchased a pump of riot-control calibre. Bloody brilliant!

I hastily shut the pump down, seizing the brief window of time it took for Maggie to gather her wits, pick herself up, and process the watery assault. In true tactical retreat fashion, I made a run for it.

The next couple of days saw me transforming a battlefield of rocks and stones, reminiscent of the Somme, into a space fit for a lawn. Three days later, five substantial sacks of grass seed arrived, which I enthusiastically scattered, like a seed sower of old. Watering became a far gentler affair compared to Maggie's rude awakening, as I aimed the water skyward, letting it fall like a monsoon rain.

CHRISTMAS DAY IN APRIL

Journal entry from April 2016 – *I am the proud owner of a tractor. But only a small one. For some reason the bloke brought his family over with him to deliver the gear. Not sure whether he thought we could give them a short holiday break. But for one we don't have the beds – though I got the impression they'd be happy with the floor – and secondly their son, who I'm thinking was about ten, reminded me of Damien, that scary kid from the film The Omen. There was clearly something not right with that lad. I'd normally say it's all in the eyes but his were a bottomless black. Anyway I think the dad got the hump with me when I didn't offer, so much so that he's left me with all this gear and I have no idea how it works. How hard can it be? I'll find out tomorrow.*

Good to see Gérard again and we've been invited to Beryls for supper next week. Went to his for aperitifs (apperos) in his little Hobbit house and had my first – and last – try of his homemade eau de vie (water of life). More like eau de la mort. I'm not sure whether he was pleased or surprised that he'd had the same bottle for quite some time – years in fact. We tried to speak French all evening, as per our rules, though to be honest it was more Franglais. But at least we tried and he seemed happy that we did. Maggie stayed at home under the pretence of looking after Jack, as I think she finds Gérard a bit creepy. We told hm we were going to Beryl's for supper which he didn't seem to be too envious about.

This place never seems to disappoint. The walk from Gérards to ours is only less than five minutes but that's all it took for me to realise how many more stars there actually are in the sky. You read about this stuff, and see on TV those programmes about the night sky, but I swear, until just a few minutes ago I had not appreciated how much there is to marvel at, when there are no street lamps, or other lamps to pollute your view. Not sure I'll become a stargazer though. Too much to do on earth just now.

***

The tranquillity of Saint-Barthélémy enveloped me like a comforting blanket. Folks often describe absolute silence as "deafening," though I've never quite grasped that concept. What I can tell you is that, particularly on that night, it was wonderfully peaceful. Save for the owls, the occasional wild boar crashing through the undergrowth (truly heart-stopping), and the amorous foxes serenading the countryside with their high-pitched yelps.

The night sky put on a spectacular display, a celestial extravaganza that I'd never witnessed before, even after living so long in rural England. The sheer number of stars prompted a strong urge to want to buy a telescope, a temptation I managed to resist. As I was reminded of the telescope I bought for our son when he was a boy – a spur of the moment gift that seemed inspired at the time. I envisioned us spending countless hours together, my arm draped casually over his shoulders as he peered through the lens, eagerly naming constellations while I jotted them down in a little notebook. In reality, after just one outing, the telescope found a permanent home under his bed, alongside a host of other 'great idea' gifts, rarely seeing the light of day. A few years later, I discreetly sold it to a father and son duo, spinning tales of our many celestial adventures, to fetch a good price. When our son eventually asked about his telescope while packing for university, I merely shrugged, feigning ignorance, in case he got any ideas about claiming a share of the proceeds.

***

I had purposefully turned down Alan's generous offer to mow the grass in the potager and verger, which had grown to a formidable metre in some places, despite him having cut it just six weeks earlier. The reason? My own, albeit miniature, tractor and an assortment of accessories had arrived from England – and I was really excited. The prospect of teaching myself how to operate it all was slightly less thrilling. But there was no way I was going to let that creepy kid stay in the same house as a sleeping me.

Enter YouTube, my saviour. I found a treasure trove of instructional videos, all playing in slo-mo – not so much to help me grasp the instructions, but because our sluggish Wi-Fi was struggling to keep up. The signal didn't extend as far as the hangar, requiring an annoying routine of to-ing and fro-ing to the tablet PC in the kitchen – the outer reaches of the network's realm.

Eventually, Alan arrived. After he had his hearty laugh at the diminutive size of my mini Kabuto tractor and its so called Toytown accessories, he graciously got down to business, teaching me the basics. This included hooking up various implements, such as the topper, which was destined to see the most action.

'I am the proud owner of a tractor. But only a small one.'

***

As we prepared to leave for our home in England – what would be our final reference to any home in England – the grass on the Somme was just beginning to sprout. I gave it one last deluge with the water cannon before securing everything or stowing it in the barn, still awaiting its new roof. Maggie seemed quite content to be departing, but she announced, out of the blue, that she wanted to give France a try, meaning she wouldn't pursue further education but come live with us, at least for as long as she could tolerate our company. This was a topic for a lengthy discussion once we returned to England. Jack, meanwhile, seemed blissfully unaware of the impending car and ferry journey, his recent car rides limited to short trips to the Blavet for our daily walks.

Clare and I, on the other hand, carried out our respective lock-up duties in silence, trying to conceal our sorrow at leaving a place that wasn't quite our home yet. We stayed mostly silent during the short drive to St Malo, anticipating the day long journey to Portsmouth.

Despite it being a daytime crossing, we had access to a cabin, which Clare, Maggie, and Jack utilised, emerging only for meals and the occasional drink. The highlight of my journey back was finally securing a full English breakfast sans tomatoes. However, my request for scrambled eggs (*œufs brouillés*) was met with two delightful fried eggs (*oeufs au plat*). Win some, lose some, I suppose.

'...the Blavet for our daily walks.'

Journal entry from end of April 2016 – *Sitting in my usual place on the St Malo, Portsmouth ferry, right at the back, outside, overlooking a fading France coastline. This is a sad day, though tinged with some happiness. The next time we come over it should be with the removal truck. Curious how Maggie suddenly decided she wanted to come to live in France with us. See how that plays out over the next couple of weeks. Going back home to no work is still a strange feeling but one that I have increasingly gotten used to over these last few weeks. I thought I would miss it, but I really don't. Although in reality what we've just experienced was little more than an extended holiday. I have, I hope, at least another couple of decades to fill, which might require a bit more planning. I've often thought I might write, and I have to say that keeping this journal has given me a bit of an appetite for it. But I have an old farm to put back together first. We certainly covered a lot of ground once more and managed to get out and see some more of Brittany. I did like Vannes and think that's somewhere I might want to go again. Though the Landy was a problem. Its height meant we couldn't park in the underground garage and with its turning circle of an oil tanker I really struggled round those tiny streets. Now I know why most French cars are so small.*

    How Clare manages to pick exactly the right paint colours I'll never know but then I don't get asked. Pleased that oak floor is finished downstairs. Man that was a hard job. But then none of the jobs in that place are easy. I just need to man up a bit I reckon.

***

The day before our departure, following Hélène's suggestion, we embarked on the hour long journey to Vannes. Not the most accommodating place for our Land Rover Defender, but after a mildly exasperating search for parking, we discovered the town and its harbour were well worth the effort. It managed to distract us, albeit temporarily, from the imminent return to England.

Vannes was just one of many charming places we explored, most of them dotted along the picturesque Brittany coast.

Back in England, we had circled the 1st of June 2016 on our calendars as our emigration to France date. This gave us a tight four week window to sort out our affairs, finalise details with the removal company, bid our last farewells, and tackle a whole lot more.

'... following Hélène's suggestion, we embarked on the hour long journey to Vannes.'

**Picture courtesy of the internet

PART SIX

THE FINAL MOVE

Immigrant – *a person who has come to a country that is not their own in order to live there permanently*[1].

That would be me (us) from this day forward.
Interestingly (or not), the Brits we encountered in France – whom we artfully avoided – insisted on calling themselves expats, despite having resided there for many a moon. Apart from familial ties, they had no real base to return to in Britain, should the fancy take them. If you're unfamiliar with the commonly accepted distinction between an expat and an immigrant, allow me to enlighten you: An expat is someone who resides outside their native land, typically for a limited period and with no firm plans to return home. An immigrant, on the other hand, relocates with the intention of settling permanently. Regardless, both expats and immigrants are generally viewed as foreigners in their adopted countries.

One can only surmise that these folks find the term expat more palatable, sparing their delicate sensibilities and the stigma of being labelled immigrants. This term frequently

---
[1] Source – Cambridge dictionary

conjures images of people – often, but not exclusively, desperate people – leaving their homelands in search of a better life for themselves and their families. Much like us, really.

We arrived a few hours ahead of the removals truck, allowing us precious time to open up the house and prepare to receive our belongings from England. The previous week had been a whirlwind of farewells to friends, neighbours, and relatives. My goodbyes to friends, in particular, were brisk and efficient. Clare, however, turned each parting into a mini epic. We concluded the week on Sunday, the 29th of May, with an all the trimmings Christmas dinner in the garden of our particularly good friends, Graham and Julie. Why a Christmas dinner? The reason escapes me now, but it was perfect. Unlike our departure from England.

I'm not sure what I expected, but there were no streamers, no fireworks, no music or entertainment, no speeches and toasts, and no photos. Just the usual mix of novice holiday goers and seasoned travellers – scrutinising each other's trailers and caravans – waiting to board the Portsmouth to St Malo ferry. None of them had the slightest inkling of the significance of this journey for us, one that would undoubtedly shape the rest of our lives.

The Land Rover was crammed to bursting with items we deemed far too precious to entrust to the removal company – chief among them, the kettle and tea supplies, which we firmly believed, had they been packed into a box, would otherwise vanish into oblivion. There we were: Clare, Maggie, myself, and Jack, packed like sardines. And making its maiden and likely solitary voyage was our cat, Nettle, the tabby of considerable self-importance. Nettle treated all with a level of disdain that was bordering on the aristocratic, reserving an extra dose of contempt especially for Jack.

The crossing, you could argue, was a bit choppy. In our day

cabin, Jack adopted his familiar guise of panic-stricken hound, Maggie transformed into the resident grumbler, and Clare teetered precariously on the edge of seasickness. Meanwhile, Nettle, with typical indifference, commandeered the bunk designated for me. I, true to form, took my post at the ferry's stern, watching dear old England recede into the mist while attempting to pen something profound and worthy of literary acclaim in my journal. A lofty aspiration akin to *Robert Burns's* immortal *'The Emigrant's Farewell,'* no less. Unfortunately, fate (and an empty pen) conspired against me. The prospect of purchasing a souvenir Brittany Ferries pen held little allure, given the improbability of me crafting an inspirational piece of verse that people would pay tribute to, hundreds of years later.

Resigned, I succumbed to more mundane pursuits – sleeping, reading, and nibbling on snacks – resolutely avoiding the return to the chaos of our cabin.

Arriving in St Malo was also another exercise in anticlimax. No welcoming brass band, no jubilant streamers – only the undignified scramble of passengers eager to reach the car deck the moment the disembarkation announcement crackled through the public address system. It was as if they believed that by being first to their vehicles, they would somehow accelerate their exit from the boat. Much like those frantic souls on airplanes who leap from their seats and haul luggage from the overhead lockers the instant the 'seatbelt' sign extinguishes, only to clog the aisle with their impromptu bag ballet.

Our ferry compatriots, naturally, ignored instructions to keep their engines off, sitting instead in their vehicles with engines humming in defiant anticipation, awaiting the car deck attendant's grand wave off. Having long learned the futility of such haste, I took my sweet time shepherding our party down to the car deck, ensuring everyone was loaded just as the cars ahead of us were signalled to disembark. Experience, my dear reader, is priceless.

The novices, in their rush, would then speed to the passport control kiosk as if in a rally. Meanwhile, the seasoned travellers, like ourselves, would meander casually, ignoring the arrows directing 'Cars Only', instead heading to the 'HGV Only' kiosk. There, passports in hand, we'd usually find a couple of amiable Gendarmes, awaiting the arrival of the lumbering lorries – and us. We also knew better than to follow the GPS's southbound route, which would inevitably lead through the town or onto a commuter rat run. No, our knowledge of the land gave us the upper hand – every twist and turn memorised in the mental map of a hardened voyager.

***

Alan and Hélène were already 'on-point' at Saint-Barthélémy to greet us as we rolled in around mid-afternoon. The house was open, and although delighted to see us, Alan wore a look of profound concern. After exchanging the usual pleasantries, Alan gently guided me to the kitchen / dining room – the room that had undergone the most dramatic transformation. Demolition, rebuilding, new kitchen, full redecoration, new oak flooring, the works.

As we entered, the cause of Alan's consternation was glaringly apparent. The oak flooring, which I had meticulously stored and laid according to every available instruction – quite a feat for me – looked as though I had buried a small farm animal beneath it. We had a wooden wave, about thirty centimetres high, cresting along one edge of the room. Compounding the issue, just as I was pondering how to tackle this wooden phenomenon, the removal truck arrived. And these fellows were on a mission, needing to turn around swiftly to catch the ferry back to Portsmouth. This left no time for niceties or commiseration over my flooring fiasco, as they rapidly offloaded our belongings with military precision. Despite some of Clare's room labels being followed – beds in bedrooms, that sort of thing – the majority of our possessions ended up in the very room where I was grappling with the oak floor.

Determined to rectify the situation, I wielded a crowbar with little finesse. At last, the floor yielded to my efforts, accompanied by a resounding crack and an involuntary shout from yours truly. The crack signified the release of pressure as the boards separated from the wall, and the shout was my exclamation as the sudden release caused me to topple backwards and wind up winded on the floor. For reasons beyond comprehension, this sent me into a fit of manic laughter.

Amazingly, despite the whirlwind of activity, we managed to squeeze in a cup of tea. The two removal chaps then vanished as swiftly as they had appeared, leaving us amidst the customary chaos that follows moving into a new home. Alan and Hélène soon made their farewells, but not before extending a most welcome invitation to supper, an offer for which we were immensely grateful.

Feeling rather like a third wheel as Clare and Maggie industriously stashed the contents of boxes into cupboards, I ambled up the yard, passing the hangar where the corrugated metal roof sheets creaked in the gentle breeze – with Nettle, our arrogant tabby, already claiming my tractor seat as her new throne. I continued on to the verger, where Jack was blissfully snoozing in the shade generously offered by the trees. Simply being there had an immediately calming effect, as I let the sounds of the verger and the surrounding calm wash over me.

It was as the sun dipped behind the still overgrown laurel hedge – prompting thoughts of yet another necessary gardening toy – that a wave of melancholy swept over me. By all rights, I should have been ecstatic, joyful even. After all, our long journey, conceived as a mere idea three or so years ago, had finally become a reality. This was the dawn of our grand adventure, yet I felt anything but elated. The reason for my discontent eluded me then and still does to this day, but the feeling soon lifted as I made my way back to the house. There, I was greeted by the cheerful sounds of music – Maggie had unearthed the iPod music system – and laughter.

It would take quite some time before our French dwelling felt like home, but while I was adjusting to the notion, there were a multitude of events and experiences to navigate. Each day brought its own peculiar adventures, turning the mundane into a mixture of delightful absurdities and unforgettable moments. Our journey to familiarity was punctuated by the comical and the profound, transforming our new residence into a tapestry woven with stories that would one day, no doubt, become the stuff of legend. Albeit a legend of our own making.

THE IMPROMPTU APPEARANCE OF A NEW BARN ROOF

The early days of June, and at an unholy hour of the morning, a monstrous skip trundles onto the drive. Bleary eyed, I peer out of the window at the commotion and are greeted by an overly cheery, frantically waving Christian.

"*Bonjour! Je suis venu pour commencer votre toit.*" Something to the effect of, "I have come to start your roof."

"*Était-ce arrangé?*" (Was this arranged?) I shouted back.

"*Oui, c'est parfait, je prendrai un café s'il vous plaît. Sans lait.*" (Yes, that's perfect. I'll have a coffee, please, without milk.) He then turned to converse with the skip delivery driver. Naturally, it hadn't been arranged – par for the course with getting any work done in our adopted land.

"What's going on?" a drowsy Clare inquired.

"It's Christian and a skip."

"Christian the roofer?"

"Do you know any other Christians then?" Recently, we'd taken to appending trade titles to names, owed largely to a trio of Daves – Alan's friends – who'd invaded our lives in recent weeks. Dave the aerial man had fitted our satellite dish, Dave the tree man had dealt with a large tree split in two, and Dave the chimney sweep had handled the flues for our new wood burner. A merry band of English immigrants Alan trusted, and which we had now adopted. The fact that we didn't know any other Christians seemed beside the point.

"What did he say?" she asked.

"He's come to start the roof and he'd like a coffee without milk."

"Was this start date arranged?"

"Of course it wasn't." And with that, I trudged off to make coffee for us – plus one.

Clad in my usual tea-shirt and shorts, I ventured forth to

deliver Christian his coffee, finding him already perched on the apex of the barn roof, having torn off his own makeshift polythene repairs. Safety harness, helmet, or shoes? Pish posh! Clearly, these were surplus to his requirements.

Christian's exact age eluded me, but a wild guess would place him in his mid to late forties – no spring chicken, indeed. Like most Bretons, his clothes were less about fashion statements and more about practically covering one's skin. Much like my own recent clothing choices, I might add.

Here was a man clearly built for his trade. Thin and nimble, he moved across the skeletal remains of our barn roof with an agility that bordered on the enviable. Spotting me with his coffee, he greeted me with a jubilant *"bonjour"* and *"merci,"* before descending to ground level with the grace of an acrobat. He accepted the proffered mug (sans lait) with a broad, toothy grin that stretched across his weathered, sun-kissed face.

"Alors, combien de temps pensez-vous que le travail prendra?" (So, how long do you think the job will take?) I inquired, more to break the ice than to elicit any actual commitment. Predictably, Christian merely shrugged, a gesture that conveyed an entire philosophy of nonchalance. Born into every French tradesperson it would seem.

Without further ado, he turned and ascended the heights once more, this time with coffee mug in hand, not spilling a single drop. I watched as he stood, almost regally, on the apex of the roof, surveying the countryside. In that moment, he seemed to bask in a triad of joys: the coffee, the view and, apparently, his very existence.

Christian, became our sunny-day friend. For nearly a month, he'd grace us with his presence, provided the heavens weren't throwing it down. The weather, that summer, for some odd reason, had an obsession with raining on our parade, but Christian had an aversion to such weather-related mischief – he stayed at home – except for one notorious day.

The skies unleashed a storm of epic proportions, complete with thunder and lightning. Christian, caught off guard, attempted to brave the elements like some heroic warrior, until the squall conspired with fate, leading to an unexpected blackout. This time, the culprit wasn't the weather but Christian himself. In a desperate bid to save himself from an unceremonious tumble, he latched onto the nearest object – a rather large electrical supply cable. With one hand clutching the hissing cable and the other gripping a wooden rafter, he resembled a man wrestling an angry eel. My long dormant electrical knowledge sprang to life, and I swiftly cut the main power. Christian, freed from his predicament, expressed his relief in a flurry of colourful French expletives, probably with a dose of Breton flavour – none of which I understood.

I rang Stephane, our go to electrical contractor – and beneficiary of all the plumbing and electrical works we had done in the place – who, while not exactly leaping at the chance to rescue us, promised to lend a helping hand – though typically making no commitment as to when it might be. I pondered bringing our generator into action, but thankfully, an electrician arrived within a couple of hours. As for Christian, he departed, none the worse for wear, undoubtedly with a newfound appreciation of the dubious relationship between rain and electricity.

***

The day our new barn roof was handed over to us, and we parted with a cheque for twenty thousand euros, coincided with the Brexit result. Which, of course, you know about already.

But on that fateful morning of the 23rd June 2016, I took Christian his usual morning cuppa, sans lait, when I heard a shout from the top of our barn. *"Terrible,"* pronounced in the French way, by a genuinely distraught looking Christian. He was, of course, referring to the referendum result. To be honest, we had kept no more than a very lazy eye on proceedings in the UK regarding the whole Brexit thing, thinking it was something the Tory party had agreed to just to appease a few moaning Eurosceptics. But it clearly wasn't.

Not being too sure what it was Christian was raving about, I rushed back into the house and fired up the laptop. Ten minutes later – the time it took for the Wi-Fi to connect me to a search engine – I found myself staring, unbelievably, at the screen. Clare came down the stairs and asked what all the commotion was about, and having told her that the UK had voted in favour of leaving the EU, she responded accordingly and, in hindsight, appropriately. "Silly buggers. What shall we have for breakfast?"

In case you're wondering about her casual attitude, it had nothing to do with a lack of interest on her part. It was, and always has been, her way of dealing with things outside of her control. As far as she's concerned, there is no point in wasting energy or time on moaning or trying to find solutions to things that you have no influence or control over. Far better to use that energy on the things that you can, such as family and, in this case, fixing breakfast. Which she was, and always has been, right about, of course.

Over breakfast, we discussed – or rather, I talked about – the likely impact of this decision by the British public on our being there, all of which was pure supposition on my part and pure patronisation on hers, as she sat quietly listening to my cogitations. When I had finally run out of steam, she simply and gently brought me back to earth. "Will Christian be finished today? Because we need to go shopping at some point."

'...and at an unholy hour of the morning, a monstrous skip trundles onto the drive.'

'The day our new barn roof was handed over to us... coincided with the Brexit result.'

'NORMAL' IS AN INEVITABILITY AND IT'S OKAY

It's rather astonishing how, as humans, we tend to chase after entertainment, excitement, and a whole parade of other pursuits that amusingly start with the letter 'e'. Yet, the truth is, we equally revel in the humdrum, the routine, the everyday stuff. It's a condition we naturally drift into and find ourselves quite content with. That is, until you wake up one morning and realise you've been plodding along in an unremarkable existence, and the status quo could use a good shaking up.

Despite our grand adventure of emigrating, there was no way we wouldn't eventually slip into a routine. Even the most intrepid adventurers must pause from their escapades to cook dinner, wash a few clothes, or pop out for groceries – or in their case, perhaps go hunting, foraging, fishing, for provisions.

The funny thing about life's little rituals is that they sneak up on you. One minute, you're – metaphorically speaking of course – scaling mountains and exploring uncharted territories, and the next, you're contemplating the merits of different laundry detergents. And therein lies the charm. While we crave the thrill of the extraordinary, we equally find solace in the comfort of the ordinary. It's the delicate balance between the two that keeps life from becoming either too mundane or too chaotic. After all, who wouldn't want to experience the exhilarating rush of a grand adventure, followed by the simple pleasure of a well cooked meal and clean clothes? It's these everyday moments that anchor us, providing a steady backdrop to the extraordinary tales we live and tell.

During that first proper summer as starry-eyed immigrants, our days were a balancing act between making essential repairs and performing necessary upgrades to our new home. Of course, there was always the humdrum task of cutting grass to contend with. Yet, despite these domestic drudgeries, we still had the looming task of transforming ourselves into bona fide residents of our adopted country.

One such thing involved obtaining a national insurance number, which, if I recall correctly, was somehow entwined with acquiring the much coveted *'Carte Vitale'*. Or perhaps it was the other way around? Details, details. The Carte Vitale, you see, is the golden ticket to the French health insurance system. For those lucky immigrants who qualify, it promises to cover around sixty to seventy percent of medical expenses, including appointments, scans, and prescriptions. In more serious cases, such as heart disease or cancer, this coverage impressively rises to a full hundred percent. Any remaining costs, unfortunately, come from one's own pocket.

All good but inevitably there's the tedium of bureaucracy to contend with! Even as we embarked on this adventure of ours, it became evident that routine and red tape were inescapable companions in our adopted country.

And so, we found ourselves navigating a maze of paperwork, all while continuing to make our new home liveable as well as learning the rhythm of daily life in a foreign land.

Notwithstanding the bureaucracy there was, like most things in France, a few more hoops to jump through before we were to get the Carte Vitale. I'm not going to bore you with the entire process, as that would make for really dull reading.

In summary, it involved us making several pilgrimages to a special office in Pontivy. Each visit required us to present a plethora of documents, much like contestants in some bureaucratic quest. Our first attempt ended in a humiliating defeat when we were turned away for failing to prove three months of actual residency. But, in a rare moment of French leniency, they allowed us to commence the process by submitting all manner of information, ready for our three month milestone. Apart from the usual suspects – bank account details, proof of address – the most important element was proof of income, which, in our case, consisted of our pensions. This, of course, was fine, except for one minor hiccup: everything was in English. So, we had to provide a precis in French, alongside the English versions.

Consequently, the dance continued. With each visit, we inched closer to our goal, navigating the labyrinthine corridors of the French establishment. But, in the end, we emerged victorious, though we would have to wait, – for some unspecified amount of time – for our cards to be issued.

***

There were one or two other things that still needed sorting out. Nothing extraordinary but no less essential. Finding a dentist was one of those unavoidable tasks. Back in England, we had the same dentist for nearly thirty years, a fine fellow named Mr. Nick Dobbs – whom the kids delightfully dubbed 'Dick Nobbs' (much to his chagrin, I'm sure) – until he retired.

But we loyally stuck with the same practice and welcomed the bright young replacement, a lady with an utterly unpronounceable name. Along with her came an array of modernisations, starting with the transition from the soothing tones of the BBC to something called KISS FM, which left us both bemused. The beloved comedic poster of the old Giles family – a classic by arguably the most famous cartoonist of the twentieth century – was swapped for a cartoon hedgehog frolicking with a caricature of a portly Italian chap. My kids informed me it was from a computer game.

In the short term however, there was no pressing need for a French dentist. We ingeniously altered our English address to that of Clare's parents and scheduled our dental appointments to coincide with our biannual visits to theirs. It wasn't a long-term solution, but it sufficed for the time being.

Next up was the quest for a hairdresser, which I naively assumed would be straightforward. But here's the catch; in Brittany, hair styling seemed to be more of an afterthought. Take Alan, for example, who alternated between his local barber and his wife's clippers. Both options left him looking rather severe and with a decidedly asymmetrical head.

Now, I'm not one for a full on grooming routine, but I do appreciate a tidy barnet. Unlike Clare, I couldn't take advantage of our biannual trips to her parents for a trim, so I decided to embrace the home cut lifestyle. Over a few glasses of wine – never the ideal setting for serious discussions – we agreed that Clare would keep me trimmed and groomed. After all, how hard could it be? A few days later, during one of our shopping trips, we acquired a gentleman's grooming kit.

With instructions in hand, Clare called me to a straight-backed wooden chair she had positioned in the hangar. "Something for the weekend, sir?" she quipped, channelling the classic barber's query, which historically referred to a packet of prophylactics. Whether she was attempting to calm our collective nerves with this bit of humour was unclear, but with one of the old dog's towels – normally used to dry Jack after muddy walks – draped around my shoulders, she set to work with surprising and reassuring confidence.

Though not needing a shave as there was no beard to contend with, as I wasn't allowed to have one. I did attempt it once, inspired by ruggedly handsome men with facial shadows, convincing Clare that she might wake up next to a

George Clooney lookalike. After a few days of stubble, she promptly told me to shave it off, as I resembled less of a TV doctor and more of an inebriate.

Two minutes in, with hair cascading into my lap, I found myself drifting into a rather hypnotic state. That is, until I heard an alarming sound from Clare, the sort of sound one dreads to hear when someone is wielding sharp cutting implements near your head. "Oops!"

Immediately on high alert, I asked Clare to clarify what she meant by "Oops!" Her response, unfortunately, did little to calm my nerves, but I decided to let it slide. "Don't worry" – which, naturally, got me worrying – "I just used the wrong attachment. All good now."

This was followed, sooner than I would have liked, by a second "Oops!"

With the haircut presumably complete, Clare had me stand in front of, not just any mirror, but a full-length mirror still attached to an old wardrobe door, along with an apology. Staring back at me was a scruffy bugger, unshaven, sporting a haircut reminiscent of some poor sod destined for transportation to the colonies back in the olden days.

GÉRARD CLEANS UP

"Monsieur Colin, could I borrow your jet washer, if it's not too much trouble?" Gérard's request was delivered with the same casual charm as a door-to-door salesman. He had a knack for appearing unannounced, frequently under the guise of checking on our well-being but with an ulterior motive of enjoying a whiskey or two before drifting homeward for his afternoon siesta.

However, today's visit seemed genuine. Gérard had a pressing need – not just for a chit-chat over a dram, but for *my* jet washer. The allocation of our household items had always been clear cut. Anything mechanical or needing maintenance, like the car engine, was distinctly mine. The rest, save for a few shared electricals like the TV, were Clare's domain. Our unspoken agreement, with the terms clearly defined – by my wife – seemed to work well.

"So, Gérard, what on earth do you need the jet washer for?" I inquired, comfortably reverting to English since we were on home turf.

"I've been assisting a friend, and now the inside of my car is very horrible," Gérard declared.

I took a peek inside his little Renault, with the rear seats folded down, and he wasn't exaggerating. It was a proper goat pen, littered with what appeared to be farmyard excrement. "What kind of help were you giving your friend that could have possibly resulted in this?" I asked, taking in Gérard's dishevelled appearance, which was no cleaner than the interior of his car. And the smell? Let's just say it was beyond anything remotely pleasant – he reeked.

"My friend needed help moving some goats from his small garden to his friend's much larger one. His van was broken, so I agreed to take them in my car, as it was only a two-kilometre journey. I folded the seats down to make room for his four little goats. But there wasn't enough space for my friend, so he decided to cycle and meet me there," Gérard explained, pausing to catch his breath. It was clear that not only was his car in a shambles, but he was genuinely traumatised. "So, with the goats loaded, off I went, with him cycling behind me," he continued, pausing again, clearly gearing up for the climax of his tale. I remained silent, allowing him to continue. "What my friend failed to mention was that one of the four little goats was a man goat, and the other three were lady goats. Within a couple of minutes, the goats started leaping around my car because the man goat was trying to fuck them! I, of course, shouted at them to stop immediately, but they didn't seem to understand and just carried on with their fucking. So, I pulled over to let them out. They quickly jumped out of the car, but not before each had relieved themselves many times, creating this mess you see. That is why I need your jet washer, please."

How could I refuse? I even suggested rigging it up on our drive so he could utilise our well water. But, being the self-sufficient Frenchman he was, Gérard told me he had his own well. With a nod of gratitude, he took the jet washer, hopped back into his little Renault, waving cheerfully, as he drove the small distance to his little house. "I will return it soon, and then we can have some whiskey, yes?"

A couple of hours later, Gérard reappeared – this time looking refreshingly clean and considerably less pungent – with my jet washer in tow but noticeably without his car.

"I thought you would bring it back in the car, Gérard," I remarked.

"The car will not start. I think there is water in the electrics. I will try again tomorrow," he admitted with a resigned shrug.

"Did the jet washer do its job?" I asked, curious about the

outcome of his chaotic episode.

"Yes, very good," he replied, with a hint of satisfaction. "But now I need a new *doublure de toit*." I had to quickly consult my internal dictionary to realise he meant the roof lining of his car. "The jet washer is very powerful my friend." he continued, almost proudly. "It also removed the top of *le tableau de bord* [the dashboard]."

Clare, ever the gracious hostess, poured him a supersized whiskey while I reluctantly transported the now filthy jet washer back to my workshop.

***

During that summer, our first in residence, we found ourselves in the delightful company of Gérard more often than not. He was not just good company but a genuine fountain of knowledge, especially when it came to all things garden related. He taught me the fine art of crafting hornet traps from plastic bottles to hang in the fruit trees and how to prepare the soil for our potager. Gérard was also an enthusiastic forager, often returning with a car boot full of assorted goodies. Most of these he assured us were edible, and most of which Clare received with a grateful but sceptical eye, particularly the unfamiliar fungi.

Our lives were undoubtedly enriched by Gérard's frequent visits and willingness to lend a hand. He was always ready to assist, and we reciprocated when we could, although perhaps less often due to our own rather more frequent needs. Gérard, however, was a magnet for mishaps – the goat episode being a prime example.

Take, for instance, the well incident. Like us, Gérard had a well, and like us, he had a pump to water his garden for free. Unfortunately, after indulging in a bit too much of his homemade *eau de vie*, Gérard showed up one morning to announce that he had lost his pump down the well. When I asked why he hadn't secured it, I was met with the classic

French shrug – a gesture that conveyed everything and nothing.

On another occasion, he arrived in a flurry, speeding into our drive in his little Peugeot – the Renault having never recovered from its jetwash ordeal – executing an emergency stop, and leaping from the car, all while shouting for help. *"Aidez-moi, aidez-moi, j'ai été piqué par des guêpes. Sur ma tête et dans mes oreilles,"* which roughly translated means, "Help me, help me, I've been stung by wasps. On my head and in my ears." Clare sprang into action with the first aid kit, expertly applying lotions and antihistamines to Gérard's partly bald head, which rested childlike on her chest. He seemed to experience, relief, embarrassment and contentment, in equal measure as she tended to his stings.

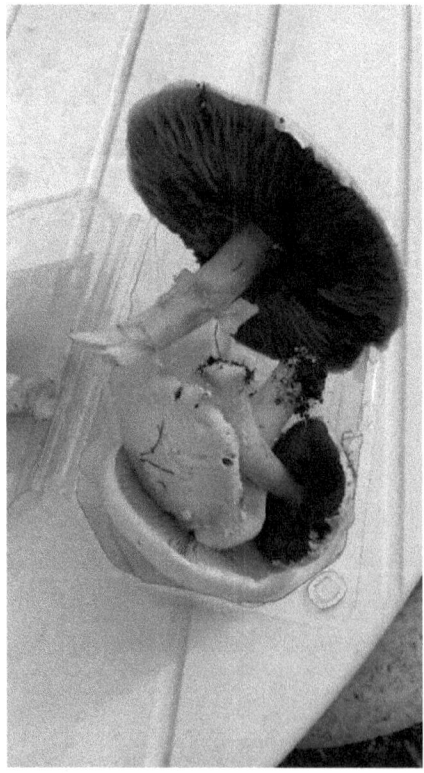

'... which Clare received with a grateful but sceptical eye, particularly the unfamiliar fungi...'

THE ADDITION OF HENS (POULES)

Back in England, we had the delightful, albeit chaotic, experience of hen keeping during the kids' formative years. This was one of Clare's brilliant ideas, which, predictably, translated into a mountain of work for yours truly. Such was the nature of Clare's grand plans, I have to say. Keeping chickens, especially when your neighbours are in close proximity, requires transforming your garden into an impenetrable fortress. For us (and by us, I mean me), this meant constructing a timber framed, wire meshed enclosure – otherwise known as a run, for our feathered friends. Within this grand enclosure, a hen house was a necessity – a regal residence for roosting, egg-laying, and other avian activities.

Of course, there's also the expense of keeping our clucking residents content – food by the sacksful, hay for bedding, a water feeder, and a variety of elixirs to maintain their well-being. On the bright side, if you acquire hens at the optimal age – around twenty weeks at point of lay – they'll reward you with a bountiful supply of eggs for at least five years. In their first year alone, it's not uncommon for a healthy hen to lay over two hundred and fifty eggs. We had four of these industrious birds back in Dorset. I'll let you do the maths. This was precisely the number Clare insisted we should have on our farm in Brittany, despite my gentle reminders that previously, we ended up giving away more eggs than we could consume.

The good news was that there was already a designated domain for the chickens. However, it needed a thorough clearing and the existing fencing required a lot of fortification to fend off poultry pilfering predators like Mr. Fox. I delegated the task of sourcing the chicken house to Clare and Maggie, and it arrived a few days after I had finished taming the hens new living space. A splendid piece of kit it was too, styled after a New England clapboard house. Naturally, Clare and Maggie insisted on painting it in a dazzling spectrum of rainbow colours – a visual feast that our new tenants would never fully appreciate. I kept that thought to myself, of course.

In addition, and this was a non-negotiable on my part, we introduced a fully automatic door. This ingenious contraption would close in the evening – when the hens would, hopefully, be snugly tucked in for the night – and open in the morning – when any nocturnal marauders would, hopefully, be tucked up for the day. This lesson was learned from our previous chicken keeping escapade, when it wasn't unusual, in our frantic rush to get ourselves and the children out of the door in the morning, to forget to liberate the chickens. Conversely, it was not uncommon to receive a prod at some unearthly hour because we'd (I'd) neglected to secure them in for the night.

The next task on the agenda was to acquire the hens, and for this venture, we enlisted the invaluable assistance of Alan and Hélène. They brought with them not only their local know-how but also their linguistic prowess. Despite our French improving in leaps and bounds since mingling with the locals, this hen buying escapade – complete with the prospect of some good old-fashioned bartering, as Alan ominously informed us – was uncharted territory.

Now, unlike the straightforward English perception of a chicken – as either a delectable meal, an egg laying machine, or a symbol of cowardice – things in France are a bit more nuanced. Here, a chicken destined to lay eggs is referred to as a *'poule'*, which also carries the less flattering connotation of a coward. On the other hand, *'poulet'* refers to the chicken meat we (though not Maggie or Jamie) would request in a food shop.

And then there's the *'coq'*, which, needless to say, isn't relevant to this particular tale.

So, while this book might not be the ripping rollercoaster of entertainment you were hoping for, it's at least to some extent, educational.

The following Saturday, we trundled off to the local market, armed with Alan and Hélène. Alan, ever the man of the hour, set about locating the *'vendeur de poules'* – which he did with remarkable speed. In no time at all, a deal was struck, and we found ourselves the proud owners of four hens, each around eighteen weeks old.

The hen seller, a man of considerable gusto, did not merely place the hens into a box – oh no, that would be far too normal. Instead, he loaded each hen, with the finesse of a magician wearing boxing gloves, one at a time, into a single box scarcely larger than a shoebox. He then slammed the lid shut and proceeded to assault the box with a large knife. This, he explained with a casual shrug and a *"pour l'air"* (for air), as if entirely normal.

Upon our return home, the new feathered residents were introduced to their splendid new residence. Clare, with her usual optimism, declared that they looked positively ecstatic. Personally, I had no notion of what a happy hen looks like, nor indeed an unhappy one. I found myself thinking it might be an opportune moment to give my French shrug a try-out.

Our new residents wasted no time in getting into the groove, leading to an unsurprising abundance of eggs. Alan and Hélène gratefully accepted the predicted surplus, while Beryl and Gérard, too, got their fair share. Speaking of Beryl and the egg deliveries – well, they returned to us in a variety of ways. Mostly in homemade cakes which, like much of her culinary endeavours, embarked on their journey with good intentions but often found themselves lost along the way. To Beryl, a recipe was merely a set of loose guidelines, susceptible to whims and flights of fancy. Apart from our precious eggs, everything else in the cake seemed to be conjured straight from her imagination. And she was never shy about entertaining us with tales of her culinary disagreements with recipes.

One day, she presented Clare with a Victoria Sponge. It was unfashionably rectangular, because, as Beryl confidently declared, "it was easier to slice." The biscuit base, she insisted, added 'something' – though she was rather vague about what that 'something' was. And so, Beryl's creations graced our table, each a testament to her rebellion against conventional baking.

'Naturally, Clare and Maggie insisted on painting it in a dazzling spectrum of rainbow colours – a visual feast that our new tenants would never fully appreciate.'

***

But I soon discovered that chickens, while appearing to be the epitome of indifference, are secretly plotting their great escape. Early autumn I think it was – yeah I know we're getting ahead of ourselves timewise, but it is a chicken related story (kind of) – I embarked on a quest to locate the elusive hole in the fence through which one of our cunning chickens had made a break for, day after day. Another lesson in chicken behaviour revealed that despite their escape artist prowess, their attention span is akin to that of a goldfish. Once through the fence, instead of making a beeline for the nearest road or railway station, our feathery escapee stopped at the first food source she encountered – in this case, the adjacent field where the farmer had recently harvested his corn crop, leaving a few kernels scattered on the ground.

It was relatively easy for me to track her down and return her to the run, but the hole in the fence remained as elusive as ever. This escapade coincided with a visit from our eldest daughter, Jamie Ann, and her potential fiancé, whose name now escapes my memory. There I was, pacing up and down the fence in my pyjamas, wellington boots, and an old coat – any semblance of fashion sense long gone – determined to find the hidden escape route.

Out of the corner of my eye, I noticed Jamie Ann's suitor, let's call him Douglas for now, lurking nearby. Thinking he was offering to help, I attempted to engage him in conversation. But he remained tight-lipped until, finally, he burst out with what had been weighing on his mind.

"Colin, can I have a word?" he asked.

"Sure thing, Douglas, what is it?" I replied – Wish I could remember his actual name.

"I'm thinking that I might like to marry your daughter, Jamie Ann," he declared, as if for some reason I might have forgotten my own daughter's name.

Now, I don't know about you, but when a bloke – or whoever – requests a conversation about wanting to take your daughter's hand in marriage, one would reasonably expect that person to be unequivocally certain about his intentions. To hear someone using terms such as "I'm thinking" and "might" didn't exactly instil a great deal of confidence, to be frank. And I told him so in no uncertain terms.

"So, Douglas, what you're telling me is that you're only thinking about it, and even then, you only 'might' want to marry my daughter. Have I got that right?" I inquired, unashamedly savouring his subsequent speechlessness. To rescue him from the self-dug hole, I continued, "How about when you're one hundred percent sure that you really do want to marry our daughter, then we'll talk again. How does that sound?" He chose not to respond, simply thanked me, and retreated back to the house. They, our daughter and he, could, of course, just elope and get married, so despite my need for some assurance, I credit him for having the gumption to at least broach the subject with me.

As it turned out, they didn't marry. They, in fact, separated halfway through the following year. Meaning he couldn't have been so sure after all. Or perhaps it was our daughter who wasn't so certain. Who knows? And, frankly, it's none of my business.

That said, there was still a silver lining amidst this small pantomime, I managed to find that elusive hole in the wire.

Indeed, as chicken stories go, this one might seem a little tenuous. It was, of course, more about the ill-fated attempt of my daughter's suitor to ask for her hand in marriage than the antics of our feathered residents. But I had to capture it before it fluttered away from my memory, much like a chicken escaping through a hole in the fence. See what I did there?

THE ORCHARD (LE VERGER)

High summer and the verger is in a lazy, sun dappled haze, the trees were sagging under the weight of their fruity bounty. The apples and pears, in particular, were so burdened that they seemed to groan in exhaustion under the weight. Enjoying a whiskey one afternoon, Gérard, shared tales of the farm's cidery history. Back in its heyday, the apples and pears were transformed into delightful, cider, (or '*cidre*' if you're feeling particularly French) and the somewhat cheeky '*poiré* for pears.

Those olden days were evidenced by an erstwhile press – long since redundant – now gathering dust, and an array of oak barrels and bottles lounging in the barn, a reminder of cider days gone by. As for the prunes (or plums if you're British), they had long since vanished. We had devoured tons and shared equally generous amounts, yet the memories were preserved in a multitude of glass jars, brimming with plum jam, lining the larder shelves.

As for the peaches, they wouldn't win any beauty contests or taste awards. But they were palatable, let's leave it at that. The walnuts? Well, they were playing the long game, still in no hurry to mature, nevertheless offering a promise of future harvests.

Walking up to the verger and standing amongst it, was one of my favourite things. Whilst we had done some necessary sprucing up – trimming here, pruning there – the verger still called for more attention. This, however, would have to wait until I'd properly boned up on horticulture and the arrival of autumn and winter, for that much I had gleaned.

For Jack, the verger was his sanctuary, his escape from life's so-called pressures. A typical day, for him, consisted of the arduous tasks of rising from one of his many beds, enjoying a prepared meal, embarking on a leisurely walk – Jack didn't do brisk – returning home to a treat (or two), followed by a series of naps, another round of delicious food, probably another treat, and back to bed. Truly, the life of a stressed out canine.

Another unsung hero in our verger – the hornet traps. Gérard, had instructed us in the art of repurposing old plastic drink bottles, which dangled from the fruit trees like miniature, irresistible confectionary kiosks for insects. A splash of some sugary concoction lured these marauding beasts – and their buzzing cousins, the wasps – into a sticky demise.

Though, to be clear: we weren't aiming for insect genocide. The few hornets we managed to trap were but a drop in the entomological ocean. But having experienced the agonising sting of a hornet, a creature determined to sink its venomous prick into any person it deems to be an intruder, our sympathies laid firmly with the traps. To put it in perspective – for the unaware – a hornet sting is like a wasp sting multiplied by five and sprinkled with a slam of viciousness. Unlike wasps, which might occasionally display a bit of seasonal peevishness, hornets exist in a state of perpetual fury, their default setting being 'irritated'.

As much as I celebrated our bountiful harvest of fruit, the question remained: what on earth to do with it all? Back in England, when we had an excess of eggs and a modest glut of plums – nothing on the scale of our verger here in Saint-Barthélémy – the kids would box or bag them up. These were then placed outside our cottage, where any passersby could purchase them by dropping the requested amount into an honesty box. At the end of each day, the leftover produce would be brought in, and the money counted and shared among each of them.

France, however, played by different rules. Not only did we lack foot traffic, but selling our homegrown produce was also prohibited, something about unfair competition with local farmers. I recall an old couple nearby who set up an honesty box, as we did in Dorset, and were promptly rebuked by the local mayor for their entrepreneurial spirit.

This topic came up during one of our many drinking sessions with Gérard. We were discussing the old cider production on the farm, and I asked how the previous farmer sold his produce. Gérard explained that the old farmer's business model involved delivering bottles and barrels directly to locals and bars, collecting empty containers and cash as he went – one of his customers being none other than the local lady mayor (*la mairesse*). According to Gérard, the farming community operated by its own set of rules, and any attempt to sell our eggs, plums – or any produce for that matter – however small, would be seen as a threat – a smouldering ember needing to be stamped out with the local mairesse's help, no less.

Similarly, there were restrictions on car boot sales (*Vide-greniers*). Known as *'Puces'* to us, these sales in France were considered commercial activities, with any money from our home produced goods seen as taxable income. And let me tell you, dobbing in unsuspecting Brits was quite the local sport. If you wanted to offload some of your English junk, you were limited to doing so twice a year. This is why such events were infrequent but massive and popular when they did occur. None of which solved the problem of what to do with our fruit harvest.

'High summer and the verger is in a lazy, sun dappled haze, the trees were sagging under the weight of their fruity bounty.'

'Those olden days were evidenced by an erstwhile press – long since redundant – now gathering dust...'

In Need of a Fix, a Football Fix

I'm not going to lie to you; there were quite a few things I increasingly missed about England. Most were tolerable, many insignificant. But one was really hard, and that was my football fix. Actually, no, not so much a football fix as a matchday fix. Brittany purportedly played football, though from what Alan and his son told me, the matchday experience there was a pale shadow of England's lively antics. And so, with Clare's generous agreement, I set off for Portsmouth for my matchday medicine.

Clare kindly deposited me at St Malo to catch the overnight ferry to Portsmouth for Saturday's game. Upon arrival, I strolled from the port through the city, eager to reunite with our eldest daughter, our son, my brother, and brother-in-law.

We then embarked on our well honed ritual: meet at a pub (generally the same one), down enough ale to become excessively optimistic about the result of the impending match, exchange copious laughter, engage in politically incorrect banter, laugh some more, and then proceed to the ground to purchase and devour dodgy burgers or a fried chicken meal. Given, what I thought to be a wise decision to forgo the Brittany Ferry breakfast, I required sustenance beforehand, so partook in a bowl of pub cooked, overly spiced chicken wings. Which my body subsequently expelled in the most violent of ways a few hours later.

Talking of chicken, brings to mind one particular occasion when our son, still feeling the effects of a nocturnal outing with his pals, continued to drink with gusto before the match. The result? His bag of fried chicken became ensnared in the turnstile, and he dozed off for the entire second half of the game.

Post-match, we returned to the pub, consumed more beer, laughed a great deal, discussed anything but the game, and then sought solace in a curry house for dinner. My brother's wife then dropped me back at the ferry port, and I slept like a log, blissfully unaware of the wind and rain storm that gripped conversations and newspaper headlines the following morning.

A couple of hours out of St Malo, I rang Clare so that my disembarkation would, more or less, coincide with her arrival at the port.

Now, Clare's sense of direction, particularly when driving, is somewhat...adventurous. And the Land Rover Defender, bless it, boasted as much technology as a stone age wheel. Nonetheless, she'd been back and forth to St Malo enough times that I was confident, and so was she, that all would be well.

An hour after my arrival, I was still kicking my heels – alone – in the arrivals hall. No sign of Clare. Traffic, perhaps? Unlikely, being a Sunday. Two hours later, I called her again. She apologised, admitted to a wrong turn, but assured me all was well now. Another hour passed, and both hunger and worry gnawed at me, so I rang again. This time, Maggie answered

"Everything okay, Maggie?"

"Yes, we're fine now. Mummy came back home to get me so that I could read the map on my phone for her. She got all the way to Questembert and then turned around."

"But hang on," I said, "Questembert is in the completely opposite direction to St Malo. Due south, in fact."

Just over four hours later, my wife and daughter finally arrived. I took the wheel and drove us home, managing to avoid Questembert by about one hundred kilometres.

Despite doing a number of football fixes, it was never enough to make me regret our move to Brittany. Even with all the niggles and hoops we had to jump through to accomplish even the most basic of tasks, the charm of our new life was still undeniable.

CUTTING BACK AND THE SCRUMPERS

Soon enough, summer was giving way to autumn, and our focus shifted to the imminent winter preparations. This being our maiden winter in Brittany, we were flying blind, save for the assumption that a storm or two was on the cards. We weren't to be disappointed. No sooner had we bid farewell to September, October stormed in with a vengeance – wet and angry. Very wet, in fact. This, we soon discovered, was Brittany's winter signature.

Though often no colder than southern England, Brittany had a particular affinity for persistent dampness, replete with abundant rain and relentless wind. On those rare occasions when the heavens withheld their watery bounty, we were treated to one or two crisp, frosty days – delightful respites, albeit as rare as a hen's teeth in comparison.

'...October stormed in with a vengeance – wet and angry. Very wet, in fact.'

***

It was also that delightful time of year for apple and pear gathering. One morning, as we were savouring a boiled egg for breakfast, four aged individuals came marching purposefully up the drive and past the house. Three women and a bloke, all lugging an assortment of bags, taking a moment to admire the improvements we'd made, particularly our shiny new barn roof. Clare and I exchanged puzzled glances. I rose from the table and stepped out onto the driveway.

"Bonjour. Puis-je vous aider?" – (Hello. Can I help you?) I asked in what I hoped was a congenial tone.

The chap turned and smiled broadly. *"Bonjour messieurs-dames, Comment ça va?"* No translation needed for that greeting.

"Oui, ça va," I replied, before inquiring about their intentions. *"Qu'est-ce que tu fais?"* – (What are you doing?)

"Nous sommes venus ramasser des pommes et des poires comme nous le faisons toujours à cette période de l'année." – (We came to pick apples and pears as we always do at this time of year.)

Clare and I pondered whether this was some quaint local tradition, though we didn't voice it. We stood there, looking at each other, not quite sure what to do next. As we turned back to address our would-be scrumpers, they had already lost interest in us and were heading towards the verger, where Jack, was napping. Chatting cheerfully, they wandered on, and Jack, ever the vigilant guard dog, greeted them with a tail wag and enthusiastic licking of their hands.

Less than an hour later, their bags now brimming with apples and pears, the foursome retraced their steps back down the farm, wishing us a cheerful *"au revoir"* as they passed.

Later in the day, Beryl arrived with one of her infamous

'landfill' cakes – so named because much of her baking ended up there. After gratefully accepting the cake, we recounted our visitors' tale. Beryl explained that their actions were less about tradition and more about opportunism. Apparently, during the years when the house stood empty, she frequently saw people passing her house to raid the orchard. Many were local cider makers capitalising on the old farmer's absence.

We never saw those people again, which was a bit of a shame, as we had more fruit than we could ever use and no easy means of giving it away.

THE CLOCKS GO BACK, BUT WILL THE IN-LAWS?

Autumn was very much upon us, much like the arrival of the in-laws – Clare's mum and dad. It was also the first time in ages that I had dusted off my journal. Determined to establish a Sunday writing habit once again, I succeeded – though only for a few fleeting months. Despite my ability to display discipline in so many areas, journal keeping proved to be my Achilles' heel. So, as we ushered in 2017, my journal entries continued to dwindle. Consequently, the tales within these pages from this point onward are largely the product of Clare's and my recollections.

***

Journal entry from October 2016 – *With the clocks due to go back tonight I guess we've officially come to the end of summer, but more precisely our first summer of retirement and as immigrants in our adopted Country of France. This week has been good to us from a weather perspective as indeed has the whole summer. Chilly damp and misty mornings giving way to pleasantly warm and sunny afternoons where even butterflies have taken advantage of the few blooms, seeking whatever sustenance there is on offer from those flowers that have yet to concede to the forthcoming chill. I think I might leave the deckchairs out for another week.*

It has also coincided with a visit from my in-laws, cutting back and pruning were very much on the agenda with my father-in-law Ron's help, guidance and experience being of particular value to a garden rookie such that I am. What to cut, how much to cut and what to leave to die back dominated lesson one.

Resulting in the production of a considerable amount of garden waste, which was duly added to the huge amount already accumulated, as a result of us simply trying to tame land that had been left to overgrow and unkempt for goodness knows how many years. Good that it is now much less so, but done without much in the way of style or design, which is where Ron, my gardening guru and consultant, came in. Secateurs that had otherwise been used for cutting wire amongst other things were sharpened and put to their proper use. The result being, I'm assured, will be a garden that will grow into something resembling something like.... well a garden actually. As well as giving an impression that the owners of that garden know what they're about. We'll see come the Spring. But at present and for the foreseeable future we have a variety of what could at best be described as clusters of sticks, of varying heights, some with a hint of green, poking out of the ground around our garden. On a more positive note we did reveal some beautiful natural stone walls as well as uncovering a number of rose bushes, some small ornamental trees and other bushes that were otherwise lost.

The in-laws have now gone back to England, and I'm trusted to clear up the debris of our labours. I'm advised that gurus and consultants don't do clearing up.

***

Having the in-laws over provided a welcome distraction, nudging us off our landlocked island and out to visit one or two places we'd been promising ourselves since we arrived. St Cado, the beach at Carnac, Hennebont, and of course Vannes – our favourite day trip. It was a treat for Clare to have her parents with us, though their departure after a few short days left an air of melancholy.

Ron, a keen gardener – but rather less keen on the clearing up – was like a kid in a sweetshop. His gardening enthusiasm was almost contagious, and I found myself happily tagging along as he snipped here, chopped there, and yanked things from the ground. I, in turn, made mental notes of all the gardening tasks I'd need to tackle in the coming months.

Ron was instantly smitten with the verger, much like me, but another feature that caught his eye was the woody old hydrangeas growing along the front of the barn. He recalled the hydrangeas we had in the front garden of our house in Bognor Regis, which he had once taken a chainsaw to, leaving mere inches of sticks protruding from the ground. Although it didn't seem like the prescribed method for hydrangea maintenance, Ron, the self-proclaimed 'guru,' insisted. I remember watching in horror back then, but nine months later, we had the most beautiful hydrangeas in the street.

Fast forward twenty-five years, and here he was again, telling me to fetch the chainsaw. And once again, he was spot on, as the hydrangeas came back spectacularly the following year.

He also found himself transfixed by our barn, concocting plans that ranged from the mildly ambitious to the unsettlingly personal. First, he suggested we could transform the old barn into a quaint holiday retreat, an absolute gold mine, he suggested, provided we poured in a small fortune for some necessary renovations. Which seemed all well and good, but then Ron, in his typical forward-thinking fashion, proposed an even more audacious idea: converting the barn into a cozy residence for himself and Ann. Or rather, a snug nest for Ann to inhabit once he had permanently checked out. Not that he had any imminent plans for such an exit, of course.

We had already entertained the notion of a holiday let months prior, even going so far as to engage an architect who discovered the barn's illustrious past as being the original farm dwelling, dating back nearly three centuries. The sketches looked promising, but the thought of having holidaymakers traipsing across our land, disturbing our tranquillity during the loveliest time of the year, was simply too much. The idea was unceremoniously shelved.

As for the prospect of hosting Ron and Ann, and later just Ann, a mere twenty meters from our doorstep? Well, that was an entirely different kettle of fish, one that required a delicate touch in handling.

"What did you think of Dad's idea?" Clare asked one night as we lay in bed, serenaded by the persistent buzz of mosquitoes.

"The holiday let? We've already dismissed that, but I'm willing to reconsider if you are," I replied.

"No, I meant the idea of them living in the barn, especially after Dad's, departure," she clarified.

"Absolutely not! Good night," I declared, hoping to end the discussion.

Nevertheless, Clare's resolve led us to revisit the architectural plans, reimagining the barn as a permanent residence. During one of our frequent calls with Ron and Ann, I cunningly mentioned our numerous house moves over the years. From such humble beginnings, the seed of doubt was planted, casting uncertainty over our long-term stay in the house.

A few weeks later, Ron and Ann had a change of heart, realising that their affection for France did not extend to actually living there. Thus, we skilfully dodged the proverbial bullet, and peace was restored once more.

'...nudging us off our landlocked island and out to visit one or two places we'd been promising ourselves since we arrived. St Cado...'

'...the beach at Carnac...'

'...an architect who discovered the barn's illustrious past as being the original farm dwelling, dating back nearly three centuries.'

***

Ann, the mother-in-law, was less a gardener – even less a planner – and more a matriarch – a mouse that frequently roared. Her idea of enjoying the garden involved having Ron place cushioned chairs, a table, and an umbrella in a prime spot, allowing her to dispense advice and opinions from her veranda perch. When she visited us, it was my turn to be summoned into service to set up the terrace in her very prescribed manner, periodically moving the pieces as the sun's position shifted.

But our very own colonial stereotype experienced quite a thrill during a visit to Bertrand's, our favourite Brocante.

Housed in a dilapidated former office building, it was typical of Brocantes across the country, filled with old stuff the French no longer wanted but we Brits seemed to romantically covet. Clare and I had been introduced to Bertrand by Alan and Hélène shortly after we arrived in Brittany.

With our French improving, we now had the confidence to haggle with him. No matter the item or amount, he always reacted as if we'd suggested purchasing his sister for some unsavoury purpose, yet he was always willing to strike a deal. He never failed to declare, *"Je ne serai pas là la prochaine fois."* (I won't be here next time), implying that each sale might just put him out of business – again.

Ann's delight was a piece of vintage embroidery. Beautiful embroidery and linen are abundant in most Brocantes, and Bertrand's was no exception. For some reason, the young French no longer appreciated these items, much like our own children's generation. At our house, any meal involves a tablecloth, placemats, and napkins. And no, we're not posh – just proper.

This beautifully embroidered, pure linen tablecloth was priced at five euros – a steal. Clare's mother, having no French language skills, placed a one-euro coin into Bertrand's hand, closed his other hand over it, and gently patted it in a grandmotherly "don't go spending it all at once" manner. Bertrand looked at us, puzzled. I gave him my best French shrug, smiled, and turned away. I heard Ann say thank you (in English), to which he cheerfully responded, *"Vous êtes les bienvenus."* (You are welcome).

A few minutes later, Bertrand sidled up to me. *"Allez-vous ramener la vieille dame ici?"* (Are you going to bring the old lady back here?)

"Absolument pas!" I'm sure you get the gist.

Bertrand beamed, *"Merci beaucoup!"* before hurrying off to ingratiate himself with some tourists who had strayed into his domain.

***

Journal entry from November 2016 – *The sun was out earlier today but noticeably lower. As I write I look out onto the lawn that wasn't a lawn 8 months ago having now recovered from having a new septic tank placed beneath it. The sown grass is now a deep green lawn heavy with dew and in part has a covering of gold brown leaves from our silver birch tree. Another sign of end of the summer I guess along with the porridge I'm just about to tuck into for breakfast. Through those trees the sun is dappled on the stone barn wall the sky is clear blue but I know from feeding the chickens earlier this morning, that there is a chill in the shade.*

The reality of the passing of the seasons is that there is no start or finish to them, just temporary closures and new beginnings.

The next to succumb to the secateurs, axe, chainsaw and so on will be the orchard but that's a job that will require a bit more finesse than the wholesale chopping back of these past weeks.

***

With the season's randomness, Brittany transformed into a peculiar stage where summer's end mingled with autumn's introduction. It was the time of year when Mother Nature seemed caught in a bit of a quandary. Our apple and pear trees, having give up their harvest, while roses, bloomed in defiant splendour. The mornings nipped my nose, a reminder of cold months ahead, yet afternoons basked in the sun's unseasonal warmth. Our state of the art central heating system, like a dithering gambler, was unable to decide whether to stick or twist. And in the evenings, we had the wood-burner roaring, only to subsequently let it die out, as the latent warmth, amassed in our stone house walls from the days sun, released itself into the room.

You'll read how Alan is a weather obsessive – a behaviour I would often ridicule. And here I was, a novice to retirement, unconsciously finding myself developing an oddly attuned awareness to the rhythm of the seasons, the volatile nature of weather, and the peculiarities of my immediate surroundings. This newfound recognition, once dormant, now resonated with a clear, undeniable presence. Though unintended, this transformation was perhaps a cunning decision by my subconscious – an internal being calling for a necessary heightening of my awareness, without the need for any consent.

Caught in this newfound reverie, I found myself poring over weather forecasts, scrutinising frontal systems, and noting temperature variations with an almost absurd dedication – is this what happened to Alan? My daily routines altered, synchronising with this newly attuned sensibility. The revelation was profound yet welcomed, as if I'd switched lenses and rediscovered life in high definition. Within a relatively brief time, my perspectives evolved, and I embraced this shift with a surprising sense of ease. This increasing awareness had undoubtedly found its place in the pages of my next journal entry.

***

Journal entry from November 2016 *– Early morning in the orchard mug of tea in hand, my boots were getting progressively wet from the dew on the grass and the now rotting fallen apples. The sun can be seen just above the tree line but there's still a chill in the air and probably will be for a few hours yet. There's so much blue sky.*

The sweet smell of those apples is an overload to my senses. I'm even able to discern between the sweeter red apples that we had long over indulged on, to that of the other (cider) apples and the larger cooking apples, that I'm sure will continue to feature in apple cakes and pies throughout the coming months. But there's also sadness as I tread almost cautiously over what has now become a carpet of fruit.

The crunch of each apple underfoot simply serves to remind me of my delinquency and a sense of shame in not having the skill, or wherewithal to do somewhat more with them, something for which they surely deserve. I still have an ambition to make ciders and juices, not on an industrial scale – though the amount of fruit suggests for an alternative ambition – but at least something that would somehow compensate for the effort that the trees put into producing such a rich bounty. This year was always going to be difficult to realise any ambitions in the shape of cider production, as our emphasis, time and energy were all about getting the house up together and taming the land. Although Clare did manage to put many pounds of plums into the jam jars, adding to my own shame. But next year…..?

For now, I'll content myself with this sensory overload, give thanks to whoever the god of fruit trees happens to be and start to plan the inevitable pruning of these very trees, that I'm advised is due from about now and well into the winter.

I would never claim to be a man of birds. I probably know the difference between a Robin and a Blue Tit and even boast that I can tell the difference between their respective calls but that's about the extent of my understanding. But I would urge anyone to sit, clear your mind and just listen, as I did, while enjoying the unseasonably warm weather. The sound of birdsong is by far the dominant sound, even to that of the inevitable barking dog somewhere far away – there is always a dog barking somewhere within earshot in rural France, mostly by day and often by night. Have the birds always been there? Probably, but I can't ever remember taking the time, or indeed ever having the inclination, to just stop and listen. The variety of chirrups, chits, whistles, chatters and pips is almost overwhelming and inexplicably I find myself smiling. Each type of bird has its own unique voice that seems to want to be heard above all others, but as a collective it's a chaotic suite of sounds.

But whatever the purpose of birdsong is, it's not for my benefit and that's maybe the point. Whatever those sounds mean, they're not for my ears. I'm just an eavesdropper without knowledge or likelihood of understanding. My reverie is soon interrupted by a manmade noise, a tractor probably, passing by and the birds are silent in an instant. But within just a few seconds of the noise passing the birds continue where they left off. As if in a crowded room and they had been rudely interrupted, but then just as quickly dismissed the noise as nothing of importance. So they start up again. Not all at once mind you, but progressively, until they reach the same level as before. For me that brief period of silence was almost unnerving and I know, without a doubt, that even with my lack of understanding or indeed belonging I am much happier in a crowd – albeit one I have no right to be in.

I think I might leave the deckchairs out for a bit longer yet though.

Walking back to the house with pockets loaded with fallen walnuts for what I hope will be transformed into something along the lines of a coffee and walnut cake. It was time for my second cup of tea of the day and some breakfast.

***

With the larder groaning under the weight of jam jars and a greengrocers worth of apples and pears conserved to perfection – thanks to Clare's exhaustive study into the dying art of preserving – we set about tackling the aftermath of our fruity harvest. Piling the rotting remnants into barrows, we dispatched them to the soon to be constructed compost bays. Despite my guilt over the wanton waste, I couldn't deny the heady, sweet aroma that hung in the air. And as a silver lining to our effort, we inadvertently, but thankfully, shifted the likelihood of stepping on and being stung by a drunken wasp or hornet to the far reaches of the future potager.

'The crunch of each apple underfoot simply serves to remind me of my delinquency and a sense of shame in not having the skill or wherewithal to do somewhat more with them...'...we dispatched them to the soon to be constructed compost bays...'

WOOD PILES AND CHRISTMAS SONGS

It's official! I'd become a wood bore. Where my journal once shone with wit and wisdom, it had now devolved into a dreary chronicle of wood cutting, stacking, and logs maintenance. No longer the lively tales of adventure and charm, it reads like a lumberjack's manual – albeit an amateur one. The transformation from lively storyteller to timber enthusiast was complete.

***

Journal entry from November 2016 – The very term gathering winter fuel puts me in mind of the Christmas song Good King Wenceslas and a picture of some unfortunate bloke having to walk-through knee-high snow, in order to gather firewood for his family. Unlike me, who is currently going to considerable lengths to plan for winter. Signified no less by my ever-increasing wood pile which arrived earlier in the week, via Alan's tractor trailer, in the form of branches of varying lengths and thicknesses. There are few activities I can think of that gives so much satisfaction, for me anyway. I mean I'm using a chainsaw (albeit only a small one), a hand chopper, an axe and so on. It's cold but I was down to my shirt sleeves and I had sawdust and chippings in my hair and all manner of other places. And there's me thinking that driving around the place on my little tractor, cutting grass and lifting heavy things was the outdoor enjoyment I'd craved, but hell no cutting big wood is the real deal!

I've mentioned this to myself numerous times before – because Clare seems to show no interest – but such is the importance of it (wood) I have no problem in repeating myself – to myself. Wood in rural Northern France is a commodity and a wood pile is more than just a heap of logs. It's an orderly and neat stack that represents a symbol of status, masculinity and artistic prowess. None of which I can claim to have just now. I've learned the different ways to stack wood with each having a unique name or style given to them. Though typically for me, I've forgotten them all.

And then of course there are the sizes to which each log is cut so that it fits correctly, no precisely, into fireplaces and wood burners. Such sizing also adds to the neat and uniform look of these stacks. So when the 'average sizing' of my logs is commented on by man of wood, sage and aficionado of wood stacking – Alan – I instinctively know that a judgement of sorts has been made. The chin stroking, the staring and head titling, whist walking around my wood stack brought me back down to earth. Must do better my report card would read if he were still teaching.

So my log pile, although ever increasing remains in the lower league and as for the average sizing of my logs? Read; just not good enough. But I remain undaunted and soon enough I'll be back at it again, chainsaw in hand, fired up and ready to turn branches into logs…. But of a more uniform size of course.

***

I truly apologise for subjecting you to that entry. But, if nothing else, it offers a glimpse into the ever narrowing scope of my existence. A far cry from my glory days as a Global Senior Vice President in Facilities Management, whatever that lofty title might have entailed. And should you, by some miracle, decipher the true meaning of those grandiose terms, do drop me a line.

The murky gloom of November invariably signals the onset of Christmas preparation mania in our house. Or, as it unfailingly transpires in our place, a hastily orchestrated chaos. Therefore, it was scarcely a surprise to discover our ever industrious – when it comes to Christmas prep – daughter Maggie transforming the dining table into a festive craft haven one otherwise ordinary afternoon. Strewn across the table, there lay a large amount of glitter, tinsel, and odd bits of coloured paper. To underpin the festive spirit, Maggie had turned the dial on our ancient stereo to volume ten, with the raucous strains of seventies and eighties Christmas hits reverberating throughout the house – tunes we'd come to rue by the end of December, if not sooner.

Legend has it the French celebrate Christmas with a style quite dissimilar to our British traditions. Yet despite this being our adopted nation, I discovered little in their customs that urged me to alter our own time honoured ones. As far as we were concerned there seemed no earthly reason why Christmas chez nous couldn't retain its reassuringly familiar shape.

So commenced the inexorable march towards December 25th, marked by increasingly frequent episodes of artistic endeavour in the kitchen. These bouts of cutting, gluing, and the general crafting frenzy predictably ended up with my clothes being covered with glitter, at every mealtime, between then and when her industrious fever abated – sometime in mid December.

HEROES? NO, JUST REGULAR PEOPLE

Journal entry from late November 2016 – *A storm came in for a couple of days and one particularly bad night. As a result we had wind damage to one of our favourite trees, a mimosa, and further damage to two other less loved trees but nothing structural thank goodness. No cables down but our electricity supply went off a few times which to be honest doesn't seem to need the excuse of a storm in these rural parts, hence the reason why many people invest in having some kind of back-up generator. Others didn't get off so lightly, where felled trees brought down power and telephone lines and blocked roads. And here I have to make special mention of the local emergency service, which is crewed largely by volunteers, all with day jobs and all having minimal respect for lines of demarcation when it comes to helping people out of a jam. At public events I've seen these same people propping up the bar, taking a well-earned rest from putting up marquees and laying out tables and chairs. With some also being on hand to provide paramedic services, when the need arises.*

***

This modest journal entry hardly does justice to the remarkable acts of selflessness I had the privilege to witness firsthand. These intrepid volunteers, with scant regard for their own well-being, were up to their elbows in trees and chainsaws amidst the most dreadful weather conditions imaginable. They worked with the little illumination, most provided by the headlights of their own vehicles, valiantly clearing fallen trees from roads, power lines, and telephone wires.

Back in England, where the 'blitz spirit' once reigned supreme, such actions would likely attract criticism.

Detractors would brand these heroic efforts as reckless, a catastrophe waiting to happen, or even foolhardy for putting their necks on the line. Meanwhile, they'd sit comfortably on their derrières, grumbling and doing nothing to help themselves, patiently awaiting for the already swamped council workers to "get a move on."

What I witnessed, however, were selfless, single-minded, and undeniably brave actions from a group of individuals with no ulterior motive other than to help their neighbours. Undoubtedly, these very people would return to their regular jobs the next day without missing a beat.

This recollection reminded me of a recent incident in Scotland. An elderly gentleman was struck by a bus, and rather than coming to his aid, people in the vicinity merely filmed his distress on their phones, no doubt seeking recognition on that toxic dump, known as social media – a personal opinion by the way. In stark contrast, our 'have-a-go' heroes in Brittany displayed nary a phone, only a steadfast determination to help.

Consequently, when I was asked to assist in their endeavour, I felt genuinely honoured. With a touch of humility and without a moment's hesitation, I went to receive my instructions – most of which, I must admit, I barely grasped. While I wasn't assigned to the illustrious chainsaw brigade, or the A-Team, I was nonetheless pleased to join the debris clearing crew, as branches were diligently pruned away from electrical wires.

It was also time for the deckchairs to finally be put away.

ALL CHANGE

Journal entry from beginning December 2016 – December already and Christmas plans are well advanced. Though my part in those will no doubt be to do as I'm instructed and to turn up when and where I'm told to. Which, to be honest, I'm okay with. This year we also have a couple of landmark birthdays to consider. Maggie will be eighteen – middle of the month – and Sam twenty one in just six days time. In terms of planning for these two events Maggie will take full control of the planning for her own Birthday (or week as it will no doubt turn out), with the production of her mandatory list of both the occasion and expected presents. Sam on the other hand will simply turn up and fit into whatever others have planned for him. In doing so gratefully accepting any manner or type of present. Though it will be different this year as he is still back in Portsmouth, no doubt enjoying the freedom of the city now that University has pretty well packed up for Christmas.

Took a brief 'time out' this morning having finished the daily routine of feeding the chickens, refreshing their straw bedding, relining the poop tray, collecting any early eggs and so on; I happened to look down at myself and it has occurred to me how I dress these days. Far removed from how it used to be just a few months ago. Looks like I've officially become a Breton. No style just layers depending on the season.

In my later working years business dress, as I always understood it to be, became less formal as I increasingly worked from home. But it was also a time when attitudes to office attire became more relaxed, less stuffy, with suits staying in the wardrobe. Eventually finding their way to the charity shop. When I retired, and as part of our pre-move clear out, it was quite a liberating experience to see ties, suits and other such 'business' attire being bagged up for the charity shop. But I'd never thought the change would have been quite so severe once we had moved to France. I am looking like a living scarecrow and okay with it.

***

My memory of the day is etched so deeply in my mind that I can still feel the damp of the air on my face and smell the earthiness of dew-drenched leaves beneath my feet. The cold, crisp morning, with the sun just peeking over the barn's edge, teasing me with a promise of some feeble warmth.

Picture this though: Wellington boots on bare feet, paired with pyjama bottoms in a Scottish tartan that couldn't claim allegiance to any clan, living or otherwise. On top, an old tee shirt clinging to its last threads of dignity, and a threadbare sweat top that had seen better days. To combat the chill even further, I added a thermal sleeveless jerkin, zipped up to my chin, old woolly gloves, and a beanie hat that had weathered more winters than I cared to remember. Add to this charming ensemble a three-day stubble, Clare's attempt at hairstyling and a fragrant aura of the great unwashed – all before I'd had my first cup of tea.

Post-wash and fortified by my tea, my attire – for any given day – evolved only marginally. I would swap the pyjama bottoms for threadbare jeans, and a clean tee shirt might make a rare appearance. Socks, almost matching, finding their way onto my feet. Yet, beyond these minor adjustments, my day wardrobe remained a testament to my, newly acquired, rustic French flair.

Voilà! Colin Templeman, the epitome of French rural inelegance in all its dishevelled glory!

As December came around the corner, it brought with it the usual suspects: plummeting temperatures, shorter days, and our hens staging a sit-in, though in doing so, reducing egg production. Of course, it was also a time of preparation for the impending festivities. Christmas, for us, was always akin to preparing for a siege, though judging by the mountain of food and drink being stockpiled, you might think we were bracing for a full-blown apocalypse.

But Christmas wasn't the only event on our calendar. We also had the birthdays of Sam and Maggie, who were hitting the grand milestones of twenty-one and eighteen, respectively. As noted in my journal, these were landmark years, deserving of celebrations that would make even the Queen envious – particularly if Maggie had her way.

Now, when it came to such arrangements – or any arrangements, really – my input was sought more out of courtesy than necessity. My family had long since learned that my preferred role was that of a bystander rather than a participant. They knew to simply inform me of the where and when, and I'd be there. In fact, as I write this down, it dawns on me that Sam's knack for planning might just be inherited from yours truly. Along with a few other quirks, it would seem.

In the chaotic domain that is our household, where logic occasionally takes a backseat, a curious pattern has emerged. It seems that any mischief or negative behaviour exhibited by our offspring are invariably traced back to their father – me. Take for instance the time our Maggie, in an act of youthful exuberance, let loose a thunderous toot in the presence of her bewildered grandmother. The accusatory glances immediately swung in my direction, as if I were somehow the maestro behind this spontaneous wind performance.

There is little doubt in my wife's mind that Maggie's...erm, less than aromatic outbursts can only be attributed to my side of the family. It's certainly not something her kin would ever do so unashamedly and with such obvious pleasure. Accordingly, I am found guilty by association, as Clare's family remains free of guilt for such offences.

Yet, when our children showcase their finer qualities – whether it be acts of kindness, bursts of intellect, or moments of sheer brilliance – the accolades are swiftly and unanimously bestowed upon Clare. "They clearly take after their mother," is a common refrain, leaving me to wonder if my contribution to their genetic makeup is being selectively overlooked.

Nonetheless, my non-appointment to the Christmas and birthdays events committees proved to be a good decision. It granted me the freedom to immerse myself in pursuits closer to my comfort zone; constructing and mending things, taming the garden – with every ounce of my limited knowledge – and using my chainsaw with all the precision of a seasoned amateur woodsman.

With the ever increasing hubbub of forthcoming activities, I found myself gradually losing sight of what one might dub 'normal.' But, since my retirement and the subsequent move to our newly adopted country, the very notion of normality remained as elusive as my ability to grow a cauliflower.

From the time of our exodus and this newfound lifestyle, we had shed the shackles of routine with unexpected ease. Our lifestyle overhaul, geographical relocation, and altered perspective had all combined to produce days that bore no resemblance to the regimented schedules of our former lives. There was an undeniable sense of welcome disarray that accompanied our newfound freedom.

Instead, we danced to the unpredictable tune of our new existence, where even the mundane tasks like shopping and cooking played second fiddle to the more unpredictable exploits that filled our days. Not that I was complaining, but the notion of normal, as we once knew it to be, had become a distant memory, replaced by what I guess was a new ordinary. Yet to be completely figured out.

Moreover, a revelation dawned upon me: the mythical 'five-minute job' is precisely that – a myth. Tasks had a curious tendency to fill any allocated – and unallocated – hours of the day. With our lives no longer tied to the relentless march of the clock, my innate tendency for distraction flourished. In days gone by, both my professional and personal pursuits were meticulously mapped out, every minute accounted for with military precision. Weekends, particularly, were crammed to the gills with domesticity, leaving little room for idle reflection during my time off.

In retirement, however, I was to discover a different form of frustration – particularly when my meticulously defined plans, often devised over breakfast, fell by the wayside. But Clare, ever the voice of calm, would remind me with a wry smile, "there's always tomorrow," and much to my surprise, she was right. Tomorrow always arrived, fresh and unblemished, inviting me to take another swing at my to-do list with renewed vigour.

IT WAS THE WEEK BEFORE CHRISTMAS…

Journal entry from December 2016 – We made a swift run back to England this week for shopping, visiting family and collecting Sam from his Uni digs, which were predictably horrible. What is it about students, that they're able to turn, what at the outset are half decent living spaces, into squalor?

It's been a while since I've been on the ferry. No breakfast of course because it's the night sailing. The nervy, sicky bunch, Clare, Maggie and Jack have all retired to our dog friendly cabin, leaving me and Sam to catch up and talk shite, over a few beers.

The good news, for our return journey, is that I remembered to leave just enough room for one more passenger (Sam) in the Landy, which was no mean feat given the amount of merchandise we had to bring back with us.

It's not as if we're living in a third world country or anything, but there are certain things that you just can't get in France. I think I may have said before; shopping in France is a really disappointing experience – for an English bloke that is. Though shopping in England, whilst providing us with pretty much everything we had on our list, was a really horrible experience. Its one redeeming factor being the choice of produce. Or more accurately, the choice of produce more suited to my pallet at this time of the year. English ale, Cornish pasties, Twiglets, Quality Street chocolates, pork pie (of course) and a whole lot more. Not staples I know but for me, at Christmas time, I consider many of them to be essentials. Who knows, in time, as we become more native, more accepting of our adopted Country, my outlook to these essentials, and how we do Christmas may change. Or, as is likely, I might just continue to indulge myself with the best of both worlds, especially for this festive period?

***

After a night's voyage from Portsmouth to St Malo, we found ourselves back home just a week before Christmas Day. With a sense of urgency reserved for the final countdown, we embarked on the annual event of compiling our plans and 'things to do' lists – because, as anyone knows, Christmas is less a holiday and more a looming deadline.

For many, the festive season morphs into a milestone, a finishing line that compels a flurry of activity, and we were no exception. It wasn't the shopping or the wrapping of gifts that consumed our thoughts; those mundane tasks would occur regardless. No, what Clare referred to as 'extraordinary ordinary tasks' took centre stage – those peculiar chores like touching up the paintwork, hanging pictures, and installing shelves. These were tasks that could, and should, have been completed at any other time of the year. Yet, with Christmas approaching and guests imminent, our home needed to pass inspection as if it were under the scrutiny of a building inspector or would be house buyer.

And so, in the spirit of festive preparation, we get on with this seasonal ritual, ensuring our house was ready to delight and dazzle our visitors, all the while pondering why such tasks seemed to take on an air of urgent necessity only in the shadow of Christmas.

Continuing with our festive preparations, we decided that one Christmas tree simply wouldn't do. Call it an extravagance if you like, but with the layout of our house – and considering it was our first Christmas there – the big windows downstairs positively cried out for not one, but two trees. We opted for a smaller tree to snugly occupy the bay of the French doors in the sitting room, and a grander one to preside over the spacious main living, kitchen, and dining area.

Now, my contribution to the Christmas tree affair is

typically quite focused: ensuring the tree stands upright in its final resting place and dealing with the lights. Though the thing about the lights, is that no matter how meticulously I coil them up each year on the twelfth night, they seem to participate in a merry dance of entanglement while in the loft. Furthermore, once untangled, the lights – despite functioning flawlessly the previous season – often decide to play dead the moment they're plugged in. Thus begins the painstaking process of inspecting each bulb, hunting for that one elusive, misbehaving component.

In today's era, Generation Z and their contemporaries have seemingly sidestepped this festive tradition. They purchase strings of LED lights – often shipped in from China – and when they fail, they toss them aside and buy new ones, giving little thought to their ultimate fate in the dreaded landfill, nestled alongside their disposable fashion purchases. Whilst moralising as to how our generation have largely ruined the planet for them.

We, however, adhere to the old-school ethos, finding it both environmentally and economically sensible to repair and reuse our lights – as indeed we do for other items too; hair-dryers, toasters... Even hunting out replacement bulbs – that have long since ceased to be manufactured – on internet auction sites.

Once the tree was firmly anchored upright and the lights aglow, I dutifully stepped aside to allow the true artists of the season to commence their work. Enter Clare and Maggie, the dynamic duo from opposite ends of the Christmas decorating spectrum. Clare, the minimalist, subscribes to the 'less is more' philosophy with a firm stance on the tinsel embargo. Maggie, on the other hand, embraces the 'more the merrier' mantra with an unyielding passion for tinsel.

This particular year, in a moment of monumental miscalculation, Clare granted Maggie carte blanche to adorn the larger of our two trees. She naively harboured hopes that Maggie, having matured a year, might adopt a more restrained approach. Regrettably, that was not to be. The result? Our most enormous tree in years became the most festooned in living memory. Not a bough was spared from the onslaught of baubles, ornaments, and decorations. Although tinsel was mercifully absent, the sheer volume of adornments rendered the tree a dazzling spectacle. However, we all need to sleep, even Maggie. Presenting an opportunity for the 'less is more' brigade to move in, under the cover of darkness.

Personally, I thought it looked splendid, an absolute excess of Christmas cheer. Clare, however, had other thoughts, though she graciously refrained from altering too much in the way of Maggie's decoration. And so, our tree stood as a testament to the collision of decorating ideologies, a magnificent symbol of festive compromise.

***

Amongst the host of tasks that we (Clare) had ambitiously outlined to complete before Christmas, I (she) had set myself a rather noble goal: to install some shelves in the kitchen. But not just any everyday, store-bought shelves, mind you. No, I had settled on crafting them from scratch, driven by a recent triumph of transforming old wooden pallets into a pair of gates for our chickens' play area.

Buoyed by this newfound prowess, the notion of manufacturing household accessories and furniture seemed the logical next step in my carpentry career – beginning with the kitchen shelves. Following my tried and true method, I planned to use whatever timber I could scrounge up. My creative juices flowing, I pondered as to whether I could incorporate some of the old, bent, and woodworm infested timber salvaged from the barn roof's replacement, to give the shelves an authentic rustic charm. However, before I proceed, allow me to clarify my knack for creativeness. In truth, I possess no such inclination. Creativity, it seems, is a foreign state to me, where I am but a bewildered tourist. Nevertheless, I plunged headfirst into the task, determined to defy my limitations and introduce our kitchen to handcrafted rustic elegance.

Clare was positively thrilled at the prospect of not only having new shelves in the kitchen, but having them lovingly handcrafted by yours truly. In hindsight, I should have managed her expectations a little more cautiously. Unfortunately, I did not, and therefore the pressure was on to produce a masterpiece worthy of an actual artisan.

Bearing in mind also, that any artisan roots I might have, lie in the fact that I was apprenticed as an electrician. Therefore, wood, whilst a fascinating material, is not my natural forte. Nevertheless, my resolve to conquer my wood-related anxieties must have impressed Clare's father, Ron. Because, a year or so previously, he generously bestowed upon me a router, complete with an extensive array of cutters and, of all things, a book – a veritable volume of woodworking wisdom. Unbeknown to Ron, this gift, whilst well intentioned, was rather like handing a piano to a monkey. But it did offer ample opportunities for me to transform decent timber into splendid firewood.

The router had remained untouched in my tool cupboard since I'd been given it, a relic of my pre-retirement life. Occasionally, I would pick it up, examine it with a mix of curiosity and trepidation, and gently place it back in the box.

But on to the shelves! I did manage to transform some old, rough-sawn wood into something approximating smooth, shelf-like planks. Armed with copious amounts of furniture wax and a liberal dose of elbow grease, I became quite proud of the end result. With growing confidence, I even crafted some bespoke brackets – designing and building them without the need for any load-bearing calculations. The shelves and brackets were duly installed, and they stood there, almost level, ready for inspection.

As pleased as I was with my handiwork, the final arbiter of success was, of course, Clare. I am delighted to report that she was overjoyed. Once the shelves were hung (nearly straight), she set about adorning them with all manner of jars and kitchen paraphernalia. For days and nights afterward, I lay awake, ears attuned for the crash of jars hitting the worktops and floor.

To my cautious amazement, it never happened.

But, despite my satisfaction with the end product, I remain a realist. As functional as they were, the shelves never quite transcended their humble origins to being no grander than a 'D' grade school project.

***

Journal entry from December 2016 – *I got a French lesson today from a nine year old boy (Sasha), one of Alan and Hélène's grandchildren. He advised me, or rather corrected me, in the nicest possible way that only a cocky little boy can, in that 'beer' in the French language is designated as being feminine. In other words La Bière as opposed to Le Bière. The feminine masculine designation in the French language continues to be one of the many challenges that I struggle with. And to be honest the spoken French I do have, is without much in the way of a French accent, so therefore I'm thinking maybe that's why I tend to get away with not getting it right in shops and the like. Or perhaps they're too polite to correct me, or just look upon me as yet another ignorant Brit – or both. They say ignorance is bliss, but I'm still of a mind that a fish is a fish, and struggle to understand why people care so much as to whether it's designated masculine or feminine, because they all look and taste the same with chips. Obviously the French have a different view on this, though in reality – my reality – it should only present a problem if I were asked to write an essay, in French, on said fish, which is highly unlikely. But as a matter of principle beer being designated as feminine is just not right, which got me looking into other things that the French have ludicrously, and to my mind incorrectly, designated as feminine. Chainsaw, lawnmower, the television, any pie (pork or otherwise)... Oh and let's not forget credit card! WTF! The one feminine designation that I did get right was 'battle-axe'.*

***

The one blight on an otherwise good run into Christmas was the poisoning of our old cat Nettle. Well not so old at seven years but the oldest in our increasing menagerie. Coming in one morning from one of her usual nocturnal forays, Clare spotted she was lethargic, not hungry at all and after sleeping for many hours she simply tottered around as if drunk. We drove her to the vet in Pontivy and after numerous tests and a hefty bill the prognosis was that she had probably ingested something agricultural and as a result her internals were shutting down.

The vet told us that this was quite common in rural parts as pesticide residues drain from the fields, form puddles which animals such as cats and dogs will drink from. I'd never seen Nettle drink from a puddle – being out all night I was unlikely to do so – but I know that Jack was partial to water not presented to him in a bowl. Puddles, the Blavet and even the sea were his watering holes of choice.

We were informed that the next twenty hours would be crucial. Nettle, our feline matriarch, was promptly hooked up to an IV drip, with what I can only assume was a cocktail of rehydration fluids and a proper pharmacy of medications. We entrusted her delicate state to the vigilant vet, crossing our fingers and hoping for the best.

The following day, a solemn phone call delivered disheartening news – Nettle's prospects were grim. Though the medicine seemed to be working its magic, she lay motionless, seemingly oblivious to her surroundings. We found ourselves at a crossroads: should we twist the narrative and end her suffering, or stick to our guns and hold out for a miracle?

Naturally, we chose the latter, bolstered by a relentless wave of positive thoughts, fervent wishes, and perhaps even a sprinkling of prayers. To cut a long story short, by Christmas Eve, Nettle had staged a miraculous comeback! The vet reported that she was lucid, had sipped some water, and even nibbled on a morsel of food. Though not entirely out of the woods, these were the signs of hope we'd been yearning for. We resolved to continue the treatment, ensuring she stayed under the vet's watchful eye throughout the festive season.

Was this to be our very own Christmas miracle? Only time would reveal the answer.

It's a curious thing, you know. Despite my loudly proclaimed disdain for cats – those classic freeloaders who waltz in and out as they please, consume the food we kindly provide, and bestow their company upon us only when it suits them – I found myself softening. Perhaps I should give them some credit? Afterall, they are prime examples of independence, therefore deserving of some begrudging respect. Ha! Just kidding. They're freeloaders through and through.

That said, Nettle did earn her keep by keeping the rodent population at bay, even if it was more for her own amusement than our benefit. Nevertheless, when any of our animals, including the chickens, find themselves in need, we rise to the occasion and care for them without hesitation.

With Christmas now just around the corner our trusty,

laying two hundred and fifty eggs a year chickens were taking a winter break. Meaning that we had to go buy eggs from the supermarket. The chickens of course still received the utmost care, best food...despite their poor showing.

With the prospect of a white Christmas unlikely in Saint-Barthélémy I was still very much looking forward to it. Just a couple of things left to do, get the firewood in and squeeze in a bit more French language practise, before our friends Graham and Julie arrive from England.

'... and a grander one to preside over the spacious main living, kitchen, and dining area...'

MERRY CHRISTMAS A TOUS ET A TOUS

Journal entry from December 2016
Quite often you look forward to something so much that you over sell it to yourself and then come the day or event or whatever, it often just doesn't live up to expectations. As much as I'm looking forward to Christmas my natural pessimism has started to kick in. Am I over egging it a bit? Throughout my life I've had some great Christmas's and some not so great, with many that have been little more than just ordinary. Fingers crossed for this year.

***

As it happened, this Christmas will forever be etched in my memory as being a particularly enjoyable one. Our dear friends, Graham and Julie, arrived on the 22nd of December. From their noisy entrance until their departure on Boxing Day, we basked in absolute merriment. While nothing of earth shattering significance occurred, it was the very essence of good company, infectious laughter, and ridiculous games that made it so memorable. Including Scrabble – where a double word score was awarded for any profanity – reached new heights of hilarity, thanks in no small part, to the generous flow of spirits. Graham, in particular, developed an unexpected fondness for Ricard – that popular French anise-flavoured spirit – transforming him into an unintelligible Frenchman.

Our break from the mundane, and lengthy discussions about our grand plans for the garden and house in the New Year, only added to the festive spirit. Though we had Sam and Maggie with us, Jamie's absence was keenly felt amid the revelry.

Maggie thought Jack cut quite a dashing figure in a bow tie, and Beryl graced us with her presence for a few hours on

Christmas Eve – her friendliness becoming more evident, proportional to the amount of wine she consumed. Thankfully, no kitchen creation accompanied her. Upon inquiring after Gérard, I discovered he was spending the holiday with one of his Parisian lady friends. Clare, ever the compassionate hostess, invited Beryl to join us for Christmas Day to spare her from solitude. However, she had already accepted an invitation to Bernard's house, where his wife was breaking tradition by preparing a grand Christmas feast, in the British way. By all accounts Beryl had generously offered to take dessert to their house, but the offer was graciously declined – we suspected, more to do with Bernard's family's desire to maintain their digestive tranquillity than a measure of goodwill.

Our thoroughly British Christmas traditions remained unyielding, without exception. The presents that year were magnificent, unlike the typical tick-box presents of yesteryears – buying presents to merely satisfy a list. For reasons unbeknown to me, that Christmas felt different somehow. There was a relaxed, effortless charm to the festivities. Or perhaps I was simply viewing everything through a rose-tinted lens? Maybe, maybe not – either way, I didn't mind at all.

As for the age-old tradition of placing the children's stockings at the foot of their beds on Christmas Eve, my cover was blown years ago. Yet, the expectation persisted, regardless of their ages. Consequently, I continued to set my alarm for the early hours, embarking on my clandestine mission. Inevitably, I woke them up with a misplaced step on discarded clothing or a wobble while placing the stocking. It seems my stealth is not what it once was. Clare often asks why I persist, to which I respond that it's important I practice for the future generation of believers – grandchildren, of course. For now and the foreseeable future, I shall endeavour to keep the spirit of Christmas ever present in our home.

Christmas dinner, one of my favourite parts of the festive season, was an absolute triumph. Clare truly outdid herself. The spread of dishes, alongside the imported turkey Graham and Julie brought from Dorset, was a culinary masterpiece. She even served packet sage and onion stuffing, much to the delight of the kids and me, though Clare isn't particularly fond of it – yet she always partakes out of what she refers to as, "just being polite." Clare is, in fact, 'polite' about partaking in several other things she insists she's not terribly keen on – onion rings, a sit-down meal at McDonald's, fried chicken from the Colonel's establishment, and our old local pub, to name a few.

Naturally, I overindulged. To do anything less would have been an affront to the monumental effort, abundance, and quality of the feast laid before us. Between mouthfuls, I took a moment to sit back and soak in the atmosphere – the joy radiating from every corner of the table. The ludicrous paper hats, which are a classic Christmas enhancement, the remnants of nearly empty dishes, Christmas cracker debris, and the discarded jokes we've heard countless times and never found any funnier. Spots of gravy, wine and bits of food decorated the tablecloth, which had started out as a beautifully adorned and orderly piece. Laughter echoed from people with mouths full of food – an act that would normally draw Clare's stern gaze, but not today. Christmas music, a constant since November, played softly in the background, and promises of diets, abstinence and dry spells in the coming months were made in jest.

Christmas day concluded with the television flickering away, completely ignored, and a symphony of snoring around the fire. Our time with friends and Sam wound down as well. Graham and Julie departed on Boxing Day, and Sam followed suit a few days later.

I know that many of you, having read my account of our Christmas day, might declare it no different from a typical British Christmas, and you'd be right. For us, it was a classic case of "you can take the family out of England, but you can't take England out of the family". Despite our best efforts to embrace the French way of life, we found ourselves perpetually circling back to our beloved British traditions.

A STRANGER COMES CALLING

During the post-Christmas lull and just a few days after the yuletide festivities, Nettle, made her unexpected return from the vet's care. We found ourselves both richer in spirit and poorer in pocket. The vet, informed us that Nettle would still need time to recover, as indeed would our bank account. Yet, our Christmas miracle had unfolded, and Maggie was overjoyed.

With the Nettle episode thankfully fading into the background, I found the days between Christmas and the New Year to be a welcome breathing space. It was a time to pause, inhale deeply, and prepare ourselves for the upcoming New Year revelries. During this brief interlude, we indulged in blissful idleness. A bit of shopping here, a leisurely stroll around the farm there, simply because we could. We even embarked on some delightful longer walks along the Blavet with Clare and Jack. Maggie and Sam were invited but had long since tired of the novelty of walking, whether with us or in general.

Thus, we embraced the tranquillity, relishing the quiet moments before the New Year's celebrations brought us back to reality once more.

It was on one of these days, our dear Maggie, ever the disrupter, decided to introduce a stray dog into our otherwise tranquil lives. The mutt in question just happened to be sauntering along the road precisely as Maggie and Clare were driving to the supermarket.

With a heart full of good intentions, Maggie wasted no time in coaxing this vagabond pooch into their company and our car. Little did she know, this spontaneous act of charity would add a layer of unwanted pandemonium to our household.

Was this God calling in a favour for the miracle of Nettle? I wasn't to know but it was a heck of a coincidence.

Well, no sooner had Maggie and Clare returned from their abandoned shopping expedition, than we found ourselves with yet another four-legged resident. Without so much as a moment for me to object, this little black mongrel had made itself right at home, basking in Maggie's' hospitality like an old friend.

This friendly little bugger, a diverse mix of various canine breeds, looked as if it could have had three or four fathers. No bigger than Jack, but decidedly shorter in the leg department, it wore a collar devoid of any identification and despite a bit of dirt on its undercarriage, it was quite well cared for. Clearly, this wasn't a stray but maybe a runaway on some grand adventure.

As night fell, it was agreed – well, I was informed – that our newfound guest would stay for the night. Come morning, we would embark on a mission to locate its rightful owner. In the meantime, Maggie wasted no time in preparing a cozy bed in the utility/boiler room, complete with a hot water bottle for added comfort. After being well-watered and fed, our little visitor settled in for the night, no doubt already looking forward to breakfast.

The next morning, our new canine guest was let out to perform its necessaries, which it did with commendable enthusiasm. As it pottered about the garden, it soon found a willing companion in Jack, who seemed rather pleased with the unexpected company. Their camaraderie was instant, as if they had been lifelong pals. However, the one thing we had yet to discover was this little mongrel's attitude towards our resident cats and chickens. You see, we had been quite spoiled with Jack, who was blissfully indifferent to both species. Having been raised alongside them, Jack considered our feline and feathered friends to be part of the family.

Apart from the occasional foray into the chicken coop for a snack of dubious distinction, there had never been any issues.

So, with bated breath, we watched as our newest addition explored the garden, hoping that this charming stray would show the same tolerance and decorum as Jack.

Nettle was quite safe because she was on the vet advised housebound R&R. But Milo, the latest addition to our ever-expanding menagerie – a young, ginger Tom – was deemed fair game by our new lodger. Given the dog's rather short stature, it was never going to catch Milo, yet this did nothing to deter its spirited attempts. This resulted in the cat taking refuge in the barn or seeking solace up the nearest tree. One had to admire the dog's patience, as it sat vigil for hours, awaiting Milo's reappearance from hiding or descent from whatever tree it had sought refuge in. The fact that the cat had slyly exited from another door or stealthily climbed down the dark side of the tree was information we didn't feel obliged to share. This left the dog peering intently at nothing, ever hopeful.

The real predicament, however, came with the chickens. During the winter, we allowed them to roam freely in the orchard or wherever they pleased, giving their designated area a chance to recuperate from their relentless foraging. You might not know this, but chickens, when grouped together, are quite a formidable force, with few animals daring to challenge them. However, they are not the most astute of creatures and lack any understanding of the concept 'safety in numbers'. Hiding isn't a skill that comes naturally to them either.

So, when one of them chose to wander off from the flock, it presented the dog with the perfect opportunity to stir up some mischief. Within the span of a single morning, our chickens' free-range existence and Milo's carefree wanderings had been thoroughly disrupted, all thanks to our enthusiastic new addition.

'...chickens...hiding isn't something that comes natural to them.'

Our mission was clear – we needed to find the origins of this mysterious canine and return it to its rightful home. Clare and I spent most of that day embarking on a door-to-door quest among the few houses in our hamlet and along an adjoining road, inquiring if anyone owned or recognised our furry interloper. And, as luck would have it, we struck gold! It turned out that the dog belonged to an elderly lady who had taken a tumble over Christmas and was now recuperating in hospital. A friend or relative had taken on the responsibility of looking after the dog, but somewhere along the line, things had gone awry.

Though the identity of this mysterious caretaker remained elusive, we discovered where they lived. Furthermore, we discovered that the dog answered to the name of Caramel – a charmingly ironic name for a little black dog. Who said the French don't have a sense of humour? We also learned a valuable lesson: in France, adopting stray dogs is a complicated affair, with no easy handoff to organisations like our RSPCA back in the UK.

As the day wore on, we concocted a plan. By this point, Maggie had already lost interest in our (her) canine guest, leaving Clare and me to handle the situation. We trekked to the house of the elderly lady's friend, situated just outside our hamlet. Upon arrival, we knocked on the door, but unfortunately, no one was home. Undeterred, we posted a note on the door, informing the absent occupant that we had their neighbour's dog and that it was being well cared for, requesting they come and collect it. What we actually wrote was (something like) this:

M. ou Mme Templeman
XX Saint Thuriau
56150
Saint Barthelemy
Tel : 02 97 25 33 71

Chère Madame, nous avons Lé chien de vos amis. Veuillez appeler le numéro de téléphone ci-dessus. Merci beaucoup.

Roughly translated: Dear madam, we have your friend's dog. Please call the above telephone number. Thank you very much.

Reading that note, it dawned on us that it bore an uncanny resemblance to a ransom demand. So, we set about crafting something a little less threatening and returned the following day.

For the next couple of days, Clare and I made the trek back and forth, ferrying Caramel between his own house and that of the not-so-careful Samaritan. Unfortunately, there was no sign of life at either location. On one such day, we decided to take Jack for a stroll along the local canal, leaving our runaway at home. Yet, our stern instructions to Maggie and Sam not to let the stray out had clearly fallen on deaf ears. No sooner had we cleared the drive than I spotted Caramel in my rearview mirror, valiantly chasing after us. And I must say, for a dog with limited leg capacity, it could muster a decent turn of speed. However, it was no match for the Land Rover and soon abandoned the chase after half a mile or so. For a brief, hopeful moment, I thought our problem might have solved itself. But, upon our return a couple of hours later, there sat Caramel, dutifully awaiting our arrival, clearly delighted to see us just in time for dinner.

Our salvation arrived in the form of Gérard, recently returned from his mysterious Parisian liaison. As always, eager to assist, within a few hours he had unearthed all the vital information: who the owner was and, crucially, the identity of the foster carer. By that evening, Caramel was collected by a chap who may or may not have been the designated carer – I was beyond caring by that point – and life returned to its usual rhythm.

It's an odd thing, but despite the disruption caused by Caramel's brief visit, we were glad to have been of help. And, for a (very) fleeting moment, we found ourselves missing our adopted stray.

A week or so later, Caramel made a surprise reappearance. This time, he simply darted into the garden, relieved himself on a wall, and wandered off again. Perhaps he was letting us know he was alive and well, or maybe he just got caught short while out on another of his adventures. Either way, we remained hidden, as did Milo and the chickens.

NEW YEARS EVE

Journal entry from 1st January 2017 – New Year Eve dinner, fireworks and a lot of fun at Alan and Hélène's. Yannick, Steph and the boys were there along with us (me, Clare, Maggie and Sam). As always I'm a very happy man when my kids are with me. Though with one missing (Jamie Ann) I wasn't quite complete. Unsurprisingly, the evening was a triumph and although not as satisfying as Christmas dinner (it never could be no matter where and how we celebrate the New Year) we had many laughs and lots to eat amongst great friends. But man what a long evening that was.

***

Just realised I haven't yet mentioned Yannick, Steph, and their mischievous lads. Yannick, Alan and Hélène's eldest, sported a beard as formidable as his father's, while Steph, his wife, thankfully, did not. Their boys, Charlie and Sasha, aged ten and eight respectively, had a liking for correcting our French language blunders – Charlie, if you recall, once enlightening me on the feminine nature of beer – and relocating our chickens to random spots around the farm. Despite their antics, they were good lads, perfect subjects for me to hone my potential grandad skills, should the day come when I have a few of my own.

One thing we could always count on when dining at Alan and Hélène's was the sheer length of the meal. Alan's attention span – or rather, his lack thereof – played a significant role in this. We would arrive punctually for aperitifs and park ourselves on the non-operational side of their sprawling breakfast bar, indulging in a delightful array of snacks and beverages. Meanwhile, Alan would be engrossed in some culinary escapade or other, with us chattering away and watching him. New Year's Eve, of course, was no exception. But before I dive into the delightful chaos of New Year's Eve, let me attempt to paint a picture of Alan and Hélène's home for you. Now, describing places isn't exactly my forte – hence my inclination for including photographs in the book – but unfortunately, I have few snapshots of the interior of their magical home.

So, here goes nothing: Walking onto the mill (*le moulin*) is like stepping into a piece of living history. The thick, stone walls convey a sense of permanence and strength, built to withstand time and the elements. The floor is constructed from large, uneven flagstones, worn smooth by literally centuries of use. All of which has been lovingly preserved by Alan and Hélène.

The focal point of the main kitchen, dining, living area, is a large, open hearth, made from what Alan told me was, local stone, with a heavy stone beam serving as the mantel. This fireplace being not just a source of warmth but also the heart of the room. A room where meals are cooked and family and friends, such as us, gather for mostly informal dinners. There is always the scent of burning wood mingling with the aroma of herbs and ingredients from meals both past and present.

Adjacent to the fireplace is, as you might expect, a perfect stack of logs, a sizable wicker basket, for kindling and blackened fire tools in the style of a Victorian blacksmiths forge. Face on to the fireplace is a large, four seater, pre-war brown leather sofa. Covered in a woollen throw, which probably once served as an eiderdown. Either side of the hearth, almost as bookends to the sofa, are a pair of vintage wooden rocking chairs, upon which there is, on each one, a couple of homemade embroidered cushions.

Exposed wooden beams crisscross the ceiling, their dark, smoke hardened surfaces adding to the rustic appeal. The double glazed windows – the only deference to the twenty first century – small and deep-set, are framed by thick wooden shutters, which can be closed against the chill of the Breton winter or the heat of high summer.

A large wooden table, able to seat at least twelve – with three nearly matching chairs on each of its four sides – takes pride of place in the centre of the room, only a few centimetres from the old sofa. Its surface scarred and marked by countless meals prepared and shared.

Off to the right segregated by a four metre long, Alan built breakfast bar, come worksurface, come dumping ground, is the kitchen. Perfectly practical with little thought given to unnecessary fashion or style. Along the far wall, making up the galley kitchen design, is another Alan built worksurface of equal proportions and same design as the breakfast bar. Though this one having storage cupboards underneath. Each of the worksurfaces have been topped off with ceramic tiles of some Breton design, upon which, sit a variety of small, aged, kitchen appliances, a stack of old newspapers, mementos of numerous walks and holidays, an old Roberts radio permanently tuned to a single Medium Wave station – because that's the only signal they can get in the mill – and a vegetable rack. Above the worksurface on the far wall are some Alan built shelves. Lined with earthenware jars, each containing dried goods or preserves, adding to the sense of a well-stocked, self-sufficient household.

The mill machinery, located at the opposite end to the fire place, is a marvel of pre-industrial engineering. Wooden gears and stone grinding wheels, which would have once turned by the power of the, long since redundant, water wheel outside. A testament to the ingenuity and hard work of the millers who once lived there. All preserved behind an Alan installed wall of glass, with sympathetic lighting, as good as you might see in any museum, adding to the overall effect.

Hope that helps.

'The focal point of the main kitchen, dining, living area, is a large, open hearth, made from...local stone, with a heavy stone beam serving as the mantel.'

***

Back to New Year's Eve, we arrived at the appointed hour to find Yannick and his family already in situ. The fire roaring, some lively Breton music crackled from an old CD player, and Alan was in full swing, plying us with drinks and his well-worn collection of jokes.

The kitchen bore testament to the impending feast: piles of prepared vegetables adorned the worktop, alongside a splendid leg of lamb, prepped but yet to see sight of the oven. By my estimation, it would need at least two hours to roast, giving us a rough idea of when we might finally sit down for the main course. But, with it being only seven in the evening, we had plenty of time before the midnight celebrations.

Hélène, as serene as ever, was ensconced in one of the rocking chairs, keeping the otherwise rambunctious boys occupied with a book. Periodically, she'd break off to chastise Alan, reminding him that, at some point, he did need to actually cook the food he'd so diligently prepared. The scene was set for an evening of merriment, laughter, and the kind of convivial chaos that only Alan and Hélène's home could provide. As the minutes ticked by, we settled into the warmth of the fire and the camaraderie of good friends, ready to usher in the New Year with joy and a further helping of Alan's infamous jokes.

Fast forward three hours, after multiple courses of starters, a plethora of drinks, and an endless array of snacks, we had yet to sit down for dinner and our stomachs were growling in protest. The good news was that the kitchen chaos had reached a crescendo, with Alan's rising panic and a symphony of colourful profanity indicating that things were finally starting to come together, albeit with some timing mishaps and temperature adjustments.

At long last, just after ten-thirty, we gathered around the table for our New Year's Eve feast. Well, almost all of us – Maggie had to endure a bit more of a wait as Alan, in his flurry of culinary activity, had overlooked the small detail of her being a vegetarian. Nevertheless, the atmosphere was one of jovial anticipation, as we prepared to indulge in the long-awaited main course and continue the festivities well into the night.

In spite of the culinary chaos and the late hour, the mood in the room was nothing short of wonderful. The boys, being well past their bedtime, had reached that belligerent stage, while the adults, having indulged in drinks for over three and a half hours, found themselves engaged in wonderfully ridiculous conversations. Hélène, ever the epitome of grace, had worked her way through at least two bottles of the local wine and had achieved a state of peaceful stupor.

Alan, on the other hand, was oscillating between the roles of a nightclub comic and a decompressing chef, having consumed beer while cooking and now wine while eating. As other courses continued to pile up in the kitchen, his stress levels soared, and his jokes became even more outlandish. We were so far behind schedule that it was unanimously agreed we would save the cheese and dessert for after the midnight fireworks.

In case you're wondering, dessert and coffee always follows the cheese course in France.

At some indeterminate hour in the early dawn of January 1st, 2017, we arrived home. We were utterly inebriated, stuffed to the gills with delicious food, our faces aching from seven hours of relentless smiling and laughter, all wrapped in a warm layer of contentment.

That year, I decided to forgo the usual New Year resolutions, opting instead for some personal aspirations. Beyond the perennial wish for my family's health and happiness, I was eager to see my French language skills improve and to cultivate something edible from the soon-to-be-dug potager.

And so, with the promise of new beginnings and the echoes of the evening's revelry still ringing in our ears, we drifted into the new year, hearts full and hopes high.

PART SIX (AND A HALF)

BONNE ANNEE!

Journal entry January 2017 – *Happy New Year!*
Holiday over and my thoughts turn to the list of things and projects to do in the coming year, starting with the jobs I've been putting off for a while now. Such as pruning the trees in the verger and clearing many years of thorns and so on from the back of the hangar. I've just realised that I've never actually seen the back of the hangar.

Bring on the year, but for now I need to chop some more logs.

I'm still peeved about the fence between us and Bertrand's place. Still not sure why he did that.

I was glad of the dark and the need to concentrate in the thick fog as we drove Sam to St Malo. Because the lump in my chest and throat could easily have become tears. The worst thing about seeing our children is when we have to give them up to the world again. That feeling never goes away.

But I was glad he was around to help with putting up that bamboo screen. Not sure how glad he was though.

It's good that we seem to be having a proper winter at last. Cold frosty nights, sunny days and no rain, exactly what I was looking for, so I can get outside and wage war on anything that needs cutting down.

***

Something I neglected to mention earlier was the curious incident back in the summer. Our nearest neighbour, Bertrand – a disagreeable old curmudgeon if ever there was one – had inexplicably decided to remove a perfectly good eight-foot-high hedge that separated our properties.

When I confronted Bertrand about his horticultural vandalism, he nonchalantly explained that he was simply too old to maintain his side of such a substantial hedge. His exact words, if memory serves, were something like, *"Le buisson était trop haut et je suis vieux. Qu'est-ce que cela fait ?"* which translates to, "The bush was too tall and I am old. What does it matter?"

Despite his grumpy demeanour, I couldn't help but smile at his candidness. Bertrand had a way of making even the most puzzling actions seem utterly reasonable, at least in his own world. And so, with a resigned sigh, I accepted the disappearance of the old hedge, adding it to the list of oddities that made life in our little hamlet so amusingly unpredictable.

He was equally unperturbed about the possibility of Jack, leaving unwelcome deposits in his garden. After enduring a few minutes of my most intimidating hard stare, Bertrand finally relented and promised to replace the hedge with something.

However, Bertrand's interpretation of "something" turned out to be a mere string line, carelessly stretched across the now deserted gap, to mark what he believed to be the boundary. His minimalist's approach to property demarcation, was one that left me both amused and slightly exasperated. And so, our boundary dispute was resolved – or rather, redefined – in true Bertrand fashion, with a string line that fluttered in the breeze, serving as a constant reminder of our grumpy neighbour's quirky nature.

Over the years, I've observed a peculiar phenomenon among certain long-term residents of anywhere we'd lived. These individuals, having lived in a place for a few years, seem to acquire certain unwritten rights over those who have just moved in. It's as if their tenure grants them an unspoken authority, absolving them of any need to consult, discuss, or notify you about their actions, regardless of the impact it may have on you. The logic appears to be simple: they are the seasoned dwellers, and you, the fresh face.

Age often adds an extra layer to this entitlement. When the individuals in question are both considerably older and have lived in the area for many years, their perceived rights grow almost exponentially. It's as if a seniority hierarchy forms, with the long-timers at the top, wielding their unspoken privileges with ease. In this social dynamic, newcomers find themselves navigating an uncharted landscape of neighbourhood politics, where the rules are as ancient as the residents themselves and just as mysterious.

Despite Bertrand's string line strung about half a yard inside the actual boundary, I decided to capitulate, lacking the energy or inclination to argue the toss. Besides, the small patch of land he had commandeered was of no real use to me anyway. Nevertheless, my annoyance simmered, leaving me with an itch that demanded to be scratched.

True to form, Bertrand's promise of filling the gap with a fence or some other barrier never materialised, beyond the aforementioned piece of string. Fuelled by a mixture of irritation and a pinch of foolish retaliation, I set about concocting my own gap filling solution.

This, of course, is where my sanity and self-esteem came under serious scrutiny. Armed with determination and a possibly misguided sense of justice, I embarked on a mission to create a barrier that would stand as a testament to my resolve – or perhaps, my folly. The end result? Only time would tell, but one thing was certain: my feud with Bertrand had reached new, absurd heights.

My grand solution, having mulled it over for some weeks – though you'd never guess as much – manifested itself as an eight-foot-high, twenty-foot-wide bamboo screen. In the space of just a few months, it seemed I had become as small-minded as my less than dear neighbour. At the time, I was blissfully blind to this transformation, but my ever perceptive wife was not. In typical Clare fashion, she knew that any attempt to intervene would only serve to inflame the madness further.

The first part of my madcap scheme involved planting four ten-foot posts into the ground. This required me to precariously perch atop a step ladder, wielding my largest and heaviest sledgehammer, while Clare, armed with a spirit level, stood at ground level holding the posts upright. After hammering each post into the earth about two feet – mercifully without causing fatal injury to Clare – I set about stringing a series of wires and tensioners between them to support my bamboo screen.

Seizing the opportunity presented by Bertrand and his wife's extended Christmas break, I enacted part two of my plan: installing the screen. For this endeavour, I enlisted the reluctant assistance of Clare, Sam, and Maggie. Sam, the most impractical yet brilliant of souls, was dispatched into Bertrand's garden to pass cable ties back and forth between us as we secured the fence to the tensioning wires and posts. It also happened to be the coldest day of the season thus far, and the feeble winter sun provided little warmth. Poor Sam, standing in the shadow of my eight-foot creation, received none of its meagre rays. Despite his complaints and vows of never coming home for Christmas again, we nonetheless continued.

My poorly constructed bamboo screen, an attempt at retribution, was nonetheless duly installed. With a cringe-worthy sense of pride, I even encouraged friends and family to admire my handiwork. My shame reached its peak when, on a particularly windy day, my bamboo screen transformed into a bamboo sail on an immovable boat. Like a crazed sea captain, I battled to save my sails, rigging, and masts during the storm, but to no avail. When the tempest finally subsided, I dejectedly dismantled what remained of my fence, retrieving the rest from Bernard's garden.

Undeterred, and clinging to that age-old adage, "if at first you don't succeed, try, try again," I set about planning my Mark II – a design that would be tempest-proof. Then came severe frosts, making concrete mixing in order to plant concrete posts, impossible. It was at this point that Clare, with her usual grace and wisdom, made her move. Without fuss or even a hint of what a 'knob' I had been, she planted an idea.

Perhaps, she suggested, I could put up a simpler construction and, adjacent to it, grow another hedge inside Bernard's designated boundary. This would provide an easier and arguably better solution. I do love my wife, and she was, of course, right. However, at the time, I only conceded to give her idea some thought.

ONE MAN, HIS DOG AND SOME CHICKENS

Remember me telling you how, in the winter months, we allowed our hens to run free range, in an effort to allow the vegetation in their enclosure to recover. Well I came across the following journal extract.

***

Journal entry January 2017 – *Did a bit of tidying up in my workshop, which is something I like to do after I've completed a job, or the bin gets too full or I can no longer see the floor for shavings and wood dust. When out of the corner of my eye I caught movement in the form of red chicken combs just above the parapet of the stone door step. Walking slowly, purposefully and if possible for chickens, furtively, was a line of our chickens all heading off towards the freedom of the lane. All in a line headed up by one of the browns, not making a noise, until that is I happened to put my head out of the door and one of the black hens broke cover, did a couple of turns on the spot and headed back in the direction of the orchard. The line then became a shambles of chickens, as the game was up and whatever plan they had was in disarray. As escape committees go they need to work on their technique.*

***

All of which brings to mind another chicken escapade for your amusement. Our feathered friends had discovered a secret route from the back of our verger into our neighbour Beryl's garden. There, they happily scratched and scavenged in her compost heap, clearly having no intention of returning home anytime soon. Armed with a stepladder and a suitably long staff, I clambered over the five-foot fence I had erected months earlier to keep the chickens on our side and set off on a chicken round-up mission.

Expecting them to dutifully march back the way they had come was a fool's errand. Retracing their route also proved impossible, as there was no sign of a trodden path in the grass. It was as if a secret door had magically opened and closed, granting them access to Beryl's garden. Any notions of an orderly return vanished as the chickens, in a unified act of rebellion, dispersed in all directions. Their flight undoubtedly encouraged by the sight of a maniacal figure, armed with an especially long stick, ungracefully creeping up on them.

The result was a comedic scene of chaos, with chickens darting every which way and me, their flustered shepherd, vainly attempting to restore order.

Remembering the old TV show One Man and His Dog, where a shepherd, armed with nothing more than a long stick, a whistle, and a trusty hound, could herd unpredictable sheep into all manner of enclosures, inexplicably filled me with (misplaced) confidence. I fancied I could employ the same principles with chickens.

With arms spread wide and moving ever so slowly, I managed to corral the chickens into an orderly bunch. My next task was to encourage them to retrace their steps and return home. Of course, one or two made a bid for freedom, but after some one-on-one cajoling, they grudgingly fell back in line. Lacking a whistle, I adopted a unique grunt and a sing-song encouragement sound – where that came from, I haven't the faintest idea. Whether it actually helped is equally uncertain, but it definitely broke the silence and added a certain theatrical flair to the unfolding drama.

Thus, with much flapping and clucking, and my somewhat unconventional shepherding techniques, I gradually restored some semblance of order to the wayward flock.

However, a problem soon became glaringly apparent – the size of the path the chickens had taken. Simply put, it was chicken sized, and I was decidedly not. What lay before me was no more than a small tunnel through the undergrowth, a path clearly designed by and for our feathered adventurers. This might not have been such an issue, except that the chickens decided to pause halfway for a forage and a snack – such is the attention span of a chicken, I suppose.

While their impromptu picnic was all well and good, the small matter of getting them back into our garden remained unresolved. Patience quickly gave way to impatience, and I decided to charge through the undergrowth, brandishing my long stick and transforming my sing-song encouragement into a bellow.

Unsurprisingly, all I achieved was to startle the chickens, who promptly bolted further into the tunnel and closer to the exit into our garden. Which I guess I could claim as a partial success. At least they were heading in the right direction.

Enter Jack.

Now Jack, while possessing quite a few talents in absolutely nothing, excelled at being an exceptionally good-natured dog, loved by us and most others who crossed his path – especially those with snacks in their pockets. So you can imagine my surprise and, dare I say, pride when I saw him bounding through our verger, barking excitedly. In that moment, he could have been mistaken for one of those highly trained sheepdogs I'd seen on TV all those years ago. Unfortunately, Jack was nothing like a highly trained sheepdog. His enthusiastic attempts at corralling our chickens only served to spook them, sending them scurrying under my legs and back into Beryl's garden, with Jack in hot pursuit. I now faced the task of herding all our chickens and a dog back to where they belonged.

With no other option, I placed Jack under house arrest – launched him over the fence and commanded him to go home. This allowed me to once again wield my big stick and employ my limited herding skills. Eventually, I managed to get the chickens back into our garden, where they belonged.

This was but one of many escape attempts by our feathered absconders, each time successfully thwarted. All without Jack's well-intentioned, but ultimately unhelpful, assistance.

'In that moment, he could have been mistaken for one of those highly trained sheepdogs I'd seen on TV all those years ago.'

Pruning

Pruning the trees in the verger was a task that demanded meticulous planning, extensive research, ample time, and favourable weather. Having pored over countless books and articles, I felt fairly confident in my knowledge of what needed to be done, how much to trim, and when to execute the task. Yet, I couldn't shake the nerves.

One morning, as I stood in the verger, lost in contemplation, along came Gérard. Too early for whiskey and evidently not looking to borrow anything, he had come to impart some advice. Though he'd never owned a verger, he regaled me with tales of his youth spent working on fruit farms across the region. His motivation? Not money, but the numerous ladies who frequented such places.

According to Gérard, his employment history was as colourful as it was varied.

Among his many adventures, he had once worked on a fishing boat and was washed overboard, only to be rescued by a boat with a female skipper. Naturally, she fell madly in love with him, and they enjoyed endless romantic escapades on the high seas, punctuated by copious amounts of fresh fish and lobster. He fondly reminisced about her whenever he prepared Coquilles St-Jacques.

Gérard's exploits didn't end there. He claimed to have been the mayor of a commune – though he conveniently forgot its name – and a gardener on a large estate, where he had a dalliance with the lady of the Château. That particular tale seemed lifted straight out of *Lady Chatterley's Lover*, but it was undeniably entertaining. As I listened to Gérard's fantastical stories, my nerves about pruning the orchard momentarily faded, replaced by amusement and intrigue at the life of my colourful neighbour.

Standing in our verger, Gérard regaled me with an endless stream of stories about found and lost love. Between these colourful chapters, however, I discovered that he was quite knowledgeable about pruning trees – accordingly, he would say he was a fountain of knowledge on lots of other things too – offering a couple (or three) pearls of wisdom that would stay with me long after the tales of his romantic escapades had faded. According to Gérard, there should be no crossing branches, the centre of the tree needed to breathe and have sunlight, and however much pruning I thought was sufficient, I should double it.

A job best done on your own and with no interruptions or distractions. So I was pleased that Gérard found diversion in the smells of banana and choc chip muffins emanating from our kitchen. With advice imparted and the smell of baking too much to ignore, Gérard left me in peace, while I set about decimating our verger.

Many, if not all, of the trees had been neglected for years, meaning I couldn't accomplish everything they needed in a single year. As one of the many books advised, doing so would risk 'shocking' them. Patience, as they say, was the order of the day.

As I've previously told you, our verger had an abundance of differing trees – from plums to peaches to pears, with apples of various types and sizes reigning supreme. Sadly, I had no clue about any of them, other than the fact that each required its own unique triage before I could even consider hacking into them. My grand plan was to tackle each tree individually, assess any major work requirements, and then follow up with some lighter pruning, snipping, and shaping.

And so, armed with Gérard's pearls of wisdom and a trusty pair of pruning shears, a selection of saws and my small chainsaw, I set about rejuvenating our neglected verger, one tree at a time.

We had upward of thirty trees – hardly a forest or industrial orchard, but enough to keep one bloke busy. Despite my fondness for family, friends, and (a few) people in general, there was something profoundly satisfying about being alone in the verger for hours on end. And yes, I admit, I did find myself talking to the trees now and then. I shared my prognosis, diagnosis, and intentions as I set about both heavy and light cutting and shaping, much like a doctor might do before performing a medical procedure. I adhered to my plan of tackling each tree individually, sometimes revisiting one or two to ensure I hadn't missed anything.

The result of applying all this newfound wisdom was a verger full of trees that were almost shadows of their former selves. But at least I had a good supply of fruit wood – logs and kindling – to burn in the following winter.

All that was left for me to do was hope. I hoped the trees would survive my attentions, crossing my fingers for a healthy show of blossom come Spring.

I still had much to learn.

I spent much of that winter walking the verger, gazing upon our stunted trees and contemplating ways to cause Gérard some physical discomfort, should his advice prove to be horticultural homicide.

Spoiler alert: Every tree not only came back from the dead but also flourished, adorned with superb blossom and once again yielding plentiful fruit. While the quantity wasn't quite what it had been, the quality of the crops was certainly higher, with larger, more impressive produce.

PERFECT DAY

Perfect days are a rare thing and often sneak up on us when least expected. We might meticulously plan a perfect day – like a wedding or a seaside excursion – eagerly anticipating its perfection, only to find it can be a hit or miss. For me, the best perfect days are the ones that come upon you and which are rarely grand.

Tackling the brambles and all manner of rampant vegetation at the rear of our hangar was a task I'd been persistently postponing since we bought the place. The 'out of sight, out of mind' approach sufficed for a while, but eventually, I ran out of excuses. The brambles in question were particularly wicked, with stems as thick as a thumb and tentacles that sprawled into trees, under eaves, and along the ground. They snagged clothing, scratched skin, and tore through even the most industrial of gloves.

This tangled wasteland was littered with discarded concrete blocks, large stones, old tree stumps, and trees of various sorts that had been allowed to run riot. The area itself wasn't vast – perhaps twenty-five metres by five – a narrow strip of land serving as a barrier between the back of the hangar and an adjoining field.

On day one, Maggie joined me in the fray. Despite her grumbles about the cold – justifiably so – and the inevitable snags to skin, hair, and clothing, we managed to clear about a quarter of the area. Day two saw Maggie return, and together we cleared another quarter. However, I must admit, we had tackled what was arguably the easiest section, though the cuts and torn clothes might suggest otherwise.

Nevertheless, we were making progress, and a pile of concrete blocks and debris, possibly for burning, stood as a testament to our labour. By day three, Maggie had opted out, leaving me to tackle the remaining brambles solo. Armed with an arsenal of cutters, shears, my chainsaw, and a colourful vocabulary, I set about clearing the lot. Though the air was still cold, the sun made a rare appearance, prompting layers to come off as I worked up a sweat.

By day's end, I had orderly piles of debris ready for burning or dumping – I still hadn't quite decided yet. The trees I chose to keep were trimmed and pruned to perfection, my clothes were thoroughly snagged, and my tools cried out for sharpening. But the job was done, and for the first time, I could see the back of our hangar. As the sun began to dip, signalling the end of the working day, it still managed to provide a modicum of warmth, despite it being late January.

I sat down on one of the old tree stumps, remnants from an age when larger trees adorned this space. It was one of those rare moments when I wished I smoked. Not cigarettes, mind you, but a pipe – yes, a smouldering pipe would have been just the ticket. But instead, I simply sat there, basking in the setting sun, taking in the view across the field to the valley that housed the canal. A quietness surrounded me, with no sound but the blood coursing through my veins as my heart calmed after its exertions. Small birds, seizing the opportunity to explore the newly cleared ground, added to the tranquillity. The occasional 'chit, chit' from a Robin perched in one of the saved trees made me wonder whether it was thanking or reprimanding me.

Tired, sweaty, scratched from head to toe, and with a muddy bottom from the tree stump, I couldn't help but think – was there ever such a perfect day as this?

If there's a God, then I offer my thanks. If there isn't, well, thank you anyway.

'...a narrow strip of land serving as a barrier between the back of the hangar and an adjoining field...'

BOYS TOYS

Boys and their toys come in every conceivable shape, type and size. I'd already amassed a modest collection, but that fateful February, I became the illustrious one-third owner of a chipper machine. The other two shareholders? Alan, and his mate Barry, a lively Geordie chap.

Now, the theory behind this marvel of engineering was simple enough: you feed branches in one end, and out the other, voila! Chippings! These chippings, so I was assured by various online videos and glossy pictures, had multiple uses. But the real thrill was all in the chipping – happily reducing bits of trees into delightful, bite-sized wooden chips.

Our first challenge: assembly. It seems to be a modern curse, doesn't it? Gone are the days when you could simply unbox a piece of furniture or, in this case, a substantial tool, and commence playing with it immediately. Instead, we were faced with the formidable task of putting it together ourselves. Mercifully, on this occasion, there was no patronising image of a beaming woman on the instruction manual, wielding tools and a smug smile, as if to declare, "Look, even a woman can do it!" That woman, always there to ensure that when you're scratching your head in bewilderment, her cheerful visage is on hand to exacerbate your sense of inadequacy.

No, this occasion was different. Our guiding light was a set of instructions, in the form of a monochrome booklet, possibly produced by a diligent Chinese child, illustrating the chipper in various stages of assembly. Accompanying these were numerous bags of nuts, bolts, and washers. And then there were numerous metal panels – of all shapes, sizes, and hues. Alan and I set to work, guided by the colour neutral picture book. If the coloured panels held any special significance, the black-and-white images certainly didn't enlighten us. But with British pluck and a bit of ingenuity, we began to decipher what went where.

To cut a long story short, we breezed through the four pages of instructions with relative ease, each step bringing us closer to what the pictures promised. Yet, by the end of the pamphlet, we were left with a perplexing assortment: a yellow metal panel, some mysterious clips, and a handful of nuts and bolts, all of which seemed to belong nowhere. Clearly, the adding of a page five and possibly six would have been a welcome addition.

Given it was a Saturday, we briefly pondered the futile prospect of contacting the supplier, knowing full well that any such endeavour would have to wait until Monday. And even then, considering the notorious unpredictability of French businesses, there was no guarantee of success. Faced with this quandary, we did what any self-respecting blokes would do: we began attaching bits and pieces wherever they seemed to fit. Our desperate efforts led us to consult an online video, artfully produced by the Chinese manufacturer. The soundtrack, presumably Chinese, was complemented by English subtitles, undoubtedly crafted using a knock-off version of that ever popular translation site.

The machine in the video bore a passing resemblance to our contraption, this one being hitched to the rear of a tractor. The man operating it, an epitome of rugged masculinity, without a hint of job satisfaction on his face whatsoever, stoically fed branches into the chipper. We replayed the video countless times and, after much perseverance, managed to complete the assembly. Miraculously, we had no leftover nuts, bolts, or washers – an indication, we dared to hope, that we had done everything correctly. The machine even looked the right shape. We were poised and ready to chip.

And then the heavens opened. Rain descended in torrents, day after day, for best part of a week. During this deluge, Alan discovered that the drive to his tractor was the wrong size. He was then out of commission for at least another week due to other commitments. Therefore, despite being a proud one-third owner of a chipper, I had to wait nearly a month to see it in action.

Eventually, the much-anticipated day did arrive, albeit after a rather unfortunate incident you'll read about soon enough. Remembering how all three of us shareholders convened at Barry's place, eager to transform branches into chips. I would still have no clue as to what the chips would be used for, but that seemed irrelevant. I was like a child at a party, experiencing cake for the very first time.

There is more to this tale, but I need to leave it for now – chronology and all that.

A BIT OF A BLOW

February was a month where, aside from the chipper, we found ourselves somewhat adrift. Quite literally, considering the deluge we endured. The rain poured relentlessly, turning our days into a soggy, endless wait. Yet little did we know, our preoccupation with the weather was only just beginning, with it destined to be more brutal and last far longer, than we could have ever anticipated.

***

Journal entry, end of February 2017

Walking the dog is one of Clare and mine's nice to do's and I know Jack enjoys it too. We still tend to walk along the canal most days, but sometimes it's good to mix it up a bit; a country walk with a canal walk. Either way it's something we enjoy and the uninterrupted tranquillity allows us to have proper conversations. Nothing mind blowing just things like our future plans for the house, the garden or for life in general.

We talk about news we've read or heard about, the English weather compared to ours, that type of thing. Nothing too taxing, just chit-chat and laughs. But these walks also allow the luxury of just losing ourselves in our own thoughts. And even though we frequently tread the same path, there is always something new to see. Often as a result of the changing seasons. With the winter brown of the woodland and canal side trees starting to change to a slight greenish hue, followed by some early blooms of mixed blossoms, on trees that I have no knowledge of – not even their names. Clare is much better at these things as she is able to put names to many more trees and plants than I can. Her efforts to educate me just fall on stony ground as names are forgotten in a moment. But even an ignoramus like me can feel the season changing, as the sun, when it appears, is warmer on my back these last couple of mornings, as it seeps through my coat tempting me to loosen a button or two. Though geographically, we're only a few hundred miles south of Dorset, the weather and in particular the seasons are like craie et fromage.

Today we talked about plans beyond the spring and in doing so I shared my thoughts on the need to replace some of the timbers on the small hangar. These last few months I've had to make quite a few temporary repairs, despite the tin roof being sound. Unlike our two small wood sheds where I will need to probably strip the old tin off and replace it with good second hand or perhaps even new sheeting. But, as anyone reading this can see, our conversations, by and large, are not likely to win any Nobel prizes for extraordinary contribution to mankind or the world in general, but this is now the extent of our world and pretty much the shape that retirement has taken for us. Are we boring?

Alan, our compulsive weather watcher, has told us there will be a bit of a blow coming in off of the Atlantic tonight and into tomorrow plus of course rain – no doubt lots of rain. Nothing much to worry about by all accounts but expect (another) rainy play day tomorrow.

***

As predicted, Alan's 'bit of a blow' arrived that very night, and we awoke to find it still raging like some invisible savage beast. Ignoring Clare's wise advice to stay indoors, I donned my largest coat and wellies to survey the overnight carnage. To say I wasn't disappointed feels like the wrong choice of words. Lying in bed, I'd listened to the wind roaring through the slate tiles of our roof like a rip tide, thankful yet astonished that our roof wasn't scattered across Brittany.

Our large hangar, with its geriatric corrugated tin roof, fared much worse – though not as bad as I first feared. We could hear the metal sheets waging a valiant but losing battle against the tempest, lifting and falling in sync with each gust of wind. After a couple of hours, we were met with a series of ominous sounds – a creak, a groan, then nothing. This undoubtedly signalled that a sheet or perhaps multiple sheets had surrendered and were now lying who-knows-where.

Surveying the damage, with the wind doing its best to relieve me of my coat, I was, naturally, unsurprised to see multiple areas of the hangar roof revealing the wild grey sky above. The errant sheets of tin, as I would later discover, had found new homes in an adjoining field. The remaining sections of the roof were putting up a commendable fight, but for how long, I couldn't be certain.

The other unsurprising casualty of Alan's 'bit of a blow' was my unloved bamboo screen. That once symbol of my childish tantrum, it now flapped like a sail on a broken mast, on some shipwrecked galleon. With that barrier gone, the roof of one of our wood sheds – the one I had planned to repair in the Spring – was now languishing in Bernard's garden. Similarly, a portion of the tin roof from what we affectionately called our small hangar – primarily a wood and junk shelter – along with its assorted woodwork, was now artistically strewn about the verger and beyond.

As I trudged to the back of the hangar, I spotted another piece of corrugated tin threatening to free itself. If it lost this battle, I knew more would soon follow. I arrived back at the house just in time for the power to go off.

Although the storm had spent its fury by evening, we would continue to have no power for the next two days.

***

Journal entry February 2017 - *Trees are down, with quite a few broken. I'm making my notes for this journal entry with the drone of our generator in the background, which is keeping our heating and freezers going, as we enter our eighteenth hour without electricity. Shops are closed due to there being no power; roads are blocked by fallen trees, so, the chances of getting out to buy petrol for the generator looks bleak. I noticed earlier how the chickens, including feeding troughs et al were pinned against the barn wall by the still strong wind. The rain is still lashing down and my new lawn is under water. I've always fancied a water feature, but not Lake Windermere.*

Note to self; Need to speak with Alan in order to fully understand the subtle difference between a 'bit of a blow' and a bloody full scale storm!

***

I actually find myself looking back at those forty-eight or so hours with a certain fondness. Whether it was our bulldog spirit or some primal instinct, our situation galvanised us into a state of defiance, manifesting itself in various ways. First things first – a throwback to our Neanderthal ancestors – I ensured a fire stayed alight in the sitting room. This not only provided us with warmth and a bit of light, but also a means by which to cook. Unlike our cavemen cousins, the fire wasn't needed to keep any wolves at bay. On that subject, they say that our domesticated dogs are derived from wolves, but if you had ever met Jack, you'd most definitely question that notion.

Anyway, Clare swiftly whipped up some batter while Maggie assembled the other ingredients, and between the two of them, they set about making crepes on top of our recently installed wood burner. From goodness knows where, a small camping kettle was also unearthed, allowing us to brew that quintessential English remedy for all disasters: tea.

Games were played by the flickering light of candles and the warm glow of the fire. Come bedtime, the generator was reluctantly switched off, despite the risk of our freezer contents defrosting. With no clear idea of when power would return, we had to ration our precious petrol supply.

As it turned out, the power played a tantalising game of on-and-off throughout the night, preserving the integrity of our frozen provisions. By the end of the following day, power was more or less restored, albeit intermittently, as the electric company brought in their own generators while they set about repairing cables and re-erecting fallen poles.

Funny how people's priorities come to light when adversity strikes. For me, the pressing concern was always the next meal. Maggie, on the other hand, was fixated on when she might next enjoy a hot shower. Clare shared this particular need as well. Fair enough, I suppose, as blokes and ladies often have markedly different priorities when it comes to hygiene, hardship or not.

I warmly remember recounting a story from my granny about her wartime washing routine, a tale that never failed to elicit a mix of disgust and incredulity from our youngest. In one of her many "you don't know how lucky you are" moments, gran detailed her method: standing stark naked in a bowl of – not necessarily – warm water, washing as thoroughly as possible with a hand flannel. Most of the water, along with whatever came off her body, would naturally fall back into the bowl. After stepping out, drying herself, and presumably putting on some clothes – though she never specified – she would take the contents of the bowl into the garden and pour it over whatever vegetable required sustenance the most.

By day three, we managed to venture out for shopping and restocked our petrol reserves. But there's no doubt we had learned a great deal about ourselves during that brief period of adversity.

- Though we fancy ourselves advanced, civilised even, how woefully unprepared we are, both practically and mentally, for even the smallest of upsets. This storm, and others like it, proved as much.
- Our Western European pampered lifestyles give us an unreal perspective of what true hardship means when compared to less fortunate and less well-off peoples.
- Should a real disaster befall us, we would undoubtedly flounder and likely starve within days.
- Lastly, if Alan were ever to say to us again, there's a bit of a blow forecast, or a bit of an anything for that matter, multiply it by a factor of ten.

As I write this tale for you, the radio is prattling on in the background. The BBC solemnly informs me that some parts of the UK have experienced a whopping two centimetres of snow, resulting in the closure of over two hundred schools. I rest my case.

The next few days were given over to clearing up and assessing the storm damage. What needed repairing and what was beyond economical repair. To my amazement, the large hangar emerged relatively unscathed, requiring only minor repairs despite the missing pieces of tin roof. The small hangar, however, needed major surgery, much sooner than anticipated. I had to reinstate most of the roof, much of the woodwork, and all of the guttering, which was meant to be part of an elaborate irrigation system for my yet to be built potager.

With the repairs and the planned works on the verger, it was clear that most of my immediate tasks would be heavy-duty for the foreseeable future.

***

Apart from the structural damage to our farm buildings, the trees around the place took quite a battering too. None more so than one of the largest of the lot – a colossal fir tree at the far corner of our front garden. The top third had been mercilessly removed, leaving our once majestic tree with a decidedly flat top. After a quick discussion with Alan and an inspection by Dave 'the tree' – one of the Daves I mentioned previously – the prognosis was grim. Not only had our tree lost a third of its height, but it had also split the remainder of its trunk, rendering it unstable. With heavy hearts, we agreed that the best course of action was to have it taken down completely.

For Alan, and his eager chainsaw, the 'bit of a blow' turned out to be his perfect storm. In his attempt to put a positive spin on our loss, he predictably mentioned the amount of timber we'd get from it once logged. Many people frown on the idea of burning pine, but it's fine as long as it's seasoned – which it does much faster than other wood varieties – and used alongside other types of wood due to its low heat and quick-burning characteristics. Meaning that compared to, say, oak, you need a lot more pine wood for the same amount of heating. But, as Alan pointed out, space wasn't something we needed to worry about. Smells good as well.

"And that concludes our thrilling broadcast on 'Explosive Timber Varieties and Their Prime Utilisations'. Heartfelt apologies are extended for the increasingly mind-numbing tediousness of this book."

***

The silver lining, if there was any, was that none of the fruit trees had been severely affected by the storm. Aside from one or two snapped limbs on a couple of apple trees, we got off lightly. When I relayed this news to Gérard, I added how fortunate we were to have that three metre high laurel hedge around the perimeter, acting as a natural windbreak. He agreed, but only to a point, preferring to believe that the lack of damage to our fruit trees was due more to the expert pruning advice he'd given me.

'...and an inspection by Dave 'the tree'...'

'With heavy hearts, we agreed that the best course of action was to have it taken down completely.'

THE FALL AND FALL OF THE CHIPPER

As a result of the 'bit of a blow' quite a few other trees around the place took quite a battering, but adopting Alan's optimistic view, we now had a lifetime's worth of winter fuel. Admittedly, most of it was sprawled horizontally across vast swathes of our farm. The other notable point was the plethora of branches that begged to be chipped. And naturally, we had the perfect tool for the job – still sitting in Alan's garage, eagerly awaiting its debut.

With the stars aligning (me, Alan, and Barry), we set up the chipper in Barry and Stella's (Barry's wife) garden for its maiden voyage. What an anti-climax it turned out to be. An hour into its first challenge, we were met with smoke, broken belts, and a chipper that clearly had an aversion to sappy wood. More precisely, the funnel through which the chips were supposed to be expelled kept blocking up. As it turned out, that was the least of our problems. After removing guards and plates to investigate the source of the smoke, Barry quickly diagnosed that a pulley had moved out of alignment, causing the drive belts to run askew, hence the smoke. To add to our woes, two of the five belts were now broken. The atmosphere was tense; you could cut it with a chainsaw. Alan seethed, Barry pondered, and I looked on in sheer disappointment. Our French-bought, China-manufactured contraption had faltered at the first hurdle.

It's during times like these that one hopes for a game-changer in the team, and that hero was Barry – a real-life engineer. Not the sort who fixes washing machines, but the kind who builds bridges in his spare time. A misaligned pulley was nothing more than a splinter for someone of Barry's calibre.

Within ten minutes, the guilty pulley was off and in

Barry's workshop, undergoing a complete rebuild. In no time at all, it was back on the machine. But alas, even Barry, with all his mechanical prowess, couldn't stop the sun from setting (though I bet he's tried) and with the light fading, we called it a day, agreeing to reconvene the following afternoon. By then, Alan assured us, new belts would be procured from one of the many farmers' outlets in the area.

However, the next day brought a minor setback – naturally, the belts weren't a standard size and needed to be specially ordered. Undeterred, Barry set the chipper up to run on just three belts. After all, we had nothing to lose; if the three belts couldn't cope, we had a whole new set on order.

As it turned out, it was a triumphant day for Team Chipper. The newly refurbished pulley – and its three belts – handled everything we threw at it. We even showed a bit of respect to its frailty by setting aside the small sappy branches for burning.

Here's the thing though; don't let anyone ever tell you that lifting and feeding branches into a chipper for hours on end is anything but sheer hard work. And I would love to see a picture of the woman they use to demonstrate these products after she's shifted a pile of lumber for a few hours. I'm pretty sure she wouldn't be smiling, that's for sure.

The last I saw of the chipper, it was quietly rotting away in the corner of Alan's wood yard, a sad monument to our investment. That was until the local scrap merchant came and whisked it away some months later. Despite our (or rather, Barry's) best efforts and even with new belts fitted, it remained a heap of garbage. The modest cash we received from the scrapman, a paltry seventy-five euros, was promptly invested in wine to drown our sorrows and while away the time flipping through magazines, hunting for our next grand purchase.

They say experience and memories are priceless, and in many ways, they are. This particular episode, however, cost us quite a few thousand euros – not an insignificant sum for us three old fellas. However, we subsequently learned that a decent chipping machine, one not deemed 'cheap rubbish' by forestry folks and Barry, should cost at least double the amount we'd paid for our Chinese machine.

THE BIRTH OF THE POTAGER

Journal entry March 2017 – The good news is that the weather is turning warmer. The clocks are due to go forward in a few days time so it is nearly officially Spring. Mybe my changing mood is one of the reasons why I've picked up this journal again. Though my appetite to draft reams, as I used to, just doesn't seem to be there anymore. Maybe it's because, now that I'm living it, I don't have the need to record it? Need to think on that one. Or better still, do something about it.

One of the sure signs of winter coming was of course the shorter days and longer nights coupled with the drop in egg production by our hens. Over the course of the last week or so I've noticed the sun setting later in the evening which I hope is a sign of warmer days to come. But the real sign is that we are now getting between five and six eggs a day from our now six hens. This has to be a sign that we've turned a corner and we're definitely the right side of winter.

***

Why my journal entries continued to tail off remains a mystery and a regret. Spilt milk and all that – so no point in dwelling on it any longer. But I did make a concerted effort as can be seen within the next few episodes.

For some reason I got talked into adding two more hens to our collection. With production already outstripping demand I questioned the decision. But as we live in a democracy, where my vote counts for little and Clare's for everything, I was easily outvoted.

Anyway, moving on to the potager.

One of the many promises I made to myself when we relocated to Saint-Barthélémy was to have a serious go at growing things. We had the space and the time, but not necessarily the know-how. Don't get me wrong – we had grown things before in our reasonably large Dorset garden, but that was limited to easy-grow produce such as potatoes and runner beans. Low maintenance and almost foolproof. And when the harvest did fail us – which was more often than you might think – such things were easily bought in.

One of our annual events used to be the potato competition, the brainchild of my father-in-law, Ron. The same Ron who would come into our garden, execute some robust pruning of practically every plant, and then leave the detritus for me to clear up.

Every year, the children and their grandad would plant a couple of seed potatoes in a suitable pot. Then, a couple of months later, we would have the grand reveal. One by one, grandad and the kids would turn out their pots, with Clare on hand to do the weigh-in. There were no prizes, just lots of finger-pointing, accusations of cheating from the losers, and plenty of laughs. Inevitably, grandad was the primary cheat, one year turning up with two pots, claiming that his harvest was so abundant he had to separate the plants. However, the truth was that one pot contained the product of his potato seeds, while the other, buried under some earth, held two kilos of shop bought potatoes, still in their bag. He was, in equal measure, both a good and not-so-good role model for our children, and we all loved him for it.

Another annual event, still ongoing to this day, is the pumpkin carving competition. One year, Maggie happened to be staying over at her grandparents' at the time of the competition, so grandad thought he'd join in. While we typically carved our pumpkins with knives, grandad had other ideas. From his garage emerged an assortment of woodworking tools and a battery drill fitted with an auger bit. This was some fifteen years ago, but to this day, Maggie has tears of laughter in her eyes as she recalls bits of pumpkin being flung up the walls, onto the curtains, and all over grandad. For weeks afterward, her nana would find pumpkin seeds in the most unexpected places. True to form, grandad denied all knowledge and, of course, blamed Maggie.

Having invested in multiple gardening books and binge-watched countless episodes of gardening programmes, we were finally ready to construct our potager. We had a fair idea of what we wanted to attempt growing. My ambition, as you now know, extended to cauliflowers – even a single cauliflower would have sufficed. You may have different thoughts, but to me, they are the most spectacular of vegetables. If you have ever seen a cauliflower seed and marvelled at what it transforms into, you might well agree. But then again, I suppose the same can be said for pumpkins.

Our lineup also included potatoes – obviously – carrots, onions, and salad stuff. Following the available advice, we also decided to grow some flowers like marigolds. Allegedly, they attract bugs and pests that would otherwise invade our other produce.

We lifted the weed-suppressing membrane we had laid down back in 2015. With any unwanted growth suitably blocked, we were left with a natural layout for our potager. We had two sizable growing beds – five metres by three metres – separated by a one metre wide grass pathway from a long – one metre by five metres – growing bed. Running across the top of our three growing beds was another long – one metre wide – one. Something like the diagram over the page.

Given the amount of land we had, it could be argued that we were rather conservative in our ambitions, and you'd be right. However, we only planned to grow what we could eat. We weren't looking – yet – to be completely self-sufficient. And should it all turn to garbage, our losses, while upsetting, wouldn't be earth-shattering.

Other works required before we could claim to have a functioning potager included: a boundary fence – we were told that deer can be a bit of a bother – a water supply – the well was about two hundred meters away – and a pergola – because most of what Clare wanted to grow required some sort of climbing frame. This construction was set to run the full length of the middle, long, growing bed.

Having never built a pergola before, I was back online and leafing through books to figure out a suitable, easy-to-build type. Then, a light bulb moment hit me – a rare occurrence, I must admit – I would use some of the old barn roof skeleton, or what remained of it. Long story short, it turned out to be a perfect solution, and one I would bore people with for ages after its erection.

Many of the old oak timbers had a natural bend to them, caused, I assume, by holding up a really heavy roof for a couple of hundred years. While I had to buy the uprights and mainstays, the top was adorned with the old bent barn timber.

***

Figuring out the next steps, with the obligatory cup of tea in hand, we could hear – and smell – the muck spreading in the adjacent field. All at once, the tractor stopped just the other side of our laurel hedge, and a squat, grubby-looking fellow appeared, dressed in the local fashion statement of "anything will do so long as my skin is covered." And, of course, a bobble hat.

"*Bonjour Monsieur,*" I cheerily announced, though puzzled as to why he was there.

"*Vous en souhaitez pour votre potager ?*" (Would you like some for your potager?) Or words to that effect, as he pointed towards the large muck spreader being towed behind his tractor.

For years, Ron had told us to put manure around our roses. Not just any old manure, mind you, but horse manure. So it seemed only fitting to accept the farmer's offer for our yet to be dug potager. Whether it was horse manure or not, my French language skills weren't sharp enough to enquire. But if it was good enough for the farmer's field, we determined it was good enough for us.

"*Oui, ce serait bien. Merci,*" I replied cheerily. He then turned on his mud-encrusted heels, leaving us to ponder how on earth he was going to get his large tractor and even larger muck spreader into our garden. The tractor started up, and we stepped back, only to see him drive off in the opposite direction from our garden. Listening to the disappearing sound of the tractor, we were left rather speechless. Deciding not to offer any possible explanation, we simply gave each other the customary French shrug and carried on, as if the whole episode was some kind of shared dream.

Within a few minutes, however, we heard the unmistakable noise of an approaching tractor. No muck spreader this time, just the tractor with its bucket raised and overflowing with brown, blackish muck. He then drove straight into the garden via a gap at the end of the laurel hedge – a gap that wasn't previously there until his tractor made it so. Shouting over the noise of the engine, he bellowed, *"Où?"* (Where?). Emerging from my paralysis at seeing his tractor carve a new approach to our property, I simply replied, *"Là-bas."* (Over there), pointing to nowhere in particular. He simply nodded, moved to a piece of ground in the general vicinity of my vague pointing, and deposited a roundabout-sized heap of muck – enough to last us years.

Without feeling the need to reverse, he executed a U-turn over our neatly marked-out growing beds and drove off, cheerily wishing us a good day with a hearty *"bonne journée!"*

I ended up having to wheelbarrow the entire roundabout-sized heap of muck to a less conspicuous place. It was like moving a small mountain, and my wheelbarrow squeaked in protest with every trip.

'While I had to buy the uprights and mainstays, the top was adorned with the old bent barn timber… This construction was set to run the full length of the middle, long, growing bed.'

'…a boundary fence – we were told that deer can be a bit of a bother.

ENTER THE LOG SPLITTER

Journal entry March 2017 – Alan has been telling me for weeks that he has some wood for me. Old stuff that for some reason he can't burn on his open fire. But burning it in our wood burner is okay by all accounts. Since the 'bit of a blow' his stockpile has increased to the point where he's struggling for space. So as a result we were the benefactors of not one but three large trailer loads of timber. Not logs but timber. Large tree trunks that have been sliced up like you would a Swiss roll cake.

Which on the one hand is very generous, despite him needing to move it on to make space, but we now have half a hangar full of Swiss roll slices of tree trunk. And I have no mechanical method of splitting it into logs. All I have is the iron-age, log splitting wedge and sledgehammer, which I had a go at a couple of weeks ago and my back is still feeling it.

So even if I were to have the inclination to do such a thing again, it would take me literally months to log the amount of wood that Alan has kindly off-loaded onto me.

I'm all for giving this semi 'good life' experience a go, but there are limits. One of which is spending whole days splitting timber for little reward but bleeding hands and back-ache. I can feel another toy coming my way. I just need to get the purchase requisition past head of procurement – my wife.

***

Other than a chainsaw, lawnmower, small tractor (complete with its many attachments), strimmer, hedge trimmer, brush cutter, and a plethora of other crucial tools, the one essential thing missing from my arsenal was a log splitter. Convincing Clare of this necessity took an inordinate amount of persuading. That is, until I offloaded the problem of converting our stockpile of sizable Swiss roll slices into logs onto her. Predictably, she suggested, "Why can't you use Alan's?" A suggestion I deftly parried, having already pre-empted it. I had prepped Alan to claim his log splitter would be tied up for weeks should Clare inquire. Moreover, his splitter, much like Alan himself, was a bit of an old relic. An axe-like blade, in the same style as an old guillotine. When in use, it was attached to the rear of his tractor, employing its hydraulics to drive the axe-like blade, which was activated by a simple push-pull handle. Alan would sit on one of his yet to be logged tree stumps behind the tractor and spend hours slicing through Swiss roll-sized timber, turning them into something more usable.

The point I'm getting at, and the argument I made to Clare – with Alan's keen support – was that borrowing his equipment was simply out of the question. It would mean taking his tractor offline, when he needed it for uses other than log splitting. Though the real reason, which I'm sure Clare suspected all along, was that I wanted my own log splitter. But nothing remotely like Alan's pre-war contraption. "State of the art if you please!"

Skip forward three weeks, and there I was, the proud owner of my very own petrol-driven, eight-tonne (splitting force) log splitter. Unashamedly shipped from the UK. Southampton, to be precise. I had managed to cram in a bit of shopping during one of our planned visits to Clare's parents.

Some while later, I stumped up the courage (see what I did there) to confess to Clare that the planned visit, associated shopping trip, and even the type and model of the log splitter, was no accident. From the moment I decided I needed – rather, wanted – this essential addition to my rural existence, the die was cast and plans were set in motion.

Clare, typically and needlessly smug, told me she had

known all along. The clues to my furtive antics included my insistence that we take an empty trailer with us to visit her parents under the pretence of "you never know what we might buy when we're there," and the machine shop home page I had foolishly left up on our desktop computer.

Despite my failings at clandestine planning, I had days of fun in our hangar, turning four-hundred-millimetre-thick Swiss roll slices into logs. In doing so, I boasted multiple log piles that even Alan had to concede "weren't bad."

***

Some advice to anyone looking for a workout and stress relief: spend a few hours in your own bubble, splitting wood into logs. I mean using a proper petro-mechanical log splitter, not the sledgehammer method. That is proper therapy.

'... boasting multiple log piles that even Alan had to concede 'weren't bad'.'

CLARE AWAY AND GÉRARD COMES ROUND TO PLAY

Journal entry March 2017 – Dropped Clare and Maggie off at Auray railway station a couple of days ago. They seem to be enjoying their extended weekend in Paris with Laurence my old buddy from work. From a couple of brief phone calls and multiple messages and pictures, I know they're having the full Paris experience.

As for me its been a bit strange – my first time home alone in our French home. If this were back in England I know I would have not only gotten on with stuff – which I have – but would have most definitely taken advantage of the pubs hospitality. With at least one fish and chip supper. Here it's different. There is no pub and no fish and chip shop so instead had the pleasure of Gérard's company for dinner yesterday and in doing so continually having to convince Beryl that I had no need for her many offers of stew as I can actually cook. Albeit really simple stuff.

They're back tomorrow so I guess I ought to tidy the place and wash up. I never realised we had so many mugs to drink out of. I even got to have a cup of tea out of Sam's old Star Wars mug, tucked away at the very back of the cupboard.

Spent most of this early morning, with a cup of tea, walking the verger – my quiet place. It's all really waking up now, especially the prune (plum) trees.

***

Getting across Europe from our place was so much easier without the inconvenience of water to cross. Later in the year, Clare and I were set to venture even further afield, but I'm getting ahead of myself.

So, when the invitation came from an old work colleague and friend, Laurence, for Clare and Maggie to spend some time with her in Paris, it was an offer too good to refuse.

Unlike England, where navigating the train system can often feel like a confusing, and often disappointing, game of Labyrinth, the French really seemed to have got it right. Maybe it's easier to build a rail network when you have more open space to play with? I'm no expert, but all I know is how effortless it was for them, and by all accounts, the trains themselves are a real pleasure to board.

From our local station, Auray, to Paris in under three hours – impressive, isn't it? By all accounts, Clare and Maggie had a marvellous time, and I was, of course, delighted for them.

But the real story, for me at least, was the evening I spent with Gérard. An invitation he artfully crafted for himself upon discovering that I was home alone. I remember whipping up something straightforward – a chicken dish of some sort. Tasty, but not spicy, as he – as indeed do many French folk – does not share our British palate for piquant food. I, on the other hand, adore spicy dishes and had been looking forward to cooking up a curry before Gérard announced he'd be joining me for supper.

Nevertheless, my simple fare seemed to hit the mark, as evidenced by his clean plate. He even asked for more bread to wipe it clean – a clear sign of culinary success!

One thing I particularly enjoy, not just at meal times, but at most other times too, is music. I've amassed a decent vinyl record collection, though for meal times it's usually something playing from one of our old iPod docking stations. With no real love for CDs, except for their convenience, I took the opportunity of our move to France to transfer our entire collection of over two hundred CDs onto three second-hand iPods. The CDs were subsequently left back in England, with some going to Jamie Ann, our eldest daughter, and the remainder – the ones she didn't want – ending up at a local charity shop.

So, while preparing our supper, dipping into some apéritifs, and enjoying a beer with my guest, I had some music playing. Something that I thought might satisfy all tastes – The Beatles.

"What is this?" asked Gérard.

Slightly puzzled, not because of his English, which was, as always, rather good, but by the question itself. I turned from the stove, expecting him to be smiling in a teasing kind of way. Instead, I was met with a genuinely puzzled look.

"It's The Beatles," I said, not really knowing what else to say.

"And what are The Beatles? Are they new?" he continued, going on to ask, "Do you have any Françoise Hardy or Yves Montand?" Apparently two famous French singers from the same era as The Beatles.

Now you might think that with such an obvious cultural gulf between us the evening would be quite flat. But that would be quite a way from the truth of it.

You may also be wondering why I'm telling you all this. Even as I'm writing it, I can see that it's not exactly riveting. But the reason is, I learned a valuable lesson that evening.

No matter how wide the gulf in cultural differences, opinions, religion, or whatever else, there is always some common ground – you just need to figure it out. For Gérard and me, it was humour. Our cultural and geographical differences made things even more entertaining. You see, French humour tends to be quite slapstick – someone slipping on a banana peel, that sort of thing. Whereas British humour is known for its wit, dry delivery, and often understated style. Sarcasm, irony, and self-deprecation – the quirks of everyday life – are comedic gold to us Brits.

Over the course of the evening, with wine and whiskey flowing, we recalibrated our unique takes on humour for each other's benefit. We found ourselves laughing at things we ordinarily wouldn't. He introduced me to Louis de Funès, and I introduced him to John Cleese. The more inebriated we became, the more incoherent our language, but we still laughed. To the point where, some weeks later, Gérard took a branch to his old Renault when it wouldn't start, swearing at it in French – a twist on the classic John Cleese, Fawlty Towers clip.

Many years later, I remember that Gérard and I had a memorable, laughter filled evening, though the specific details, anecdotes, and so on, are lost in a fog. Another reason why I lament not keeping up with my journal as I should have.

I now keep a day-to-day diary and would urge anyone to do the same. Physical memories are extraordinary, but a lot of the details can still slip away.

As for our unique tastes in music? That remained an unbridgeable gulf.

UNE LETTRE DU BUREAU DES IMPOTS

Journal entry April 2017 – April already and the verger is looking spectacular with blossoms aplenty. So it looks like my enthusiastic pruning didn't kill the trees after all. But, as last year, it's the noise of the bees and whatever other buzzing insects visit verger's, that really caught me. The only thing outdoing them is the sounds of the birds. If I was back in England I know I'd be asked to fill bird feeders, lay out assorted goodies on the bird table that type of thing. But here, in the Brittany countryside, with warm weather and sunshine, there is an all day, everyday, buffet on offer. No sign of butterflies yet though.

Got a letter from the tax office yesterday, reminding us that we need to do our tax return. Our first French one. Looks like the British and French tax authorities have been talking to one another because they (the French) are uncharacteristically, quick off the mark.

According to Hélène, as it's our first, we need to go the tax office in Pontivy otherwise known as the Centre des Finances Publiques. Interesting how the tax office letter arrived the day after we were talking about getting another car. Clare has her eye on a Mazda MX5, having been sold the idea by our old neighbour Julie, who just happens to have one herself. And whose brother just happens to know someone, who happens to know someone, that has one for sale. A bargain by all accounts. Not sure if I'm being played, but if she wants it then I'm not in any position to deny her. Never have been, would never want to.

As much as we've been putting money aside for what we assume to be the likely tax bill, things such as cars and bigger projects on the house will have to wait a while. In the event of any surprises.

But the real news is the spuds I planted a couple of weeks ago have broken the surface.

***

When our first tax return loomed large, it came devoid of the digital convenience we'd enjoyed in the UK for some time. Instead we were faced with an analogue monster: An A3 sized multi-page form showing-off French bureaucracy in all its glory.

Hélène, our ever reliable mentor in such things, dispatched us to the tax office in Pontivy, and with the punctuality of the Japanese, we arrived fifteen minutes before the doors of our fiscal destiny opened. The scene that greeted us was akin to the queue for a rock concert – though highly unlikely in our neck of the woods. Just tax enthusiasts, en masse.

With the poise of the novice French tax warriors we were, we joined the winding line, utterly clueless about the protocols or any looming customs. Our plan? Simple mimicry, observing our fellow pilgrims' rituals. Surprisingly, the line advanced with remarkable efficiency, akin to a well-oiled machine. Clearly, those ahead of us were seasoned veterans in the art of tax submission. As our moment of reckoning arrived, we were summoned to the counter. Mustering our best French and with beaming countenances, we greeted the tax officer. She, detecting our foreign twang, dismissed our greetings with the grace of a night-club bouncer dealing with a pair of drunks, directing us with an imperious finger-point to another counter, manned by a chap of similar disinterest.

Undeterred, we approached our new adversary. Once more, I offered a hearty *"Bonjour!"* which was met with the same frosty silence. His sole utterance: *"Nom?"* (Name). Dutifully, I enunciated "Templeman" with deliberate clarity, not out of any disdain for his intellect, but mindful of our surname's potential verbal difficulty for non-English speakers. With gaze fixed upon his screen, he inquired, *"Prénom?"* (First name), without so much as a glance in our direction.

"Clare et Colin," I responded, being sure to point to each one of us in turn, so as to ensure no ambiguity.

From beneath the counter, our new friend, produced an A3-sized, multi-page, multi-coloured monstrosity with 'DÉCLARATION DES REVENUS 2017' emblazoned across the top. He then proceeded to unleash a torrent of French instructions, blithely unaware – or indifferent – of our language limitations. Handing us the form with the air of someone dispensing a parking ticket, he summarily dismissed us, his attention already returning to his computer screen.

Back in the car, we set about playing a makeshift game of 'tax form deciphering', reconstructing what we thought the official had babbled. We noticed, with a mix of relief and scepticism, that he had graciously circled a section in green pen. We presumed, with the confidence of the clueless, that this was the only part we needed to complete. Though, with our luck, it could very well have been the bit we were supposed to ignore.

Forty-eight hours later – on Thursday – we returned to the Centre des Finances Publiques with our completed opus. This time, we arrived even earlier. Yet, contrary to our previous visit, there was no queue. In fact, there was no sign of life whatsoever. As the clock struck nine – the designated opening hour – we remained the sole occupants of the car park, save for a gardener tending to the flower beds. Taking the initiative, I ventured towards the building, only to be confronted by a sign on the door: 'NOUS NE SOMMES PAS OUVERTS LE JEUDI' (we are not open on Thursday). For some strange reason neither of us were surprised at the outcome. Another example of the unpredictable and improvised way of life, in our adopted country.

Undeterred, we returned the following day. This time, we managed to hand in our form. Or rather, I offered it to an uninterested official, once again delivering a cheerful greeting, which she met with a look of profound weariness, as if I were some village idiot. She pointed silently to a posting box on the other side of the building, and no words were exchanged.

A couple of weeks passed without a peep from the tax office. Operating under the hopeful mantra of 'no news is good news', we carried on with our lives, though still anticipating the arrival of a tax bill.

Then, out of the blue, the phone rang.

"Bonjour, Monsieur Temple Moon, c'est le bureau des impôts, venez me voir demain. J'ai quelques questions." Roughly translated: "Hello, Mister Temple Moon, this is the tax office. Come and see me tomorrow. I have some questions."

"Bonjour, désolé, je n'ai pas compris votre nom...." (Hello, sorry, I didn't catch your name). But by then, she had already hung up, leaving me conversing with the empty air.

The next day, per instructions, we returned to the tax office, our hearts brimming with trepidation. Lacking any knowledge of our interrogator's identity, we hesitated and stammered while attempting to convey our purpose to the perpetually disinterested official. As it transpired, there was but one person in the entire building who might be expecting us. The official, with palpable reluctance, pointed us across the room to an office and motioned for us to wait outside until summoned.

Some thirty minutes later, out waddled a squat female, aged somewhere between forty and sixty, dressed in a brown ensemble that screamed practicality. Like her colleagues, she seemed to consider words a luxury. She merely confirmed our names, though continuing to mispronounce us as "Temple Moon" as she had on the phone, and employed her chin to direct us toward our destination.

The office was a barren landscape, save for a large, solid, dark brown desk that dominated the room. Upon it rested a single computer monitor and keyboard, both relics from an era when Microsoft was merely a glint in Bill Gates' eye. Our host remained stoically silent as she settled into a large, well-worn leather swivel chair. Though I couldn't see her feet, I was fairly certain they dangled above the floor.

On our side of the desk stood two hard-backed wooden chairs, reminiscent of nursery school furniture. We plopped ourselves down without waiting for an invitation. The room fell into an uneasy silence as the tax official fixed her gaze on the computer screen, and we, like two miscreant schoolchildren awaiting judgment, stared at the modesty panel at the desk's rear. Our alternative views included her nasal cavities or the ceiling.

She eventually diverted her attention to her desktop and a buff-coloured folder, which we assumed contained our tax return, which she scrutinised with the intensity of a hawk eyeing its prey. From out of nowhere, a pen materialised in her hand, and she aggressively slashed two long strokes across our form. We braced ourselves for the inevitable reprimand, expecting her to toss the form back at us, branding our efforts as abject failures, much like a headmistress condemning shoddy homework.

Instead, she closed the folder and regarded us both with an impassive expression. *"Votre déclaration d'impôts est erronée. Vous ne devez aucun impôt. Bonne journée."* (Your tax return is wrong. You do not owe any tax. Good day). With a flick of her chin, she signalled that our meeting was concluded, and we were free to go.

THE SHAPE OF CHANGE

With the tax office bestowing upon us an unexpected windfall, the floodgates of spending cheerfully burst open. Clare, ever the deserving soul – so she tells me – finally got her coveted car, and I was left with an extraordinary task of planning and sourcing a suitable contractor for the next phase of our home renovation journey.

We already had three bedrooms and a sizable bathroom to accommodate the three – soon to be two – of us. But, my wife decreed that another bathroom and bedroom were of the utmost necessity. Who am I to question the boundless wisdom of the ideas department, after all? Knowing the sheer futility of challenging any notion that emerged from that sacred department, I dutifully set about my mission, being both resolute and willing to turn Clare's inexhaustible logic into a reality.

I am, if little else, a time-served exponent in the art of maintaining domestic bliss.

The first hurdle was finding someone willing to take on the entirety of our (Clare's) grand plans, not just cherry-picking the bits they fancied. Alan, bless his devoted heart, would have had me enlist the ever trusty Stephane once more, but I was determined to scout for new talent. Someone who might endeavour to do the work when we want them to.

The real challenge though, lay in securing a general builder in France, or better yet, someone daring enough to manage and coordinate the whole works – not quite a quest to crack the Da Vinci Code, but almost.

Between tracking down this elusive builder and untangling the typically complex planning process, we took on the task of clearing out the remnants of our first refurb attempt – phase one. We subsequently loaded the car and trailer with debris that had been stealthily stashed around the farm. If you recall, Stephane, ever the master of selective engagement, had drawn a firm line at removing demolition materials. Thus, another reason for hunting down a more accommodating contractor.

Enter Gérard, my self-appointed comrade, who graciously offered to accompany me to the Déchetterie. He feared the locals might take umbrage at a British-plate car attempting to offload its rubbish. According to Beryl, the gatekeepers of the tip had been known to turn away Brits – even those of us that were now resident – as if we were clandestinely transporting our refuse from the UK to France.

Before setting off, Gérard insisted on doing two things. First, he went through the entire heap of what we planned to dispose of, extracting anything he deemed too good to throw away or had some immediate use for. Secondly, once I'd repacked the trailer, he performed a thorough inspection of all my cargo straps, ignoring the fact that I had successfully transported materials and various equipment from England to France over the past few years. It was hard to be annoyed with Gérard, even when he unnecessarily tightened each strap by a couple of millimetres more.

A couple of weeks later, while returning from the supermarket, Gérard sprang out of his garden, enthusiastically waving us into his driveway. He then eagerly gave us a guided tour of his repurposed treasures.

His greenhouse now sported a sliding shower cubicle door, replacing the original door lost in the 'bit of a blow' earlier that year. The old kitchen cabinets had been dismantled, their doors repainted and leaning against his house to dry, ready to replace the plywood doors of his DIY, not-quite-fully-fitted kitchen. Apparently, some minor adjustments to the wall units were necessary to accommodate the new sizes. The remaining wood from the kitchen had been sawn up for firewood.

However, his pièce de résistance was a newly tiled garden path, previously our kitchen floor. Despite his efforts to shape tiles around corners and the like, the whole job resembled a training exercise for nearsighted tilers. Nonetheless, seeing the pride and joy on his face, I could do nothing but congratulate him on a job well done. Any trace of irony, I'm pleased to say, being completely lost on him. Clare, with her superior sincerity, cooed and smiled at Gérard's efforts, making his garden resemble an outdoor bathhouse.

***

Journal entry April 2017 – *Arrived back yesterday with madam's new toy, her Mazda MX5. It was nice to spend a couple of days in England though as a foot passenger my ability to get around was limited. But it was good to see our old neighbour Julie and her brother again, even if he is a bit of an odd fish. But he knows his way around cars so I think we were in safe hands. As for the car, it's not my cup of tea being squeezed into a space akin to a cricket in a matchbox. Plus being so low down compared to most other road users is not a good place for me. But I liked having the top down, especially once I got to this side of the Channel and the weather warmed up a bit. No satnav of course so had to rely on muscle memory for the route home – rather me than Clare.*

But the real news from my brief trip is that the server in the canteen on the ferry, once again, managed to give me a Full English, without tomatoes! Only the second time in four years.

Anyway she loved it – the car that is. Though it's unlikely to be driven as a sports car should. My wife's more of a mobility scooter racer.

We've also managed to find a builder. An English

immigrant called Lee. Came to France a few years ago and now owns a small successful building business, in the tradition of British builders. In other words we tell him what we want and he takes on the responsibility of organising everything. He, apparently, even clears the site after the works have been done. Where our rubbish goes I didn't think to ask. Out of sight out mind that type of thing. Visiting us, he came along with a couple of oddballs. One being – according to Lee – a multi-skilled labourer – never heard of such a thing but I let it slide. And the other, a one legged electrician who seemed to know what was required. I have to say I'm looking forward to seeing how he negotiates a stepladder.

I asked Lee how he gets on with the French penchant for two hour lunchbreaks. To which he told me that one or two of his men tried it on when they first started with him, and after an hour he told them to either, "get back to work or fuck off!" Apparently in English because swearing in French isn't really menacing enough.

He used similar language when his electrician told him how much the works were going to cost for our job. Listening and nodding sagely as the man – whose name I've forgotten – went through his schedule of works and finally his price. Lee looked up at him and simply said, "Fuck off!" And then in French, "Avoir une jambe ne fait pas de vous un pirate." (Having one leg doesn't make you a pirate) or words to that effect.

Negotiations complete we accepted Lee's offer to go look at a couple of his past projects and spoke with a satisfied customer, whom I suspect was primed. But his work looked okay so we agreed to give him a go. And reassuringly he liked cash in hand pricing. Though we have to watch ourselves because the French are quite hot on that sort of thing.

Good to be back at the farm though. Just need a walk in

the verger to gather my thoughts, as Clare and I had a discussion this morning during our dog walk along the Blavet, about moving the Defender on. As much as it makes us smile and considered by many as a classic, there's no getting away from the fact that it is slow, noisy, uncomfortable, guzzles gas and really awkward to park and manoeuvre around the towns we visit.

Just realised it's the last day of April tomorrow. This year and my life in general, seems to be flying by.

***

Lee the builder turned out to be a decent enough fellow and proved invaluable with our planning application. His one-legged electrician, astonishingly agile, scaled stepladders with the dexterity of a circus performer, while his multi-skilled labourer was easily one of the hardest-working individuals I'd ever encountered. As a general builder, Lee's talents were as varied as they were resourceful, often taking on tasks for which he was neither qualified nor particularly adept. Take roofing, for example. We discovered that it wasn't his forte when our boiler room roof leaked even more after the new one had been installed. Plumbing was another Achilles' heel, as evidenced by the installation of our new shower mixer valve – upside down, with hot and cold water supply reversed.

Fencing was yet another challenge. His attempt at erecting something more permanent between us and Bertrand's required immediate reinforcement following the next 'bit of a blow.'

On the plus side, Lee was ever polite and exceedingly complimentary about the copious amounts of tea we supplied.

***

As April gracefully bowed out and May took centre stage, the weather became increasingly warmer and rain practically vanished. Another reason to be eternally grateful for our inexhaustible supply of free water from the well.

In the potager, everything seemed to be growing at a breakneck speed. Our first produce – some potatoes and one or two other things – made their debut. Though not quite the bumper crop we had envisioned and certainly not enough to recoup the cost of the seed potatoes we planted some eight to ten weeks earlier, though it was still a cause for celebration.

A tiny memorable moment, from my numerous ambles around the farm was the discovery of a baby Blue tit. Scurrying around on the ground beneath one of the many bird boxes inherited from the previous owners, it seemed clear that the little fellow had taken an unfortunate tumble.

Looking decidedly peeved and emitting a faint "tsee-tsee-tsee" sound, echoed by a similar response from a nearby tree, I felt an urgent need to return the little bird to safety before Nettle – our resident bird and rodent terminator – happened upon it.

Requiring a ladder to reach the nesting box, Maggie was promptly recruited to manage ground operations. After convincing her that she couldn't adopt the fledgling, she settled for simply sitting with it. With baby Blue tit safely returned to what I hoped was its rightful place, alongside what I assumed were two siblings, my sense of affinity and responsibility towards my surroundings deepened. It was a genuinely uplifting experience.

***

Clare's little sports car had become a staple of the household, as she and Maggie seized every opportunity to make supermarket trips. The increased frequency was due in no small part to the car's diminutive boot, incapable of accommodating a large shop. But they relished the jaunts, while I divided my time between the unrelenting task of cutting grass, chasing butterflies away from my cauliflower plants, and supervising the new works.

When not joyriding through the Brittany countryside, she was preoccupied with our prodigious prune (plum) harvest. As this fruit was a communal favourite, there was no opportunity to donate or barter with the neighbours. Consequently, she produced several dozen pots of jam, froze a few kilos for prunes and custard in the winter a dish we had never before sampled – and on a, soon to be, trip back to England, she took some along for friends and family, regardless of their preferences.

Meanwhile, Maggie grew increasingly restless, her sojourn in France clearly nearing its end. She needed to spread her wings, and it was up to us to enable her flight. Though the plan remained hazy, with Sam poised to finish University in July and no inclination to leave England for France, we had the bare bones of a solution. For the next two or three months, Maggie would remain with us, earning her keep by taking on grass-cutting duties – a task she didn't seem to mind. And true to her youthful zeal, she endeavoured to mow an acre of grass, including the area around the trees in the verger, as if piloting her mum's MX5.

Additionally, she needed to pass her driving test – a significant challenge, as she had firmly declared, in a way only an eighteen-year-old Maggie could, that she wasn't doing it in France.

'Our first produce – some potatoes and one or two other things – made their debut.'

'...it seemed clear that the little fellow had taken an unfortunate tumble. Looking decidedly peeved...'

GOODBYE TO AN OLD FRIEND

Journal entry May 2017 – *Our Land Rover Defender was as much a family member as, well, a family member. Ridiculous I know but there you have it. Since the time, not so many years ago, when we went to the Land Rover dealers in Salisbury to buy a Land Rover Discovery only to come away with a Defender it has made us smile. It was noisy, slow, and uncomfortable (the kid's hated it initially but came to love it in time) and was as reliable a piece of machinery as you're ever going to come across, and practical too which we liked. We'd holidayed in our Defender, loaded it with all manner of building materials as we tracked back and forth between Dorset and Brittany to the restoration project that has become our new home. I also remember how we once rescued our friends son, stranded as he was, in a flood. Driving through winter conditions that the average Peugeot, Citroen and Prius driver could only ever dream of driving in.*

But we came to realise a possible reason why French people generally prefer their cars to be compact and easy to manoeuvre and that is because the infrastructure in most towns demand it. Even some of the biggest of towns have small roads edged with parking bays clearly not designed for large 4x4 vehicles, all with tight corners to negotiate. Underground car parks typically have height restrictions but then so do many of the over-ground ones. Meaning that even if we did manage to negotiate the twists and turns, we have all too often found ourselves excluded from parking anywhere near the town centre. We did consider buying a second car, but having thought it through we came to the conclusion that whatever we bought would become our car of choice, or necessity, for about ninety percent of our excursions. Meaning that the Defender would sit idly by becoming some kind of museum piece and reminder of happy bygone times. Added to that there was the cost of changing all that needs to be changed, in order for it to adorn French number plates and the like. Then there's the small matter of insurance. Only for us to subsequently park it up. It just didn't make sense. So we took the decision to move it on. In other words sell it. And sell it we did, back to the garage we bought it from all those years ago, who seemed pleased to see it. Not least of all because the Defender, which is no longer made, will no doubt increase in value.

I know at the end of the day it's just an inanimate object and its purpose was to serve our needs, both practical and spiritual. But seeing Clare drive it away to the ferry port for its return to England to be sold, I genuinely felt like I was losing an old friend.

That said, I was fully expecting Clare to appear anytime soon, with that familiar perplexed look on her face, of someone with no sense of direction. Having received a message as she was disembarking at Portsmouth, I'm guessing, that on this one and only occasion, she managed not to get lost.

Next stop is to buy a car here in France which will be yet another new experience. Though probably not a Peugeot or Citroen and absolutely not a Prius.

***

Seeing the Defender drive away for the last time was quite the emotional farewell. In stark contrast, fetching Clare from St Malo was utterly farcical – Toad of Toad Hall collecting Mrs. Tittlemouse in her MX5. One of my pet irritations is seeing elderly gents clinging desperately to their long-lost youth by driving sports cars. And there I was, embodying that very cliché.

Now, it's one thing for mature ladies like Clare to cruise about in such vehicles – they somehow manage to pull it off with a little panache. But as I made my way to the ferry port, I couldn't have felt more self-conscious if I'd tried. With my Panama hat – an essential sun shield – and old Ray-Ban sunglasses, I must have looked every inch the sad old biffer I felt.

In June, we took delivery of our new car – a sleeker, more agile, more comfortable, more speedy, and less fuel-guzzling Land Rover than the Defender. Despite our ongoing linguistic challenges, the sales process progressed with surprising ease. However, as with all things in France, a considerable amount of information was required before they deemed us worthy customers. The selling experience was as fuss free as buying a washing machine – no coffee, no fawning, just a straightforward exchange of particulars, a cheque handed over, a receipt issued, and a brisk farewell, as the sales guy clearly had more pressing matters than peddling luxury cars.

Six weeks or so later, a call came from the dealership in Lorient. And if you think I'm somehow condensing the whole affair, you'd be mistaken. The phone rang, and I answered with my usual polite *"bonjour"* and first name. The caller curtly informed, *"Bonjour, votre voiture est ici. Au revoir."* (Hello, your car is here. Goodbye). The line went dead before I could inquire further.

"Who was that?" Clare asked.

"It was Land Rover in Lorient, I think. Our new car has arrived."

"When can we go get it?" she replied.

"I have absolutely no idea."

The next hurdle was securing insurance before collection. As it turned out, this was no challenge at all, once we provided the requisite reams of information to a smart expat English lad. Blessed with perfect French and a refreshing disregard for excessive admin, he liaised directly with the dealership on our behalf and accepted our payment online. Or rather, over the phone.

The following Friday – why I remember it was a Friday, I've no idea – we drove to Lorient to collect our new pride and joy. Having done this countless times in England, we braced ourselves for the usual fanfare. Land Rover in the UK typically bestowed multiple freebies, flowers, and a bottle of something celebratory. In Lorient, however, things were starkly different.

"Bonjour, nous sommes Monsieur et Madame Templeman et nous sommes venus récupérer notre nouvelle voiture." (Hello, we are Mr. and Mrs. Templeman, and we've come to collect our new car). We beamed at the first person we encountered in the dealership, hoping they were indeed an employee.

Excitement simmered as we anticipated our new car, with the old, beloved Defender now a fond but distant memory. Humans can be quite shallow I reckon – or maybe it's just me. Because the same applied to having children – the firstborn gets all the adoration, then the second and third arrive, and our attention shifts accordingly, with considerably less fawning by number three. Harsh, I know, but I'm sure there are some jungle laws in there somewhere.

Anyway, back to our new car.

"Bonjour, laissez-moi aller vérifier pour vous." (Hello, let me go and check for you), said the young lady I had been grinning at since we entered the place. If she didn't work there, she was certainly being most accommodating. From a small office emerged a trim, well-dressed young man, offering his hand in a gentlemanly greeting. Not the same person we had previously dealt with, but someone who seemed genuinely pleased to be working there.

"Bonjour, oui, laissez-moi récupérer les clés pour vous." (Hello, yes, let me get the keys for you), he said before quickly

turning away, leaving us standing in the showroom with no idea who he was. Conversely he had no idea who we were.

Within minutes, he returned with some paperwork and what we assumed were the keys. Placing the paperwork on the nearest desk, he asked us to join him in signing for the receipt of our new car, which we dutifully did. Having already paid in full, there was no need for further cheques, so we simply stood there, eagerly awaiting the fanfare.

With an air of nonchalance, he pointed outside toward a gleaming white Land Rover, handed us the keys and our copies of the paperwork, and said, *"Voilà votre voiture, passez une belle journée."* (There is your car, have a lovely day), before returning to his office without awaiting a response.

With little choice, we walked silently to our new car. I pressed the 'open' button on one of the key fobs and opened the driver's door. Saying nothing, and with nothing else to do, we peered inside. Just then, the same well-dressed young man came running out of the showroom. Surely, this was the fanfare we had anticipated. As he approached, we noticed he was holding what was unmistakably a bottle of something. *"Désolé, j'ai oublié de vous donner ceci."* (Sorry, I forgot to give you this), he said, handing me the bottle, which turned out to be some bubbly, then hurried back into the showroom.

Our new car was splendid and everything we had hoped for. The French customer service, while not quite so splendid, was nonetheless everything we had expected.

A DIFFERENT TYPE OF WARMTH

With blazing June well into full swing and with caterpillars feasting hungrily on what was left of my cauliflower plants, my brother Alan and his wife Alison paid us a visit. Generally keen to stay within a ten mile radius of his house in Portsmouth, it was great to have my seventy year old brother and his wife come stay. Regarding my brother's age. he's been seventy for quite a few years now. Even in his forties he was seventy, such is the kind of bloke he is – really old fashioned. As for Alison, she is one of life's nice people. Though avoid her cooking. Her fork to plate gravy is legendary.

The reason I'm sharing their visit with you is because one of our evenings together was – and still is – one of the nicest I've ever had.

It started out pretty much as most of our evenings did during the summer in Saint Barthélémy. Apéritifs outside just as the sun was thinking of packing it in for the day. But on this occasion and with no preplanning I decided to move the old table – the one I told you about much earlier in the book, inherited from the previous owners and used for our very first outside meal – to the verger. Around which I placed an assortment of chairs purchased from our numerous visits to Bertrand's, my mothers-in-law's favourite Brocante. For some reason my wife likes an old wooden chair. So much so she's bought quite a few over the years. Many of which never actually get sat on but end up residing in the garage. What can I say? Other than it's a madness that shows no signs of abating.

Clare placed a white linen tablecloth – another Brocante purchase – over the table with me and Maggie proceeding to cover it with plates and bowls containing an assortment of nice things to snack on. Beer and wine was also brought up from the house to add to proceedings, at which point Beryl and Gérard appeared. Neither of whom were invited but then they never needed to be.

So there we were, the seven of us, with no need for false pretentions, the conversation, laughter and apéritifs just flowed. With Gérard regaling Alan and Alison with stories we'd heard many times before, Maggie feeding Jack under the table and Beryl sharing, with Clare, the intimate details of a recipe she'd recently discovered – knowing that one day soon we'd be invited round to try it out at hers – gave me an opportunity to just immerse myself in the unfolding evening. With Gérard in full swing my services, conversations or anecdotes were not required. Allowing me to be a temporary observer. And what I saw was as close to perfect as I could ever have imagined. The setting, our fruit laden verger, was wonderful. Even the teeming buzzing insects seemed to respect the occasion, by pausing their usual biting antics until later. The sun, creeping toward the horizon, was still warm as I gazed across at it, through the gap in the perimeter, made a few months earlier by our manure angel. Most of which still sat as a pile and being home and place of continued fornication for a million or so flies.

It was Alison who brought me out of my reverie, by saying how it all reminded her of *The Darling Buds of May, a book by H E Bates*. Recounting the piece in the book where the family are having Sunday dinner, in all of its understated extravagance, in their orchard.

Jack, having had his fill of potato crisps and cheese, soon fell asleep under my chair and I didn't want this evening to end. And in my mind it never will.

Maisie

For quite a few weeks – possibly months – we had been toying with the idea of getting another dog. Not that Jack craved company, mind you; it was more of a notion that Clare, in particular, was keen to explore. There are many qualities I both like and love about my wife, but once she gets a bee in her bonnet, in this case about getting another dog, she's unstoppable.

We agreed – or rather, I was advised – that our second dog would also be a Border Terrier. While I was still processing this announcement, I was informed that she had already found the perfect candidate: a seven-month-old lady dog. Yes, I know, lady dogs are generally referred to as bitches, but I've never been comfortable with that term unless it has been justly earned.

The dog in question was being sold by a breeder near Cambridge, who specialised in producing show dogs for various UK dog shows, culminating in Crufts. Maisie, our soon-to-be seven-month-old addition, was deemed unfit for the show ring due to a 'slight overbite.' To be honest, when we finally met Maisie, I saw nothing amiss. The breeder, on the other hand, possessed a set of teeth that could frighten small children. It made me ponder whether we should adopt the same level of detachment with humans as some do with animals. If they don't look right, perhaps rehoming might be in order.

Photographs had been exchanged, a deal struck, and with a collection date arranged, we set about planning the logistics of our journey to Cambridge and back from Brittany. The first step was depositing Nettle at a local cattery, which she took in her stride. After all, she would have her own room, zero chance of having her food pilfered, and her own private area to promenade and poo in.

As for Jack, he had to endure another dreaded car and ferry journey, though thankfully not all the way to Cambridge. He was left in the lap of luxury at Clare's parents near Southampton, where he would be royally fed with the finest M&S offerings and allowed to sleep wherever he pleased. The only downside to this haven of overindulgence was having to share the humans' attentions with their own eccentric Schnauzer.

In late June 2017, after a sleepover at Clare's parents, we set off towards Cambridge to collect our newest family member, ready to part with six hundred pounds plus other disbursements, such as a dog passport. My first, and lasting, impression of Maisie was that, while she bore a facial and physical resemblance to Jack – not surprising given they were the same breed – she was his polar opposite in terms of behaviour, which, in many ways, was a blessing.

Maisie was a confident and accepting traveller, perhaps a result of the numerous journeys she had made to dog shows. She was a delight – no panting, no fretting, just peacefully looking out of the car window or sleeping. On the ferry, she would promptly find the cosiest spot and settle down with ease.

Moreover, where Jack would often retreat into a day-long hibernation, Maisie insisted on multiple episodes of the 'zoomies'. This delightful trait, which many dogs possess, was entirely foreign to our Jack. Maisie would dart here, there, and everywhere at breakneck speed, often with a toy clutched in her mouth. She could change direction with enviable immediacy and leap gazelle-like over any obstacle in her path – thankfully sparing Clare's flowers. When Jack, not wanting to be outdone, decided to join in on a 'zoomie' session, he also displayed impressive turning abilities. However, instead of gracefully leaping, he would barrel through flowers and vegetation, leaving a trail of scattered blooms in his wake.

Maisie was also quite vocal, especially when she deemed it time for us to rise. Most mornings, Jack would nuzzle us awake when his bladder was bursting, ever the gentleman. Maisie, on the other hand, simply barked – loudly!

But Maisie was an instant hit with the family, even winning over our other newest addition, the large ginger tom, Milo – who I think I mentioned earlier in our story. Nettle, however, was a different tale altogether. She harboured a disdain for anything that hinted at disrupting her meticulously ordered day, which consisted mainly of coming and going as she pleased and claiming any high ground as her rightful sleeping place. To Nettle, coexistence meant that anyone entering her domain did so by invitation only.

The other three – Jack, Maisie, and Milo – got along famously. Maisie even picked up a trick or two from Milo, such as how to slide open our larder door, a skill Milo had honed soon after his arrival, along with his knack for attracting fleas.

Having Maisie around certainly injected a new energy into Saint-Barthélémy, which was a most welcome development.

'Maisie was an instant hit with the family, even winning over our other newest addition, the large ginger tom, Milo...'

ROAD TRIP

July 2017 was marked by a ludicrously ambitious mini-adventure, a marathon road trip from our home in Brittany to the distant city of Gothenburg in Sweden. A casual 2,800 miles, give or take a few detours and wrong turns.

We were to pass through five countries in a week – France, Belgium, Netherlands, Germany, Denmark, and back – much to the astonishment of our friends and perhaps our own common sense. The purpose? To spend some time with an old school chum of mine and his wife in Sweden.

We had been talking about making the trip for some time and having taken delivery, or rather unceremoniously collected, our new car, we felt we were as prepared as we were ever going to be to make such a journey.

With the needs of our menagerie being taken care of by Maggie, we set off full of optimism with the road being our stage for the next couple of days. Unfortunately however, our experience was anything but exhilarating.

I wish I could regale you with tales of extraordinary escapades, but in all honesty, our time on the road was rather... underwhelming. Our sole points of interest were a pit stop in Lübeck, Germany, and the jaw-dropping Øresund tunnel-bridge hybrid from Copenhagen to Malmö. Beyond that, it was just a blur of monotonous driving. Could we have paused to savour more of the countries we passed through? Absolutely. Did we? Absolutely not. So as travel logs go this isn't going to be much use to anyone looking to get some insight into places to visit, and so on, between Saint-Barthélémy and Gothenburg.

As for the much-lauded German autobahns – vast, bustling, and entirely berserk. When the satnav lady cheerily informed us to "Please stay on this road for four hundred and eighty miles," we knew exactly how our day would unfold: a mind-numbing marathon of tarmac. The only respite from the tedium was the occasional crash site, a ghastly reminder of the autobahn's notorious lack of speed limits. We amused ourselves by guessing the makes of mangled vehicles – before they became mangled – a macabre pastime that occupied our brief stint in Germany.

Upon reaching Lübeck, a mere twelve hours since departure, exhaustion had turned me into a zombified driver. Opting for sleep over sightseeing, we checked into a hotel, consumed some forgettable food, and collapsed into bed. The next morning, however, we explored the charming old town, which was right up my alley, with its abundance of medieval architecture. An eager tour guide informed us (for a few euros, naturally) that Lübeck was once a powerhouse in the Hanseatic League, a coalition of merchant guilds and market towns in Northern Europe. Clarifying from the outset, that the Hanseatic League, had nothing to do with football, much to my initial disappointment.

Breakfast beckoned, and Clare graciously tipped the guide before we discovered Café Fräulein Brömse. Whether the café shared its name with the owner, we never inquired. Instead, we enjoyed an hour of people-watching, feasting on Brötchen with butter and conserve – what you might call bread and jam – and sipping the local coffee blend. Two cups in, and with our teeth having gained an unpleasant fur, we set off to hunt down a purveyor of marzipan, courtesy of our tour guide's recommendation. Apparently Lübeck is famous for the stuff. The sugar rush was, to say the least, unnecessary after the breakfast we'd just had.

Reinvigorated and back on the road, we journeyed to Denmark. Multiple bridges and seven hours later, we arrived at our friend's house to a warm welcome.

Roger, a schoolmate with whom I'd forged a curious bond

(largely thanks to my unrequited crush on his sister), and his charming Swedish wife, greeted us with open arms. Despite my wife's inexplicable urge to mimic a Swedish accent while phoning home – "Hay Maggie, just so you know, ve are in Sveden" – Roger's wife remained unflappably gracious, displaying a patience known only to the Swedes.

For three splendid days, our hosts were the epitome of perfection, whisking us off here, there, and everywhere in between. We indulged in a veritable piscine parade – fish, fish, and more fish. Cooked, uncooked, pickled, and prepared in ways that defied culinary conventions. One particularly enchanting stop was Tjörnekalv, a picturesque coastal gem in Bohuslän. The residents' pride in their little town was evident in every well-maintained corner, and for a change of pace, we had some fish for lunch.

Our wanderings also took us into Gothenburg – or Göteborg, as the locals insist on calling it. Having frequented Stockholm on business, I was keen to see what Sweden's second city had to offer. As it turned out, not much, to be perfectly frank. Gothenburg, much like its capital counterpart, was clean (naturally), orderly (of course), and predictably overpriced. We dined on beef steak – a welcome departure from the endless seafood – and sipped on beverages that were alarmingly expensive. Only difference this time was that I couldn't reclaim it from my employer as expenses. But Göteborg had the most outrageous treat in store. A gin and tonic for the price of what I considered to be the equivalent of the waiters daily wage. So no, not impressed.

We encountered many of their Swedish friends, each with impeccable manners and a warm, welcoming demeanour. Their sense of humour, while different from ours, was refreshingly self-deprecating and charmingly understated. They didn't take themselves too seriously and had a knack for laughing at their own imperfections, which made for a remarkably pleasant atmosphere.

However, after three days of sanitised living, unyielding conformity, and an abundance of rules, we were itching to get back on the road. Don't get me wrong, there's plenty to admire about Sweden, especially its people. But as a full-blooded Brit, I struggled with their unwavering adherence to authority. Speed limits, drinking limits, restrictions on where to wash your car – the list was endless.

And so, with a mix of fond memories and a sigh of relief, we hit the road once more.

Now, I don't know about you, but when holidays draw to an end, all I want is to teleport home. That's precisely how our return journey felt. No sightseeing (not that there was much to behold on the outbound trip), just hitting 'fastest route' on the satnav and off we went. Necessity dictated a pit stop, and we opted for Liège in Belgium – a city renowned for its beauty, though you wouldn't know it from our fleeting visit. For us, Liège's allure was its proximity to the motorway and its selection of hotels. After a fourteen-hour driving marathon, I was ravenous and yearning for bed. We checked into our hotel with surprising ease, strolled across the road for a quick, forgettable meal, and promptly retired for the night. Thing is, no matter how exhausted I am, I've never managed to sleep well in hotels, a lifelong affliction.

The next morning, still groggy and fatigued, I suggested Clare take over the driving. Her response was an impolite decline. And so, we soldiered on, clocking up another ten hours and two rather unceremonious pit stops, before finally arriving back home.

Thus concluded what was arguably the most uneventful road trip in the annals of travel history. And, as they say, there's no place like home.

'..particularly enchanting stop was Tjörnekalv, a picturesque coastal gem in Bohuslän.'

HIGH SUMMER AND A PAUSE FOR THOUGHT

Journal entry July 2017 – *With little else to do with it being so hot outside I thought I'd take some time to reflect. My journal entries are becoming increasingly rarer these days despite promises to the contrary. Which raises a question that I've been thinking about for quite some time now. In fact before we went off to Sweden. What will our life look like once the house and all that comes with it, visa-vie the other buildings and land, are done? Of course they'll be ongoing maintenance, maybe one or two new projects to keep us occupied, but what about the gaps in-between? What about the future? What will we do with ourselves, given that neither of us are inclined to 'just be'? We don't do stability.*

Reading back on that and what I've subconsciously done, is to open up a debate, albeit with myself, as to what our future will look like. And I don't have an answer. Being so absorbed with getting on with stuff, the next job, the next visit to somewhere, the next social event and so on, we've given no time to thinking about the longer term.

I guess while the remaining projects keep us occupied and the various calendar events keep us entertained then we have nothing much to think about. Which reminds me we need to respond to Laurence – she's inviting us down south to stay at her father's place.

***

High summer brought with it high temperatures. In what turned out to be a relentless summer in all of its not so sizzling glory. It was so hot that we had no option but to retreat indoors after noon and either nap or ponder, a practice that went completely against our active nature. However, one silver lining was that the parched weather meant the grass didn't grow so much, therefore sparing me the ordeal of having to get the mower out.

Not that I mourned the lack of lawn maintenance; in truth, the job of mowing had become a fairly tiresome thing. While I took pride in tidy lawns, the tedious ritual of retrieving the sit-on mower – or for the front lawn, the laborious push-along model – and traversing up and down, punctuated by periodic breaks to empty the grass catcher, was becoming a dreary charade. Then, of course, there was the post-mow clean-up, driven more by my compulsive tendencies than necessity. I was adamant that the mower was meticulously cleaned using the air compressor – a legacy of my apprenticeship days where the mantra "care for your tools and they'll care for you" was drilled into me.

With the grass-growing postponed for the foreseeable future, and more leisure time on our hands, Maggie also found herself with fewer horticultural obligations. Consequently, this translated to frequent shopping escapades in the blessedly air-conditioned car – too sweltering for the sporty MX5 – a venture in which I was gladly excused from participating.

Meanwhile, the potager had taken on a wild, unrestrained life of its own, primarily, I suspect, due to our overenthusiastic irrigation regime – no water restrictions for us, thanks to our well's generous year-round supply – and the abundant application of complimentary manure which we dispensed liberally.

Despite the profusion of growth, much of our produce had either gone to seed or fallen victim to a wealth of pests. Nevertheless, the potager's output had been remarkably abundant, and the continuous learning process, invaluable.

It was also that time of year again, the dreaded mosquito season, which meant I was frequently summoned to the bedroom – not for romantic endeavours, mind you, but for the noble quest of eliminating the annoying insects. There was a peculiar satisfaction in ridding the room of these tiny tormentors, wielding any implement that came to hand or, in the absence of such, resorting to the swift and decisive slap of my palm.

I soon determined that there were two categories of foes: those that had already dined and those that had not. Squashing the former on the bedroom wall invariably resulted in a stern reprimand and a trip to the bathroom for a moistened tissue to clean up the ghastly crimson smear I'd left on the wall. The latter, however, earned me a stay of execution. Clare, during these skirmishes, made a concerted effort to maintain her distance – whether to avoid the unflattering sight of my naked mosquito-battling contortions or to escape the risk of being caught in the crossfire, I never asked.

Returning to the conundrum posed in my infrequent journal entry, it was a topic that we deliberated during our many evening strolls along the Blavet. Despite our best efforts, an answer eluded us. Our strategy, or rather our avoidance tactic, was to consign the issue to a metaphorical back-burner – a decision that would come back to haunt us in the near future, much like the mosquitoes.

My intention in sharing these thoughts with you is to revisit the topic of adapting to 'normal,' something I touched upon previously. If you recall, back in 2016, I was grappling with the concept of our new normal. At that time, the new normal was intertwined with grand ventures, fresh experiences, places yet to be explored, and a myriad of other, often unusual, opportunities waiting to be embraced. It felt like a boundless tunnel with no end in sight – an exhilarating prospect. However, in the present, we found ourselves glimpsing the light at the end of the tunnel, a reality we were unprepared for.

Rather than formulating a plan to manage the

forthcoming stability, we found ourselves yearning to extend the tunnel, to prolong the uncertainty. With no solutions materialising, we chose to bury our heads in the sand. It was evident that we needed to return to the planning stage, but we hesitated. As the summer progressed, although not unpleasant, a subtle sense of unease began to creep in.

'Nevertheless, the Potager's output had been impressively abundant...'

A TRIP SOUTH

Remember me telling you about my old work chum, Laurence? She's the one Clare and Maggie visited in Paris earlier this year. A fluent French speaker, thanks to her dad, but had spent her informative years in Chicago, meaning her French has a charming American twang to it.

So, in early August, Laurence, with her unlimited generosity, invited us to her père's holiday retreat just outside Aix-en-Provence – commonly known as just Aix. Joining us were Dan, a boisterous Chicagoan with a personality larger than life, and another of Laurence's old friends, whose name unfortunately escapes me at the moment.

Now, you'd think, after our last pilgrimage to Sweden, the long haul drive – two days, to be exact – would be a chore. But this time, even with Jack and Maisie in tow, the journey down through the heart of France was a wonderful experience. No slight to our Swedish escapade, but comparing the two is like comparing a sunny day with a rainy one. Sweden's charm was there, but this trip, with our friendly companions and lively locales, was in a league of its own.

We finally approached our rendezvous point – Châteaurenard, if memory serves – a stone's throw from Aix, as the afternoon sun dipped in the sky. A message from Laurence popped up on Clare's phone, saying they were still out shopping for provisions but would be back soon. She instructed us to let ourselves in, giving us the precise location of a hidden key. She also provided the address: 63 Rue De, something or other.

Arriving at the provided address, to say we were underwhelmed would be an understatement. The place was a petite, single-storey dwelling that looked like it would struggle to accommodate two people, let alone five and two dogs. We consoled ourselves with the hope that its modest frontage concealed a Tardis-like interior.

As we pondered whether to sit tight or embark on a key-hunt, the door creaked open. Out stepped an elderly gentleman whom we presumed to be Laurence's father. Despite his frail appearance, he was immaculately dressed, with an attention to style and quality that surpassed anyone I'd encountered in Brittany. This elegant fellow surely couldn't be Laurence's father, given that I distinctly remembered being told he resided in another town, some miles from our location, closer to the city. Perhaps he'd made the journey to grace us with his company on our first evening, I remember thinking.

While we deliberated the origins and intentions of this dapper chap, he beckoned us to exit the car, arms spread wide in a gesture that clearly said, "Welcome to my home!" Without further ado, we obliged.

"Bonsoir monsieur. Nous sommes Clare et Colin." I said. No need for translation, I'm sure you get the gist.

"Bonjour et bienvenue chez moi. Vous êtes anglais, oui?" (Hello and welcome to my house. You are English, yes?) he said with a warm smile, stepping aside to let us pass into the house.

We inquired if we could leave the door open to keep an eye on our dogs. To this, he suggested we bring both inside. Ever the sociable canines, Jack promptly watered the old gent's flowerbed and Maisie the small lawn, before trotting confidently into what we hoped would be our cosy abode for the next few days.

Once inside, it became glaringly clear that the house was just as small as the modest frontage had suggested. Before we could question the spatial logistics, our host offered refreshment. *"Quelque chose à boire?"* (Something to drink?). Without waiting for our reply, he generously offered food as well, *"Puis-je vous apporter quelque chose à manger?"* (Can I get you something to eat?). We gratefully accepted a glass of wine each. As for the food, it seemed a simple yet full meal for one was already laid out on the table. He diligently divided it into three equal portions. I wasn't entirely sure what it was – perhaps a pâté of sorts with black bread – but it was both welcome and as it turned out, delicious!

The room served as kitchen, living, and dining space. The walls, barely painted white, with a small kitchenette tucked away in one corner, consisting of a sink atop a unit – its front concealed by a curtain, hiding anything stored underneath – some workspace, and a small electric cooker. An aging potbelly wood-burning stove took pride of place on another wall, its rusting flue disappearing through the ceiling. Beside the unlit burner was an armchair, draped with a blanket that hid its age and condition. In front of it stood a two-seater sofa, once adorned with a floral design, now faded to muted shades of brown and green. Behind the sofa, filling the remaining space, was a dark wood table with a chair neatly placed under each of its four sides. Various electrical lamps dotted around the place, lit even in the late summer afternoon, to combat the room's low-ceilinged gloom. Strangely enough, the little place exuded a serenity, a practical kind of homeliness that didn't require clutter or unnecessary adornments.

As we sat comfortably in the cozy, albeit compact, living space, I couldn't help but admire the rustic charm of the place. Our gracious host, began to regale us with stories of the region, or at least that's what we thought he was saying, as most of his language was lost on us.

The simple meal and wine seemed to work their magic, and soon enough, we felt right at home. The fading afternoon light filtered through the windows, casting a warm glow on the timeworn furniture and adding to the cosy ambiance. Despite its modesty, the house had a humble elegance that was hard not to appreciate. And I liked it.

Just as we settled in, Clare's phone rang. It was Laurence. "Where are you?" I heard her ask.

"We're waiting for you," Clare replied, adding, "But we're fine as your father is spoiling us with wine and food. How long will you be?"

There was a pause – a really long pause. "We left my father's house about an hour ago, and we've been back ages. We're just waiting for you to arrive before we crack open a bottle," Laurence said, then repeating her initial question in a distinctly puzzled manner. "Where are you?"

Clare scrolled through her phone, found the address we had been given, and read it out. Another long pause followed. "Clare, I'm so sorry, I gave you the wrong house number. We're at number thirty-six. Large orange house with iron gates and a long driveway."

I heard all this unfold as I placed the last piece of black bread and pâté into my mouth.

"Everything okay?" I asked, knowing full well that it wasn't, while smiling at the old man who clearly wasn't Laurence's father after all.

"We need to leave – now!" Clare hissed in stage-whisper tones. Luckily, the old man's English was practically non-existent, as he simply smiled at us while feeding cheese to our dogs.

"Merci pour votre hospitalité. Nous devons y aller maintenant" (Thank you for your hospitality. We have to go now), I said as I rose from my seat, looking at Clare to do the same. As for Jack and Maisie, they continued to look longingly at the cheeseboard.

"Merci d'être venus, ce fut un plaisir" (Thank you for

coming, it has been a pleasure), the old man replied, moving away from the small table to open the door. He shook my hand as we left, bidding us a good evening and safe onward journey. Adding, that if we found ourselves passing by again, we were free to call in. Little did he know we only had a few hundred yards to our final destination.

***

Over the next few days, we finally met Laurence's father. Equally genial, he was something of a local celebrity, an artist of some renown – allegedly. Though I couldn't quite see the talent that others clearly did. To my uncouth eye, I'd seen better art on our fridge door, back when the kids bombarded us with endless pieces of unintelligible drawings and paintings from school. Of course, we cooed and congratulated each one as if it were a masterpiece. Even those I inadvertently hung upside down, given their unintentional abstract nature.

The weather was superb as we toured the cities of Avignon – Palais des Papes (Palace of the Popes) – Aix, and a few local towns. I enjoyed every moment, mostly due to the casual nature of it all. We'd simply stop for coffee, beer, wine, and food whenever the mood struck us. For a few days, it was the polar opposite of Sweden, as we existed entirely without the need for rules a bank loan or itinerary. It was marvellous.

The only fly in the ointment was dinner on our last evening together. Arranged by Laurence with the best of intentions, but she didn't account for the heathen in her midst – me.

It was the first – and possibly the last – time I suffered an *Expérience gastronomique*. To my boorish character, it was little more than a long, drawn-out sequence of small, overly elaborate dishes. Allegedly designed to showcase the chef's creativity and skill. Or to my mind: Showing off. There was also what was theatrically called wine pairing: really expensive wines meant to complement each course. All of which was tolerable, had it not been for the tiny portions and the waiters' insistence on explaining the inspiration and ingredients behind each dish, adding unnecessary narrative – and increasing the meal time.

All the other diners, including Clare, seemed to enjoy the experience. I, on the other hand, had no appreciation of it whatsoever. A few times during the meal, probably sensing my lack of enthusiasm, I was told it was all about indulging in the sensory pleasures of food, drink, and the environment, making it a memorable culinary journey. By the end of the evening, there was no doubt I'd remember the experience – hence its inclusion in this tale – but the only lingering sensory impact was tiredness and an unfulfilled hunger. The evening's saving grace was spending many hours around a table with a great bunch of people.

The following morning, just before our departure, Laurence unveiled one last surprise – a visit to the local vineyard, Chateau Constantin, some thirty minutes north of Aix-en-Provence, for a spot of wine tasting. Having been through a few of these in my time and always left underwhelmed, I wasn't exactly brimming with excitement. But you'd never have guessed, as I readily agreed that it was a splendid idea.

Considering my lukewarm response to the previous evening's *Expérience gastronomique* and my begrudging participation in wine tasting, you might think I'm a bit of a bore. And you may well be right. But I assure you, I'm not. I find joy in simple pleasures, as long as they're not wrapped up in pretentiousness. If a wine tastes good, I'll drink it, regardless of its pedigree or price. I'll pair it with whatever food I fancy and at whatever time of day suits me. The same goes for food. Serve it up, tell me what it is, and if I like it, I'll eat it. To me, good food and drink don't require theatrics.

As it turned out, the wine tasting was a lot of fun, and I enjoyed most of what was on offer. The atmosphere was unpretentious, as was our host – a delightful young man with a refreshing sense of humour. I enjoyed hearing about his and his wife's vision for the vineyard – to produce only organic wines – and his positive attitude towards life in general. He was also indifferent as to whether we bought any wine, which is probably why we ended up purchasing a whole case of Rosé.

All too soon, it was time to head home, already looking forward to our next adventure. The one where we would take Maggie back to England to kickstart her young adult life, and where she would be living with her brother, Sam – once they, or rather we, had found an apartment for them.

'The weather was superb as we toured the cities of Avignon – Palais des Papes (Palace of the Popes)...'

MADAM KERJOUAN COMES VISITING

A quiet Sunday dawned with a predictable dose of French sunshine, as Clare and I, continued in our endeavour to tame the plant life of our disorderly Eden. Before the heat drove us indoors.

Little did we know, our sanctuary was about to witness a scene straight out of some rural drama. Madam Kerjouan, the diminutive but formidable former proprietress, had, unbeknown to us, taken up residence in an old folks' home in Baud soon after the house sale. Fate, or perhaps a burning sense of nostalgia, compelled her to talk her daughter, Chantal, into making an impromptu pilgrimage to her erstwhile residence. They parked, not in the driveway, but at the end of the lane – providing for a literal and metaphorical stroll down memory lane.

Madam Kerjouan once again found herself in familiar surroundings, arm in arm with Chantal. I'm in little doubt that her eyes would have drifted over the small houses lining the lane, each one a repository of memories. She likely recalled the days when she knew every resident by name, stopping now and then for a friendly chat. Back then and with the resilience of youth, maybe, I would like to think that friendships would have blossomed with ease. Yet, as Gérard had informed me, those once familiar faces had long since departed, replaced by newcomers who neither knew nor cared to know her.

Such is the fate of many older folk; their world shrinks until it fits within the confines of their own memories. Here she was, revisiting the house where she, Thérèse, and her husband Honoré had raised their family. Each step no doubt a bridge to the past, a delicate balancing act between cherished memories and the inexorable march of time.

Fortified with her daughter's arm for support, Madam Kerjouan ambled towards our home.

Spotting us in the garden, Clare's diplomatic instincts kicked in immediately. She greeted them with the warmth that I have come to admire over the many years we've been together. Madam Kerjouan, with all the humility of the olden days, apologised profusely for the intrusion. We, with the grace befitting our new status as custodians, assured her that no such intrusion existed.

Declining our offer of refreshments, they chose instead to meander through the farm, heading towards the verger now resplendent with fruit. Like two ghosts revisiting their haunt, they moved slowly, uttering hushed comments, pointing at reminders of the past. In the verger, they paused, as though trying to imprint the scene onto their souls.

While they wandered, Clare and I retreated to the kitchen – our safe place and beating heart of our home – to prepare tea. It was during this simple domestic ritual that Chantal, her head peeking through the open French door, asked, *"Serait-il acceptable que ma mère entre dans la maison?"* (Would it be alright for my mother to come into the house?).

"Bien sûr. Entrez," I replied, catching Clare's approving nod.

Tentative steps echoed on the newly laid wooden floorboards as they entered. Wearing expressions of respectful intrusion, the weight of their visit palpable in the air. Once more, we extended the offer of tea, which they politely declined.

Then, the moment happened. Thérèse, with tears streaming down her weathered face, broke from Chantal's side and approached Clare. *"Tout est si beau,"* she murmured, her voice laden with emotion. *"Tout est si beau,"* she repeated, as if the words were a chant warding off some deep sorrow.

With heartfelt gratitude and one final apology, they took their leave. Clare and I, hand in hand, watched them walk back up the lane, neither looking back. The final chapter of Madam Kerjouan's life at the farm was complete, the weight of their visit lightened, we hoped, by the knowledge that the new custodians have honoured the past.

EMPTYING THE NEST

Nearing the end of August, and my odds of producing a cauliflower in the summer of 2017 had evaporated like some mirage. Sadly, my cruciferous dreams were dashed, but the butterflies – or more accurately, their ravenous offspring – feasted royally. Our garden, however, yielded an abundance of other delights, which were now gently bowing out as summer's curtain was beginning to fall.

I found myself often in the company of my own thoughts during those days, occupied with the endless tasks of splitting logs and mowing grass. Anything, really, to divert my mind from the impending pilgrimage to the motherland. England called, and I was in no rush to answer, especially as it meant leaving our daughter behind on that isle.

The journey promised to be anything but fleeting, for there was much ground to cover. We were on a quest for a residence in the district of Southsea, the chosen sanctuary for Maggie and Sam. This also entailed furnishing it comprehensively, since their inventory of household goods amounted to little more than a couple of cushions and a kettle. Oh, and an abundance of computer technology.

Accordingly, with the canines vaccinated to the hilt, the car groaning under its load, and the house shut up, we embarked on what was to be the lengthiest stay in England since our exodus to Brittany.

Using Clare's parents' house as our command centre, we commenced our flat-hunting crusade the day after our arrival. To that end, we thought it would be a good idea to enlist the help of Sam, being still shackled to his student digs in Portsmouth, to scout ahead. Much to our disappointment, it turned out that, despite living in the city for nearly three years, Sam's knowledge of Portsmouth was as scant as my nan's grasp of the off-side rule. However, if we needed a pub rating or the whereabouts of some budget-friendly fried chicken, he was our man. Beyond that, he was of no use whatsoever.

So, we were left with no choice but to resort to the old-fashioned method of legging it around town. During our tours, we navigated the complex world of letting agents, deciphering their cryptic words. Their mastery of saying everything and nothing simultaneously was truly a spectacle. It's astonishing how little these intermediaries know about the very properties they are meant to be showcasing. As it turned out, we got lucky. After a mere three days and countless viewings, we stumbled upon the ideal flat – a real showstopper – the top-floor of a Victorian townhouse. It boasted two bedrooms, a kitchen, a bathroom, and a living/dining area. Located in a charming part of Southsea, it afforded them splendid views across the common and the seafront. Our next mission: furnish the place. Cue the grand pilgrimage to the Swedish furniture mecca.

Not an enthusiastic supporter of the labyrinthine store, I must admit that for those seeking a budget-friendly way to outfit a living space, it is without equal.

Choosing what was needed, wanted, and desired was entirely above my station, so my role was relegated to trolley pusher and debit card handler. Our trolley was one of the grand, flatbed behemoth types, which became progressively heavier with each circuit of each floor of the store. In doing so , we adhered to the conveniently placed arrows on the floor; woe betide any who dared defy their path, inviting a chorus of tutting and disapproving glares from fellow shoppers. Interestingly, the staff were indifferent to my directional changes – it was very much a customer-enforced code of conduct.

Sam, due to his utter disinterest in shopping and declared

lack of taste – as determined by Maggie – was commandeered to push trolley number two. Yes, two colossal flatbed trolleys, both filled to their brim with goods well beyond recommended weight limits. Being a Swedish enterprise, the store was festooned with a plethora of warning signs, instructional signs, and a surplus of 'danger of electric shock' signs – predictably on electrical goods!

Even the promise of Swedish meatballs for lunch did little to raise mine or Sam's spirits. We quickly learned that questioning any item placed on the trolleys by Clare or Maggie was an exercise in futility. Despite my seemingly robust argument against the necessity of multiple packs of fifty tea lights, my protest was dismissed.

The next day, it was all hands on deck emptying the large van we hired. Load after load of flatpack furniture was hefted up three flights of stairs. Suddenly, the much-admired view from the kids' flat seemed considerably less enchanting. After wrestling a three-seater sofa – yet to be assembled – up those flights, I would have gladly traded the view for an underground dungeon.

By day's end, the flat began to resemble a home, and we were all satisfied with our efforts. Even Sam, not typically a hands-on kind of lad, managed to assemble a single flat-pack stool.

Once the kitchen was stocked with at least a month's worth of provisions, we were dismissed, together with a veritable mountain of cardboard – courtesy of the Swedish shop's furniture – back to Clare's parents', leaving our two youngest offspring to get on with their journey of independent living.

Twelve hours later, the phone rang with Maggie on the line and what transpired was worthy of a melodrama. She was in meltdown mode, desperate to abandon Southsea and return to France with us. We spent a good couple of hours talking her off the proverbial ledge, urging her to give it just one more day and night, as we weren't scheduled to leave until the following day.

Enter Sam, our unlikely saviour. He proposed that Maggie should experience the nocturnal wonders of Portsmouth and Southsea – an oxymoron if ever there was one. These wonders included a casino visit and a tour of some local cocktail bars. The next morning, my phone rang again. This time, it was a very hungover yet animated Maggie regaling us with tales of various cocktails sampled and her triumphant ten-pound win at the casino. In the span of a few hours, Southsea had transformed into her newfound paradise, while France had become the devil's arsehole. She concluded the call by informing us she was off to brunch with Sam and a couple of others, and wished us a safe journey home.

The drive to Poole for the Cherbourg ferry was eerily quiet. Even Jack, who typically moaned and panted about being in the car, was uncharacteristically subdued. We had come to England as five and were returning as four.

Now, we found ourselves completely childless, alone, retired, with only ourselves to look after. It was then that I recalled something I had written years ago.

> We call them our children.
> And they are, to the extent that we have certain responsibilities towards them.
> We may love them.
> But should never claim to own them.
> Accept, that when they leave you, and they will in so many ways, the loan deal is over.
> However, beware the extended warranty – hidden somewhere in the small print, never visible to parents.
> Demanding that all or any breakages, malfunctions, cause for replenishment or comfort, remain in force.
> Forever.

CRACKS

As the seasons shifted, so did our spirits. September through November, that peculiar stretch of time, where the weather becomes an unpredictable companion, and the world seems to drift into a state of semi-hibernation.

Throughout this past year or so, we had covered a staggering amount of ground. Long journeys, day trips, new towns, old towns. As well as the continued pursuance of making our home the epitome of beauty. An accomplishment we held dear, a testament to our strength and creativity.

But the burning question lingered: Was our adventure reaching its natural conclusion? This and other similar deliberations began to dominate our conversations, reflecting on how it all came to be.

Our days often began with a confab around the breakfast table, with the same anticipatory inquiry as with every other day: "So, what are our grand plans for today?" To no one's surprise, our plans often mirrored those of the previous day, with a strong likelihood of replicating tomorrow's too. Humans often crave a bit of routine, but not to the extent where our existence becomes a monotonous procession.

Uppermost were the demands of the verger, the potager, and other necessary works around the farm, dictated by the coming seasons. In short order the life to which we once had absolute control was now being controlled by an unseen force – nature. We could, in theory, break free from these shackles, but unfortunately, there was nowhere we particularly yearned to go. Our journeys across France had left no region uncharted and nowhere else held our interest.

There was little doubt that our assimilation into French life continued to be like trying to dance with two left feet – a talent that my wife often said I naturally possess. Though we didn't always voice our doubts, the frustration simmered beneath the surface. There was little joy in hearing ourselves mangle the French language daily. Some years in and our attempts at fluency were more miss than hit, often resulting in a linguistic brew that was neither French nor English, just a verbal disaster all its own. Yet, being the optimists we are, we persevered.

Alan had mentioned a couple of late summer fêtes we could attend, provided we procured the necessary tickets. Our previous encounters with these rural gatherings were met with mild amusement and inevitable disillusionment. Each fête, a carbon copy of the last: a throng of villagers gathered in an unremarkable field, seated at elongated tables, consuming industrial quantities of nondescript food, and quaffing rough wine or tepid cider – or, on adventurous days, beer. The soundtrack to this pastoral tableau provided by a local folk band, one of which included Alan on vocals and the guitar.

Our first fête was a moderate success, though conversations proved challenging. The locals weren't unfriendly, merely unaccustomed to outsiders. And our French, while passable, was not exactly fluent. As any polyglot knows, conversing in a second language can be tricky – a linguistic minefield even.

By the second and third fêtes, the charm had worn thin. The pattern was predictable, the enjoyment minimal, and the whole affair veered dangerously close to becoming a trial rather than a celebration.

So not just the governing forces of nature then. Something deeper was afoot and we needed to get to the bottom of it.

Despite our growing apprehension about what the future might unfurl, the idea of throwing in the towel never crossed our minds. We were resolute in the notion that any solution or reinvention of our grand adventure would be firmly rooted in our landlocked haven in Brittany. The thought of residing elsewhere was simply out of the question. What we needed was a cunning new plan.

In the meantime, we found ourselves grappling with the matter of the continuation of our enrolment in the French health system. Or rather the ongoing bureaucracy. The eternal adversary of any free-spirited adventurer.

***

September 2017 heralded the arrival of our coveted medical cards (*Carte Vitale*), a mere fourteen months or so after we first set out on this bureaucratic journey. The towering piles of submitted paperwork were finally approved. Besides the equally enormous task of applying for Naturalisation – which no doubt would be another prolonged venture – we were inching ever closer to the status of bona fide immigrants.

Our local surgery presented us with a choice of two doctors. Beryl, a veteran of the medical system, informed us that one doctor was fluent in English, while the other seemed to harbour a particular disdain for the English immigrant. Unsurprisingly, we opted for the former. Following the instructions enclosed with our Carte Vitales, we promptly arranged a full medical examination to inaugurate our French medical history.

The name of our chosen doctor escapes me, but I remember him as a relatively young man – though at my age, everyone seems young – with a pleasant demeanour that extended even to the most intimate inspections. A plethora of bodily fluids were collected and dispatched to some laboratory or other, and we parted ways on good terms. Despite the intimate nature of our meeting, phone numbers were not exchanged; instead, we simply proffered our French payment card for the pleasure of the experience.

Several weeks later, a letter from *l'Assurance Maladie*

informed us that our results were ready for review with our local physician. A swift follow-up appointment ensued, where we were both pronounced in good health, provided with a set of pamphlets on healthy living, and handed an invoice. Which, of course, we duly paid.

***

With autumn upon us, the final produce of the year's bounty was harvested. A rather splendid pumpkin, the unintentional product of Clare's decision to toss some expired seeds onto the compost heap, stood proudly among our crops. Clueless about what to do with this oversized gourd, we stealthily dumped it on Alan and Hélène's doorstep when they were out. When they called to enquire about the mysterious visitor, we feigned ignorance until, weeks later, we learned it had been transformed into the main ingredient for countless pies and stews.

Our apple harvest followed the same fate as the previous year, raked up and added to the compost heap. With the season's shift, our focus turned to autumn and winter chores – digging over the potager, pruning, and tackling a substantial list of repairs to fortify our home against the impending storms. It was a ritual of packing summer away, a stark contrast to the previous autumn when I waxed lyrical about chilly, misty mornings giving way to warm afternoons and butterflies flitting among the late blooms.

Looking back, reflecting on those journaled words from a year ago, perfectly encapsulated our changing mood and outlook. How swiftly the seasons and our sentiments transformed, mirroring the cyclical nature of life itself.

Thoughts then turned to the festive season. Though still quite away off, it brought with it much planning and pondering. Being notified that none of the family would be suffering the Channel crossing this year, we found ourselves at a crossroads. We could either stay put in Saint-

Barthélémy with our loyal dogs and less loyal cats, or seek an alternative. But before we could decide on our yuletide plans, we had the more immediate task of conjuring up a grand celebration for that most peculiar of British traditions: Guy Fawkes Night.

During the parched summer months, bonfires were strictly forbidden, and rightly so, given the abundance of dry, combustible crops. But as autumn rolled in, the rules relaxed, and the familiar sight of smoke plumes once again dotted the horizon.

The various demolition projects had left us with a bountiful supply of flammable material, perfect for constructing an impressive bonfire. And, with the French sharing our enthusiasm for pyrotechnics, we were able to procure a dazzling array of fireworks at a remarkably reasonable price. All that was missing were some children to justify the festivities. Conveniently enter Alan and Hélène's grandchildren, Sasha and Charlie.

Invitations were dispatched, and we busied ourselves preparing for the event. Temporary heating and lighting were installed in a recently repaired outbuilding, which had suffered during the 'bit of a blow.' A barbecue was set up, with Alan volunteering to man the grill, and Clare whipping up a selection of tasty dishes. Yannick, along with his wife Steph and their children, Sasha and Charlie, brought additional supplies.

As the night of the celebration approached, the weather could not have been more perfect: cold, dry, with a gentle breeze. The bonfire was lit, and drinks were poured. The two boys, despite constant warnings from their parents and grandparents, couldn't resist poking and prodding the blazing inferno.

They are no longer children, but young men, and I hope that one day they would be watching their own offspring revel in the same primal joy of a roaring bonfire.

Fireworks lit up the sky, eliciting a chorus of "oohs" and "aahs" from the gathered crowd, albeit not quite on par with the Bastille Day extravaganza.

As for the food, there is something about certain dishes that tastes infinitely better when cooked and served in a particular setting. Bonfire night sausages and jacket potatoes are prime examples. The ambience, the camaraderie, and the event itself all contributed to a memorable night, albeit one that underscored the absence of our own family.

In the days that followed, we made the decision to spend Christmas in England – Southsea, to be precise. And so, our seasonal journeys continue, ever evolving, ever adapting, never boring, with new adventures always on the horizon.

'...rather splendid pumpkin, the unintentional product of Clare's decision to toss some expired seeds onto the compost heap.'

CHRISTMAS ABROAD

Despite our decision not to be at home for Christmas, we hadn't abandoned tradition altogether. Our single tree – or rather, Clare's tree – stood in the bay of the French doors, austerely adorned with a spartan selection of ornaments. Clare, my Yuletide minimalist, had decreased the decorations to an almost monastic simplicity, leaving entire boxes of baubles, and my precious stash of tinsel, to languish in the loft. Whilst Clare busied herself with the art of un-adornment, I turned my attention to the exterior. I am beyond help when it comes to festive illumination! Our kids could regale you with tales of my incandescent obsession, as I endeavoured to transform our home into a beacon of Christmas cheer for our unsuspecting neighbours.

The strains of Christmas tunes, which would have ordinarily filled the air from November onwards, were conspicuously absent, creating a silent night that was more serene than usual, though not necessarily welcome.

Our pilgrimage from Brittany marked a moment of genuine excitement at the prospect of returning to England. Memories of past family holidays in France, complete with the burden of perpetual attention to our brood, designated driving, and translation duties, often left me longing for the sanctuary of home well before the holiday's end.

Our holiday retreat was a canine-friendly apartment on Southsea seafront, our seasonal headquarters until the 28th of December. Sadly, Jamie, our eldest, was unable to join us until New Year's Eve in Brittany.

During our five-day stint, we indulged in a genuine overdose of family fun, though the festivities were marred by a less than auspicious start. Clare fell victim to a bout of food poisoning – courtesy of a questionable Chinese takeaway consumed at the kids' flat. The sight of her, gripped by stomach cramps and afflicted with simultaneous expulsions from both ends, was a far cry from the radiant bride I had wed decades earlier. Those immortal vows of "in sickness and in health" were certainly put to the test.

Thankfully, she recovered in time to partake in the remaining festivities, steadfastly avoiding any cuisine that wasn't home-cooked. It's curious, isn't it, the memories that linger? Just don't ask me what I did yesterday.

Having to deal with the delightful chaos of cramming four adults, two canines, and an obscene amount of presents into our car, we set off for Clare's parents' place where we were to spend Christmas Day. It brought back memories of Christmases past, annual pilgrimages to either their house or ours, a tradition now more subdued, with everyone decidedly more adult than in those golden days.

Reminiscing about times when the house resonated with the cacophony of generations – excited children, equally enthusiastic grandparents, mums, dads, uncles, and aunties – all immersed in family classics like charades or the bizarrely named 'blow football.' Uncle Pepi, in particular, would participate with the enthusiasm of a child, despite his advanced years and equally advanced digestive system, leading to a symphony of flatulence that accompanied each enthusiastic blow.

The dining table, stretched to its limits and further augmented by a table from the garage and a mismatched assortment of chairs, would groan under the weight of our festive feast. Sadly, many of the aunts, uncles, and grandparents are now fond memories, and our numbers have dwindled, awaiting the next generation to revive the raucous revelry. But as we all know, memories live on – forever.

Dinner was a culinary collaboration between Clare and her mother, devoured with gusto by the rest of us. Crackers were pulled, jokes were read (prompting the customary groans), and Christmas pudding was forced into already bulging tummies. Post-dinner, we settled into an evening of conversation, with the elders – me included – dozing and the kids connecting with friends – both real and virtual – on their phones. It's amusing how we still call them phones when actual verbal communication has become such a rarity.

The remainder of our stay in England was divided between long coastal walks, visits to an embarrassment of pubs, and more quality time with the kids. I wish I could claim that I exhibited restraint, but regrettably, I did not. My quest for a decent pint, a useless endeavour since our relocation abroad, was finally rewarded. Numerous pubs enjoyed my patronage – some charming, some less so, some ancient, some modern, but all appreciated.

There were a few things, long forgotten, that made an uninvited but welcome return to my senses on that trip. The familiar food, the smells – mostly pleasant, though some less so – and, of course, the language. I revelled in one of my favourite pastimes: people-watching and eavesdropping. I could converse with confidence, unencumbered by the need to second-guess or meticulously craft my sentences. Though I was now a confident French speaker, the sustained unnaturalness of it continued to niggle at me.

We were like children in a long-lost playpark, rediscovering old favourites: supermarkets that sold items I actually wanted to buy, record stores, the fish and chip shop off Palmerston Road, my cherished curry house on Albert Road, the myriad coffee bars and pubs, and numerous other haunts previously consigned to memory. But above all, we relished the ease of simply being.

Epitomised by a brief time that I spent in an old traditional Portsmouth backstreet pub.

Among the labyrinth of Victorian Terraced streets of

Portsmouth, tucked away like a treasured odd sock, sits The Phoenix – a pub of such unpolished charm that you half-expect to see a Dickensian waif at the bar, clutching a lemonade. It was Christmas Eve, a Sunday no less, and the festive frenzy was in full flow. Clare and Maggie had embarked on a last minute retail rampage, their enthusiasm for Christmas shopping still undiminished. Meanwhile, young Sam was indulging in one of his marathon slumbers, akin to a hibernating bear.

Consequently, I was granted a brief interlude of liberty – a 'me-time' sanctuary in a wilderness of festive busyness. Armed with the largest Sunday newspaper I could find, I set forth to The Phoenix. There, I strategically claimed a secluded table and settled in for a session of ale-assisted reading and timewasting – perfect!

The next two hours passed in blissful tranquillity. The barman, a cheerful, though unimposing, chap exchanged a few pleasantries with me. Nearby, a cluster of Sunday regulars nodded in camaraderie – a silent acknowledgment of our shared sanctuary from the yuletide chaos.

Why this moment would etch itself onto the slate of my future, I cannot explain. Perhaps it was the simplicity of it all: no carol singers demanding attention, no gift lists needing ticking, just a man, a pint, a forest of Sunday supplements to wander through and what seemed a million miles away from France. Though hardly the cornerstone of a robust retirement plan, this fleeting respite planted a seed – one destined to flourish in the fertile soil of future retirement plans yet to be dreamed.

As a child, Portsmouth and Southsea was my playground, and as a young man, my first independent home. The geography was as familiar to me as the back of my hand, and the places to visit were embedded in my memory, as detailed in my memoir, 'Parkie Life.'

Despite the numerous changes and additions to Portsmouth Harbour, the influx of university residents – temporary though they may be – and a few alterations here and there, the city had largely remained unspoiled since my childhood. The best streets were still the best, and the worst were still to be avoided. Boundaries remained unchanged – South of Albert Road was Southsea proper, anything else, not – despite the best efforts of estate agents to stretch them.

Consequently, we often found ourselves strolling the streets, with me playing tour guide. The Victorian architecture of the city particularly appealed to Clare, as it did to me. Before long, we found ourselves perusing the windows of estate agents.

However, as country dwellers for over thirty years, the thought of city living didn't quite compute. And moving back to England, after expending so much energy and money on emigrating, seemed a baffling consideration. Yet, we couldn't deny our genuine enthrallment with our surroundings. The seafront, the open spaces, the shops, et al. But most importantly, the closeness of our family.

One quiet morning, as I sipped my coffee in our rented apartment, fresh from one of our numerous street excursions, Clare posed the question I had secretly pondered but hadn't the courage to voice, "Do you think that we've isolated ourselves?"

"By living where we do, you mean?" I replied, already knowing the answer.

The thing is, our decision to emigrate wasn't born out of any disdain for our homeland. It simply seemed a good idea at the time and one that, regardless of how our future unfolds, will never be regretted.

Yet, we weren't about to determine whether our future lay in France – or anywhere, for that matter – based on a brief visit back to England, so we let the subject drop.

Still, the spectre of isolation loomed larger each day, an elephant in the room that refused to be ignored.

All too soon, our visit was over, and with tearful goodbyes, we headed back to the ferry port.

Saying farewell to our family was a melancholic affair. We'd had the best of times, and like our children when they were young, we didn't want Christmas to end. But end it did, and we left England with tears, smiles, memories, and more questions than answers.

NEW YEARS EVE

Turning off the main carriageway and onto the single-track lane leading to our house in Saint-Barthélémy, I was delighted to see the numerous timers for my lighting displays working as intended. Like landing lights on steroids, they guided us home.

The following day and it was off to St Malo to retrieve Jamie Ann and her diminutive yet disproportionately self-important hound, Alfie. While the journey itself was nothing to write home about – a mere two-hour trip – it proved to be a golden opportunity. A rare father-daughter tête-à-tête, uninterrupted by the forthcoming domestic chaos, filled with a steady stream of quips, tales both true and slightly embellished, and an all-important catch-up on the latest dispatches from her world. Of course, as seasoned parents well know, these updates are never quite the full story. No, what we receive is the expertly curated, thoroughly redacted edition – the version that omits certain inconvenient details, leaving us with just enough to feel informed, but not too informed. A strategic art, perfected by all of our children, and one I suspect will never make its way into a parenting manual.

Then it was all hands on deck for New Year's Eve preparations. Alan and Hélène joined us, making it a cozier affair than previous years but no less enjoyable. The only marked difference was the strict adherence to Clare's programme. And let me tell you, no one messes with Clare's arrangements – not even Alan. The sole nod to Brittany tradition was the inclusion of fresh fish, particularly oysters. Alan, dedicated as ever, would set off to the coast early on New Year's Eve to fetch the freshest produce. Upon his return, he'd spend the rest of the day preparing the fish, which was gratefully received – except for the oysters, of course. They're one of those 'love them or hate them' foods. Alan and Hélène loved them; we didn't. I've tried them, adhering to my "don't knock it till you've tried it" philosophy. But to me, they're like consuming bronchitis. With the food eaten and the table cleared in good time for midnight, fireworks were naturally on the agenda. Once again, I was well-prepared, though I'd changed things up slightly from the display I'd organised for Guy Fawkes night. For New Year's Eve, I bought one of those sixty-centimetre cubes containing one fuse and multiple fireworks. I imagined lighting the fuse, retiring with the group, and enjoying the display. As midnight approached, glasses would be charged, and we'd gather outside – minus the animals, of course.

Poised to light the fuse at the final bong of the clock striking twelve on the radio, I now realise I should have clued the others into my plan. One minute to twelve, and I went outside, leaving Clare to handle the drinks. Not considering that filling five glasses might take more than a minute, I joined in the countdown as I heard the bongs on the radio. Ten, nine, eight...three to one! Happy New Year! The lighted taper met the fuse, and within seconds, the first whizz pop! A cascade of bangs and screeches followed. My fellow partiers, alerted by the noise, rushed out in what appeared to be a bit of a panic, just in time to miss most of the pyrotechnics. All of the dogs, seeking refuge from the cacophony, bolted for the nearby fields, closely pursued by Clare and Jamie through the smoke from my display. By the time they retrieved the dogs, the display had ended, and peace was restored to the new year's day. In silence, we drank our champagne and wished each other a happy new year. Like many of my mishaps over the years, this one too, is stored away in some deep retrieval system within Clare's head, to be aired publicly whenever I get too big for my boots.

PART SEVEN

SHIFTING SANDS

As you now know, one of our particular joys is a walk along the Blavet, where on one particular day in early January, the cold, dry air and our dogs, well-acquainted with the route, allowed us to amble and revisit some deep-routed questions. Part way through the stroll, Clare broached the subject I had mulled over countless times, "Have you given any more thought to Southsea?" Naturally, I had, and admitted as much. Since our return, Brittany had begun to feel less and less where our future lies.

What once felt like an exciting adventure, muddling through the intricacies of a French lifestyle, had turned into a tiresome chore. The once-exotic produce on the shelves of our local supermarkets had become alien, and the quest for those little British treats, the ones we previously splurged on for a taste of home, increasingly irritated us. Our conversations revolved around the lack of choice, energy, ambition, but above all, family.

Clare, in particular, expressed a longing for more human engagement. She envisioned herself working in a shop job in England, something to satisfy her social cravings.

Don't get me wrong, our love for each other was unwavering, and we spent an inordinate amount of time talking and enjoying each other's company. But I understood her need for social interaction beyond our home, something unattainable in Brittany.

Sure, she could have mingled with other immigrants – those who insisted on calling themselves expats – but they weren't quite our kind of people. Our interactions with them often devolved into tedious discussions about themselves, their money, the value of their houses, Brexit, and an endless stream of complaints about their French neighbours.

The scenes of Southsea, with its familiar faces and places, began to beckon us with a nostalgic pull. The continual convention barriers now felt like a shackle, binding us to a place that no longer felt like our own.

As we wandered along the Blavet, the realisation settled in: our once precious adventure had become a gilded cage. The prospect of returning to England, to the warmth of family and the comfort of familiarity, grew ever more appealing. It was a revelation that, while unsettling, brought a sense of clarity.

And so, with each step, our hearts and minds drifted back to Southsea, a place that, despite its flaws, felt more like home than our current, quaint corner of Brittany. The yearning for connection and community, for a life filled with both familiar joys, the inevitable mishaps and of course the pull of family, became our guiding star.

JOYEUX ANNIVERSAIRE SOIXANTE ANS JEUNE

Sharing a birthday with the likes of Elvis Presley, David Bowie, Stephen Hawking, Shirley Bassey, and Kim Jong-un – it does make one feel rather illustrious, doesn't it? This year, 2018, marked my sixtieth, and Clare, in cahoots with Alan and Hélène, came up with a coastal picnic, complete with Champagne and soup from a flask. A touching gesture that, in theory, should have warmed my heart. In reality, it was bloody freezing. The wind cut through every layer like an Arctic blade, accompanied by icy rain showers that seemed determined to test our resolve.

Despite the sub-zero temperatures, Clare's meticulously planned day would not be dampened. We started at a picturesque picnic spot beside some nameless river, where Champagne was served alongside cold charcuterie meats, adding a chill to my bones that rivalled the weather.

From there, we ventured to Kerguevin near Erdeven for lunch and a bracing walk along the shore. If you appreciate the Cornish coastline, with its harbours and beaches, I'd wager you'd fall in love with Brittany. In my humble opinion, Brittany leaves Cornwall trailing in its wake when it comes to coastal charm.

We spent hours at the coast, huddled in Alan's VW van with soup and bread, followed by a long, invigorating walk on the splendid sandy beach. Before the light faded, we made our way to one of Brittany's treasures, the stones at Carnac. While the UK prides itself on Stonehenge's ninety-three impressive rocks, Carnac boasts over three thousand megaliths, ranging from modest to immense and stretching across a vast expanse.

As the day wore on, my spirits lifted, and this sixtieth birthday became one of the most memorable. Come evening, we returned to the Moulin, basking in the warmth of Alan and Hélène's company by the fire, sipping wine, laughing, and marvelling at the absurd yet delightful idea of a January coastal picnic.

The superb company and the heady mix of alcohol melted away any thoughts of our future lying outside of Brittany. For a few precious weeks, the notion of moving back to England was relegated to the back of our minds, obscured by the haze of fond memories and exceptional companionship.

'...we ventured to Kerguevin near Erdeven for lunch and a bracing walk along the shore.'

PART EIGHT

APRIL 2018 – THE POINT OF RETURN

Looking out, from our potager, across the valley to the canal and with the spring time sun doing little more than make me squint. My mind flitted back to that one grand day in January, now relegated to a distant memory as faint as the echoes of laughter we'd once shared on the beach at Kerguevin.

But, our minds were made up and the die was cast – time to head back to England. Southsea, to be precise.

As we stroll through 2018, it might seem to the casual observer that I'm hastily wrapping up our story. But such an impression couldn't be further from the truth. There remained quite a few more stories, anecdotes, and experiences that I could have recounted, but, if I'm honest, they would add little value. What you've read so far, and are about to read, is a faithful and honest reflection of how our journey played out – replete with all its highs, lows, and quirks.

If we look back at the beginning, as we were planning our great adventure, we were delightfully aimless – though focused – our path lit by the thrill of the new: new faces, fresh experiences, and challenges galore. All of which I hope I have managed to convey to you.

However, as time progressed, our enthusiasm undeniably waned. The once exhilarating challenges, oddities, and differences of living in Brittany – which we had initially dismissed as mere quirks – became tiresome, even before we returned to England for Christmas in 2017. More of which I touch on a little later.

Suffice to say, it became evident that a change was necessary, and true to our nature, this change was non-negotiable, demanding swift action.

Clare joined me in my musings and together we mulled over two rather important points. One: How on earth were we going to break the news to Alan and Hélène? And two: The logistics of packing up our French adventure and moving them into a new English reality. Cue the anxiety! We knew Alan and Hélène would be crestfallen – no, probably decimated! After all, they had poured their very hearts into making our Brittany adventure come true.

Conversely, our family back in England couldn't have been more thrilled. It seemed our dear ones were already poised to wave us back at the dockside, eagerly awaiting what they considered our grand return. If only Alan and Hélène could muster the same enthusiasm...

Our future beckoned with a blend of excitement and trepidation. Question was; were our hearts ready to cope with the delicate dance between goodbye and hello?

Dinner at the Moulin was always to look forward to, filled with warmth, laughter, and superb food. Yet on that particular evening, the taste of our announcement was a bitter pill to swallow. As we broke the news that we were returning to England for good, the room seemed to hold its breath.

Alan, predictably, was rendered speechless. His silence

spoke volumes, an eloquent display of grief akin to a bereavement in his eyes. Hélène, ever the optimist, managed a smile through her sadness, wishing us luck with a grace that left us both grateful and gutted. "We will always be here for you," she assured us, her generosity unwavering, even in the face of our departure.

Ironically, their understanding – particularly Hélène's – made it all the more difficult. Had they been less conciliatory, perhaps our guilt wouldn't have felt so heavy. Yet, that's precisely why they are such remarkable friends.

Back at our little piece of Brittany, life carried on. The grass was mown, the potager was meticulously planted, and the trees were pruned to perfection – or at least as perfect as my skill allowed. Despite our impending departure, our pride and sense of responsibility would not allow the fruits of our labour to fall into neglect. We owed our adventure the same respect it had afforded us from the very beginning.

We had yet to inform Gérard and Beryl of our plan to relocate back to England. When the ominous moment arrived, their reactions were as different as chalk and cheese, yet predictably curious. Gérard, ever the stoic chap, took it in his stride. Over a quiet nip of whiskey, he confided in me, "I'll be sorry to see you both go, but it's been a lot of fun, right?" His words rang true as he added, "Better to have good friends for a short while than not at all."

Beryl, on the other hand, who wore her heart on her sleeve, took the news with a mixture of disbelief and melodrama. "How on earth will I manage without you?" she initially exclaimed. Yet, she quickly donned some armour of denial, acting as if our imminent departure was merely a figment of her imagination.

Despite the differing responses, we felt a pang of sorrow knowing we'd be bidding farewell to such good people. Principal characters, without whom our adventure would have been the poorer. Their memories etched in our minds, like the rest of the scribblings in this tale of ours.

People often ask us, "So, other than family, was there anything else that made you come back?"

Bit of an age-old question these days. Our answer, polished to perfection now, is always the same: There was no singular reason, but rather a compendium of many. Some were very French indeed, the kind that made us chuckle and think, "Oh, those French are so mad," in our early days. But as time passed, those charming idiosyncrasies slowly morphed into maddening irritations. Take the bureaucratic quagmire, for instance. The labyrinthine process of getting even the simplest of things done could drive a saint to despair. And while we could have managed those things with a bit more patience, it wasn't the root of our decision.

Having said all that, our move to Brittany was never envisioned as a fleeting escapade. Quite the contrary – it was intended to be a timeless adventure. Yet, the reality of living in a foreign land was far more peculiar than anticipated, and we couldn't have foreseen the depths of our longing for family. Our love for our adopted home revealed itself to be more of a passionate fling than a stable, enduring romance. Consequently, we found ourselves at a crossroads, requiring a redefinition of our adventure and its future trajectory.

For anyone out there considering a similar move, I can offer this insight: You'll have no real idea what it's like to live in another country until you're actually there. No matter how prepared you think you might be, and no matter how many holidays, extended stays, and so on that you've had in a place, there's still nothing like the reality of being there for good.

As you've read throughout our tale, there was a scant amount of bad and a wealth of good in our emigration experience. We're glad to have done it. The characters and the antics of those special people, named throughout, still bring a smile to my face. All the experiences you've read about – and the many we've kept to ourselves – remain priceless treasures.

***

The selling and buying process, mercifully, was less arduous than one might expect, thanks in no small part to our familiarity with both French and English methodologies. The only uncharted territory was marketing our French house ourselves. Ever intrepid, we took photos, created the blurb, and posted the whole lot onto an online real estate marketplace. Of course, we still had to appoint a Notaire. Enter our trusted friend Maître Gonan, who was ever-ready to handle the formalities, with all costs graciously shouldered by whomever purchased our place. Simultaneously, we appointed a conveyancing solicitor in Portsmouth, but that expense was a distant worry for these early days.

In our quest to sell, we were repeatedly warned, particularly by members of the immigrant community, to be patient. The French housing market, especially for older properties like ours, wasn't as buoyant as in the UK. It wasn't unusual for a sale to take up to two years – or longer.

Soon after our property details went online, the enquiries began to trickle in. One or two were French, but the majority were British. One inquisitive soul, in particular, reached out via the 'contact us' page to ask if we could drop the price. I suggested, quite reasonably I thought, that they might want to view the property before attempting to haggle. They never responded.

As it turned out, this wasn't an isolated case. Numerous Brits enquired, not about the house itself, but whether we could reduce the price, based solely on a few photos and a couple of paragraphs of blurb. According to someone in the

Notaire's office, this was typical behaviour among the British, who could be quite arrogant and dismissive of the French when it came to buying – and selling – property. We were informed, with a hint of appreciation, that we were a welcome exception to that rule.

Time passed, as it tends to do, and enquiries dwindled, prompting us to consider lowering our price. Just as we were on the brink of making that decision, we received a rather curious enquiry from a couple. They weren't interested in buying our house, per se, but wanted to get an idea of what their money might fetch them in the market. A peculiar request, indeed, but one we granted nonetheless.

The couple arrived a few days later, pleasant enough, but clearly on a tight schedule with other properties to view. We left them to their own devices, making ourselves available for any questions they might have. As they were about to leave, they peppered us with a few questions, not too taxing, but specifically about the French buying process, seeking a Brit's perspective. And then, off they went.

A few days later, they phoned us – Clare had given them our number should they have more questions – and asked if they could take another look at our place. Long story short, they wanted to buy our house, without a hint of the arrogance we'd encountered online.

We put them in touch with Maître Gonan, who ended up representing both parties, freeing us to embark on our own house hunting adventure. In a delightful reversal of roles from our time hunting for a house in France, I was dispatched to Southsea while Clare stayed behind to look after our menagerie.

Two visits and numerous FaceTime tours later, with Clare guiding me from afar, we found our new dream house. The transition was in motion, and the story of our move continued to unfold in ways we could never have imagined.

Our buyers had nothing to sell back in England, and our vendor had already secured her new home, so the process was poised to proceed rather swiftly. About thirteen weeks, if memory serves. The only fly in the ointment was extricating our money from France to pay for our Southsea acquisition. The French financial system, tied up like the proverbial kipper, posed quite a challenge. Future repatriates, take heed.

The money from our buyers went to the Notaire, as was customary. From there, it was transferred to some financial institution, where it languished until everyone in the system agreed it could be released. Despite lunch breaks, holidays, sick days, and the general bureaucratic quagmire – previously mentioned – our solicitor in Portsmouth finally received our cleared funds some eleven days later.

Forty eight hours afterwards and we're sitting outside of my favourite Portsmouth pub, The Bridge Tavern, enjoying a pint of warm beer and a fish-finger sandwich.

EPILOGUE

We've been back in England for a number of years now. Clare has found her niche working in a shop, while I most definitely do not get to chop wood anymore. Instead, I've had to reinvent what retirement means and what form it should take. Still not entirely sure if I've got it all figured out, but I still get out of bed each day with a purpose – which is essential.

We still keep in touch with Alan and Hélène, though not as frequently as we used to. One of the casualties of distance and differing lifestyles, I suppose. We did hear from the new owners of our former island and received a message or two from Alan regarding the same. He has become their go-to person for grass cutting while they're away – which, by all accounts, they frequently are – and he has also become their principal wine merchant, using his vineyard connections to get them a decent deal in return for a small commission. They even employed the services of Lee the builder, keeping him busy ripping out much of what we had worked so hard to preserve and build.

Casualties included the potager – they had neither the time nor the desire to grow anything – some of the trees in the verger – they had no need for all the fruit they produced – and most of the hangar, which was given over to a new swimming pool. We were, of course, saddened by the news of the vandalism coming from Brittany, but as we have often said to ourselves, "live and let live."

We often reminisce about our time in Brittany, acknowledging how short-lived it was. But then we tell ourselves, how awful it would have been if we had allowed the idea of moving abroad to remain just that – an idea. And there's a life lesson: Ideas are wonderful, but turning them into reality – that's the real trick.

There are, of course, things we miss. For me, the verger tops the list – my spiritual sanctuary, where tranquillity met the rhythm of nature. And let's not forget the tractor, chainsaw, log splitter, and the rest of my 'essential' mechanical ensemble. Though, if I'm being honest with you, perpetually cutting the grass wasn't exactly a highlight. Sadly, none of these tools had a place in a Southsea townhouse.

Then there's the elusive cauliflower, a stubborn resident of my bucket list. Perhaps one day, I'll conquer that verdant challenge.

***

In case you're wondering what happened to our menagerie, well, the chickens went to live with Alan and Hélène, multi-coloured clapboard chicken house and all. Milo, the ginger tom, French born and bred, also stayed behind – adopted by a young French couple. We figured he'd struggle in Southsea, given his rustic roots and lack of city savvy. Busy roads and street-smart cats could spell trouble for him, not to mention the dialect and slang of the Portsmouth Isle, which even I struggle with sometimes.

Nettle, our feisty tabby, came back with us. Having survived a near-fatal poisoning and being naturally scrappy, it was the city cats that needed to watch their backs. Sadly, she passed away four years after our return. One morning she came in for breakfast, found a spot by a warm radiator, and fell asleep – for eternity.

Maisie, Jack's counterbalance, fell ill a few months into 2018, suffering seizures and other symptoms of a defective liver. With no local veterinary hospital in Brittany, we brought her back to England for treatment. After a couple of weeks in a hospital near Winchester, we were told she was unlikely to improve. So we returned her to France, where she died peacefully, thanks to our local vet. Her ashes are buried in the yard in Saint-Barthélémy, where we hope her spirited zoomies live on.

And then of course, there's Jack, my best friend. He became a great pub dog, devourer of pork scratchings and anything else he could blag. His laid-back approach to life never wavered. Even without the verger to escape to, he nonetheless found cozy, out of the way places to snooze, including any soft furnishings and our bed. Shortly after Nettle's passing, Jack was diagnosed with an inoperable tumour on his carotid artery. Given a few weeks to live, he defied expectations, staying with us for another six months before peacefully departing one Saturday morning. His ashes remain with us.

So how did Southsea work out? Well as it turns out, it didn't. Which is why I find myself writing this tale of ours from Dorset.

BEFORE YOU GO

Do you remember these words? "I may be a bit run-down, but my promise is limitless." Surveying what we had bought, looking beyond the neglect and how it was once a cherished home. How I felt that it was, "waiting patiently, accepting its situation with no regrets or malice, just an enduring graciousness." The place seemed to be telling us that we could do as much or as little as we pleased. Because no matter what, it would still be our home.

You may recall the broken barn standing stoically, scars of past glories. The neglected orchard, with multiple varieties of fruit trees that I had yet to determined their identities. Waiting for someone to care once more. Some equally neglected land, which once thrived and hoped to flourish again under our ownership.

Allow me to illustrate how words, woven with imagery, breathed life into our reality. I hope you'll see how we endeavoured to realise its potential. Fulfilling an unspoken promise, we transformed a once-loved, yet neglected, abode into a true 'gem amidst the French countryside'.

While I could express the pride we feel in our achievements, I find it challenging to laud oneself. Such recognition is best left to others, should they be so inclined. Nonetheless, I hope we've left a distinct and memorable footprint.

Enjoy a glimpse inside our photo album over the page.

A GLIMPSE INSIDE THE PHOTO ALBUM

THE PIANO ROOM

Eating, mingling, laughing.

Going upstairs

SLEEPING

VIEW FROM A ROOM

THE FRONT LAWN

THE ORIGINAL ABODE

Colin Templeman

A STROLL UP THE FARM

LOOKING BACK

Colin Templeman

The Verger – My Special Place

-ENDS-

ABOUT THE AUTHOR

Colin Templeman was born and raised in Leigh Park, Hampshire, before carving out a distinguished career in Facilities Management—earning global recognition and success along the way. Yet, he considers his greatest achievement, and deepest source of joy, to be his family.

Diary of an Immigrant is his third book and the culmination of his storytelling craft. True to his mantra, 'practice makes perfect,' Colin is rarely one to rest on his laurels.

Now retired, he lives with his wife Clare in North Dorset, England. While he has no plans to leave Britain any time soon, that doesn't mean new adventures aren't on the horizon.

www.ingramcontent.com/pod-product-compliance
Lightning Source LLC
Chambersburg PA
CBHW061149170426
43209CB00012B/1606